LANDSCAPES OF DEVELOPMENT

THE IMPACT OF MODERNIZATION DISCOURSES ON THE PHYSICAL ENVIRONMENT OF THE EASTERN MEDITERRANEAN

T0324322

EDITED BY **PANAYIOTA PYLA**

THE AGA KHAN PROGRAM AT THE HARVARD UNIVERSITY GRADUATE SCHOOL OF DESIGN

CAMBRIDGE, MASSACHUSETTS

ISBN 9780977122448

Book and cover design by Wilcox Design | www.wilcoxinc.com
Printed and bound by Kirkwood Printing
Distributed by Harvard University Press

Cover image: Ataturk Dam, photo by Aslihan Demirtas, 1999

The Harvard University Graduate School of Design is a leading center for education, information, and technical expertise on the built environment. Its departments of Architecture, Landscape Architecture, and Urban Planning and Design offer masters and doctoral degree programs and provide the foundation for its Advanced Studies and Executive Education programs.

CONTENTS

PREFACE AND ACKNOWLEDGMENTS

This work is indebted to the Harvard University Graduate School of Design's Aga Khan Program of activities in landscape architecture and urbanism, under the leadership of Hashim Sarkis, for the sponsorship of "Landscapes of Development: Modernization and the Physical Environment in the Eastern Mediterranean," the symposium at which this project was conceived. We remain grateful for the continued support of the Aga Khan Program that enabled the production of this volume.

At the symposium, scholars from a range of backgrounds relating to the history and practice of architecture, landscape architecture, and urban/regional development contemplated the interconnections between development politics and the physical transformation of Eastern Mediterranean landscapes. This historical reflection on the mid-twentieth century seemed vital because, even though that period may register as an excessively confident era of modernity—characterized by grand reformist visions, modernization creeds, and megaprojects—it also represented a moment when architecture, planning, and more broadly the design of the built environment embodied crucial social aspirations beyond the logic of the market and the demands of consumerism. This volume's extension of the symposium's observations on mid-twentieth-century interventions thus aims to provide a critical historical perspective on the role of "the physical" in relation to contemporary forces of globalization, environmentalism, and social equity.

Current practices of development and globalization continue to strain global human relationships and threaten the biosphere, and the particular geography of the Eastern Mediterranean is faced with the agonies of an altogether new turmoil. We hope that presenting this study of the complex history of its built environment might encourage informed debate on the possibilities for physical landscapes to negotiate (or negate) current political, institutional, or environmental realities.

In addition to the authors presented here, many individuals contributed to this volume. Hashim Sarkis has been a consistent source of perceptive feedback. We greatly appreciated the insights of our keynote speaker, Wolfgang Sachs, who framed the larger debate on environmental/developmental politics and physical landscapes. Thanks also to Arindam Dutta and Ijlal Muzaffar, who along with Hashim Sarkis acted as moderators at the symposium, stimulating later revisions to the presentations. We would also like to acknowledge those colleagues who contributed to the symposium but chose not to have their papers included in this volume: Kelda Jamison, Geoffrey Schad, Georges Prevelakis, and Alona Nitzan-Shiftan. We are also grateful to Giselle Rose and Edna Van Saun for their administrative support. Thanks to Barbara Poss and Susan Johnson Roehr, who edited earlier versions of some chapters. We offer thanks to Jean Wilcox for her sensitive graphic design and to Melissa Vaughn, Director of Publications at the GSD, for editorial guidance.

PANAYIOTA PYLA

INTRODUCTION: DEVELOPMENT HISTORIES
AND THE PHYSICAL LANDSCAPE
OF THE EASTERN MEDITERRANEAN

This book examines the impact of development policies and politics on the physical environment of the Eastern Mediterranean, defined here not as a fixed region of cultural coherence but as a tentative geography where particular processes of mid-twentieth- century reconstruction, decolonization, and nation-building became intertwined developmental agendas. After the end of World War II, the countries of the Eastern Mediterranean became central to many transnational plans for socioeconomic restructuring. The various models of "development assistance" that had been offered to postwar Europe, with the goal of reestablishing economic strength and political stability for North America's more obvious trading and military partners, quickly generated multiple variants in Latin America, Asia, and Africa. The dreams of progress and prosperity for what came to be known as "underdeveloped areas" of the globe were pursued against the backdrop of larger Cold War politics. The International Bank for Reconstruction and Development and multiple variants of the Marshall Plan established the model for funding poor countries to stem the spread of communism, while the Soviet Union employed its own mechanisms for offering military and financial aid.[1] The countries of the Eastern Mediterranean possessed strategic geopolitical significance in those divisive global power politics, and both states emerging out of colonial rule (Syria, Lebanon, Iraq) and those that had not experienced colonialism directly (Turkey, Greece) found themselves receiving technical aid, development projects, and cultural exports in that "era of planning and control."[2] Oil wealth also played a part in financing development plans in some countries (e.g., Iraq and Libya as oil producers, or Lebanon as transit center), and this increased the momentum of state-led development among neighbors (Egypt, Syria),

The photographs that accompany the introduction can be read independently, as glimpses into particular politics of development entangled with built landscapes in the region. {Special thanks to Petros Phokaides for co-editing the image selection.}

The Republic of Cyprus received United Nations aid for the construction of many dams, as water management was considered key to the country's economic development and socio-political stability. A significant number of these dams were designed by the Yugoslav firm Energoproject, highlighting the local government's preference for partnerships with countries of the Non-Aligned Movement, in an effort to bypass Cold War bipolarities.

while others explored combinations of statist measures and private enterprise (Cyprus, Greece, Turkey)—all sharing visions of economic development and social welfare.

In physical terms, the drive toward development, whether promoted by international institutions (the United Nations, development banks), corporate interests (emanating from the United States or from ex-colonial centers), national governments of the postcolonial world, or western governments pursuing bilateral agreements with new nations, has been responsible for the rapid growth of metropolitan centers, the radical restructuring of rural landscapes, and the proliferation of dams, irrigation systems, and other infrastructure. Such built works were not merely utilitarian or technical artifacts but products of larger historical circumstances. Just as the project of development itself was not simply a technocratic framework for administrative reform and industrialization but an ideology, so too were dams and irrigation networks, highways, housing projects, or spaces of public recreation active participants in debates surrounding the modernizing dreams of progress, efficiency, and comfort. Competing conceptions of economic and social change, locality and globalism, resources and standards, social equity and ecology, social participation and dependency—these were contemplated on built landscapes too, just as they were debated in the realms of policymaking and economics. As such, physical interventions constitute crucial references for contemplating postwar histories of development and their contemporary impact and repercussions.

In highlighting the physical environment as an important actor in the history of mid-twentieth-century development discourse, this volume of essays recognizes the

Major General Prem Chand of India, Commander of the United Nations Peace-Keeping Force in Cyprus (right) with Lt. Col. Lauri Koho, Military Liaison Officer of the United Nations Secretary-General, pointing to Cyprus on the map. The UN was involved with extensive modernization projects in Cyprus beginning with the country's independence in 1960, intimately tying modernization to its peace mission to eliminate intercommunal conflicts between the Greek Cypriot and Turkish Cypriot communities on the island.

contribution of critiques of "the development worldview" from geography, sociology, cultural criticism, and other perspectives.[3] Modernization theorists' assumption that there existed a singular linear pattern of development that would be defined through transformations in technology, military and bureaucratic institutions, and the political and social structure has been discredited, not only for its dualistic schema of "modern" and "traditional" societies but also for its oversimplification of the processes of decolonization and industrialization.[4] Challenges to modernization theory emerged since the 1950s and 1960s, offering insights into how it promoted "dependency," "underdevelopment," or "maldevelopment," disenfranchising entire populations for the benefit of mostly the North American and European exporters of "aid." But such early critiques based on center-periphery dichotomies failed to account for the unevenness of development and the existence of not simply a "third" but a "fourth," "fifth," and "sixth world" (for indigenous peoples, the poor in rich countries, and migrant workers respectively).[5]

Recent geohistorical expositions of the assumptions of development practices have demonstrated how the "development idea" was intertwined with even more complex global power politics and economic agendas.[6] They have exposed the inequality of partnerships among development institutions, local elites, and local populations, and the politics of exclusion, repression, and exploitation.[7] Others revealed the oversimplifications of reality and the authoritarian modes of thought in modernizing agendas.[8] Thought practices that put their sole emphasis on economic growth and industrialization—as though these could viably materialize without simultaneous provisions for social welfare or political rights—have been debunked as they failed in the necessary "removal of substantial unfreedoms."[9] Similarly, the cultural powers of philanthropic practices and other circuits of knowledge have also been examined.[10] Several astute critics have demonstrated how the belief in development-as-growth advanced particular notions of nature and environment that brought on current ecological predicaments.[11] Taken together, these works have challenged the founding divisions between "technical" strategies for socioeconomic reform and political issues of governance, power, and control, and reconsider the allegedly "technocratic" processes of design, planning, and building. More challenges to "development thinking" come from feminist or labor movement perspectives, which explore how alternative institutions can assume an agency in development processes.[12] And recent critical investigations into "grassroots" or "counter-hegemonic" strategies for globalization (and its earlier versions of development) have underlined the significance of studying nuanced voices, perspectives, and locations.[13] Drawing upon these insights, the chapters presented here examine how built interventions shaped the debate on concepts of space and society, technology and nature.

Another equally important theoretical reference for this volume is the growing scholarly field situating the cross-cultural histories of modern architecture and urbanism within larger political, historical, and ideological contexts. Such studies architectural culture in different parts of the Eastern Mediterranean have exposed the ideological appropriations of built works by modernist creeds, authoritarian state policies, top-down economic agendas, nationalist aspirations, or other identity constructions.[14] Rather than treat political and ideological agendas as a blueprint from which to explain architecture and urbanism, several such studies underline the importance of

Model of the proposal for the Kuwait National Assembly by Spence, Bonnington and Collins. The John S. Bonnington Partnership, based in London, worked in the eastern Mediterranean throughout the 1970s on various architectural and planning projects.

Rural teachers training center, Syria, designed by Doxiadis Associates, 1958–59.

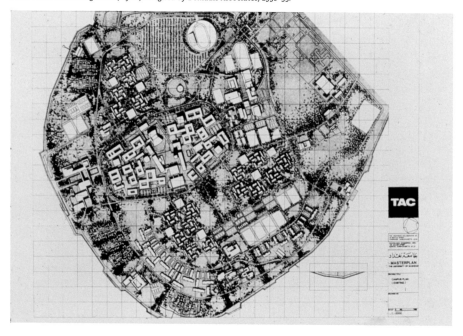

University of Baghdad Master Plan designed by The Architects Collaborative International in 1962, with architects-in-charge Walter Gropius, Robert McMillan, and Louis McMillan.

The creation of educational facilities—from vocational schools to training centers, to university campuses—targeted both economic and social modernization.

considering the complex cultural realities, ambiguities, and contradictions in the way physical design and building became intertwined with political and ideological agendas.[15] If current scholarship in architectural history has already shown us that there are many modernisms, so too there are many modernizations and more broadly, many visions of development, manifested in the physical environment.[16] This volume draws on insights of both architectural history and critiques of development to consider specific histories behind the physical transformation of multiple scales of landscapes—from dams and infrastructure to housing blocks and apartments—to highlight the nuances of the particular conceptions of space, society, science, and nature that they produced.

Just as it spans multiple disciplines, this study of physical landscapes also crosses boundaries among countries, to treat the Eastern Mediterranean as a tentative framework for grounding these nuanced reflections on the intersections of development histories and the physical environment. As mentioned earlier, the intention is not to give a comprehensive analysis of development politics in this region, and not to even define such a region as a distinct whole. The chapters presented here offer different histories of the intertwinement of development and physical landscapes, treated from the start as a "process geography" aimed at setting up a comparative framework.[17] This alternative framing interrogates the possibility of new types of overlaps, parallels, or continuities across the "Middle East," "North Africa," or "Southern Europe" that contemplate the transcultural impact of postwar development on these margins of Europe.

Eight essays examine formal manifestations of development, shedding light on urban development schemes, housing projects, and agro-landscapes and dams, from Israel to Turkey and from Greece to Syria. These contributions situate built works within the larger sociopolitical context that influenced their design and implementation, and collectively, they expose the entanglement of built interventions with national strategies or transnational discourses of expertise that were setting the rules for development. They offer new insights in the ways in which the marvelous power of technology (from dams to high-rises) opened new frontiers in the shaping of natural and built landscapes. They also contemplate how the appealing dream of human emancipation, associated with new housing and infrastructure, shaped visions of idealized futures while becoming entangled with conceptions of needs and standards and the rationalization of physical space. The analyses presented here also contemplate the roles of stakeholding communities or other localized politics as arbiters of planning/design strategies and modes of built production across the region, and they uncover the varieties of individual agency, even in the midst of grand social arrangements.

The volume is divided in three thematic sections, each of which allows possibilities for comparisons among cases. Some of the essays extend the discussion to more recent decades, precisely to underscore contemporary relevance of the debate. The first part considers dams and irrigation projects that redefined the countryside. The essay by Aslihan Demirtas, "Rowing Boats in the Reservoir: Infrastructure as Transplanted Seascape," examines infrastructure projects of the Kemalist era in Turkey and compares them to a 1950s project for hydraulic modernization, to show the socio-spatial impact and environmental excesses of postwar techno-scientific interventions. Neyran Turan's essay "The Strait, the Beach, and the Highway: Shifting Edges of Istanbul," examines how the transformations of Istanbul's seafront in the 1950s, and the underlying politics of reconceptualizing Istanbul as a modern city, compared with earlier (1930s) as well as later (1990s) transformations of that seafront. In the context of Egypt, Elizabeth Bishop in "Control Room: Visible and Concealed Spaces of the Aswan High Dam" analyzes the invisible spaces behind the Aswan High Dam that shaped workers´ roles, family relationships, and ultimately the formation of Egyptian citizenship, gendered or otherwise. The second part of the book examines the restructuring of urban fabrics caused by rapid modernization. Eleni Bastéa's and Vilma Hastaoglou-Martinidis's essay "Modernization and Its

Discontents in Post-1950s Thessaloniki: Urban Change and Urban Narratives," focuses on the dramatic transformations of Thessaloniki's urban form and the ambivalent reactions recorded in local literature. Sibel Bozdoğan's essay, "Residential Architecture and Urban Landscape in Istanbul since 1950," casts the spotlight on the transformation of Istanbul's urbanscapes, to expose how the city's apartment boom of the 1950s promoted divisions in cultural and class politics—divisions that were exacerbated within the more recent realities of postmodern Istanbul. The third section turns to another scale in the urban fabrics of Israel, Syria, Iraq, and Greece: housing projects. Rachel Kallus's analysis of the creation of a residential quarter in Kiryat Gat in "State-Constructed Everyday: Envisioning a Place for the National Community" demonstrates how modernist visions of standardization and rationalization became entangled with state goals of social cohesion and national progress. My analysis of housing schemes in Iraq and Syria in "Architects as Development Experts: Model Communities in Iraq and Syria" uncovers how state and international agendas of modernization were intertwined with architects' and planners' attempts to introduce new disciplinary goals and priorities for modern architecture and urbanism. Ioanna Theocharopoulou in "Improvising Urbanism in Postwar Athens, 1952–1974: Techniques and Processes of Another Development," examines "impromptu" housing in Athens that emerged out of back-door deals among developers and politicians, and flourished outside the professional domains of architecture and planning, beyond the official control of state sponsorship—and as such, led to peculiar definitions of development. Taken together, the histories presented in the pages that follow expand the temporal dimension within which we can contemplate the design of physical landscapes amid today's politics of development, globalization, and environmentalism.

Notes

1   For the intellectual roots of the development project and the Cold War politics behind it, see, for example, Wolfgang Sachs, "The Archaeology of the Development Idea," *Interculture*, vol. 23, no. 4, Fall 1990; and J. Timmons Roberts and Amy Bellone Hite, eds., *The Globalization and Development Reader* (Medford, MA, and Oxford: Blackwell, 2007).

2   Roger Owen, *State Power and Politics in the Making of the Middle East* (New York: Routledge, 2002), quotation on xii.

3   Wolfgang Sachs, ed., *The Development Dictionary: A Guide to Knowledge as Power* (London: Zed Books, 2010, c.1992); quotation on ix.

4   Modernization theory was a reductionist mode of social-scientific thought that had its heyday in the 1950s and 1960s, and assumed different cultures to be at different stages of a linear path, moving from being traditional or underdeveloped to being modern and developed. It was an ahistorical model of development that had shaped many American aid and development agencies' policies in the 1950s and 1960s, as it provided a non-communist answer to poverty and global underdevelopment. For recent critiques of modernization theory and its legacy, see, for example, Nils Gilman, *Mandarins*

of the Future (Baltimore: Johns Hopkins University Press, 2003), along with Sachs, ed., *The Development Dictionary*.

5   Andre Frankovits, "Development" in Tony Bennett, Lawrence Grossberg, and Meaghan Morris, eds., *New Keywords: A Revised Vocabulary of Culture and Society* (Malden, MA: Blackwell, 2006), 78–81. For an overview of dependency theory and key texts on the topic, see Roberts and Hite, eds., *The Globalization and Development Reader*.

6   See for example, Sachs, ed., *The Development Dictionary*; Arturo Escobar, *Encountering Development: The Making and Unmaking of the Third World* (Boulder, CO: Westview Press, 1998); David Harvey, *Spaces of Global Capitalism: A Theory of Uneven Geographical Development* (London and New York: Verso, 2006); Neil Smith, *Uneven Development: Nature, Capital, and the Production of Space* (New York: Blackwell, 1984).

7   Timothy Mitchell, *Rule of Experts: Egypt, Technopolitics, Modernity* (Berkeley and Los Angeles, University of California Press, 2002); Abidin Kusno, *Behind the Postcolonial: Architecture, Urban Space, and Political Cultures in Indonesia* (New York: Routledge, 2000); Irene Gendzier, *Notes from the*

Minefield: United States Intervention in Lebanon and the Middle East (New York: Columbia University Press, 1997).

8   James C. Scott, *Seeing Like a State: How Certain Schemes to Improve the Human Condition Have Failed* (New Haven: Yale University Press, 1998).

9   Amartya Sen, *Development as Freedom* (New York: Anchor Books, 2000, c.1999), quotation on xii.

10   Morag Bell, "American Philanthropy as Cultural Power" in *The American Century: Consensus and Coercion in the Projection of American Power*, David Slater and Peter J. Taylor, eds. (Oxford: Blackwell, 1999), 284–297.

11   Wolfgang Sachs, *Planet Dialectics: Explorations in Environment and Development* (London and New York: Zed Books, 1999); Vandana Shiva, *Staying Alive: Women, Ecology, and Development* (London; Atlantic Highlands, N.J.: Zed Books, 1988).

12   Manisha Desai and Nancy Naples, eds., *Women's Activism and Globalization: Linking Local Struggles and Transnational Politics* (New York: Routledge, 2002); R. Armbruster, "Cross-National Labor Organization Strategies," *Critical Sociology* 21:2, 1995, 75–89.

13   Arjun Appadurai, "Grassroots Globalization and the Research Imagination," *Public Culture* 12:1 (Winter 2000): 1–19; Peter Evans, "Fighting Marginalization with Transnational Networks: Counter-Hegemonic Globalization," *Contemporary Sociology: A Journal of Reviews*, 29:1, 2000, 230–241.

14   Selected references on modern architecture in the region: Nezar AlSayyad, *Hybrid Urbanism: On the Identity Discourse and the Built Environment* (New York: Praeger, 2001); Nezar AlSayyad, ed., *Forms of Dominance on the Architecture and Urbanism of the Colonial Enterprise* (Aldershot: Avebury, 1992); Gülsüm Baydar Nalbantoğlu, Wong Chong Thai, eds., *Postcolonial Space(s)* (New York: Princeton Architectural Press, 1997); Diane Ghirardo, *Building New Communities: New Deal America and Fascist Italy* (Princeton, N.J.: Princeton University Press, 1989); Sibel Bozdoğan, "Against Style: Bruno Taut's Pedagogical Program in Turkey, 1936–1938," in *The Education of the Architect: Historiography, Urbanism, and the Growth of Architectural Knowledge*, ed. Martha Pollak (Cambridge, MA: MIT Press, 1997), 176; Sibel Bozdoğan, *Modernism and Nation Building: Turkish Architectural Culture in the Early Republic* (Seattle, WA: University of Washington Press, 2001); Sibel Bozdoğan and Reşat Kasaba, eds., *Rethinking Modernity and National Identity in Turkey* (Seattle: University of Washington Press, 1997); Zeynep Çelik, "Colonialism, Orientalism, and the Canon," *The Art Bulletin* 78, no. 2 (June 1996): 202–205; Elvan Ergut and Belgin Ozkaya, eds., "Modern Architecture in the Middle East," *Docomomo Journal*, no. 35 (September 2006); Sandy Isenstadt and Kishwar Rizvi, eds., *Modernism and the Middle East: Architecture and Politics in the Twentieth Century* (Seattle: University of Washington Press, 2008); Wojciech Lesnikowski, *Eastern European Modernism* (New York: Rizzoli, 1996); Neil Leach, ed., *Architecture and Revolution:*

Contemporary Perspectives on Central and Eastern Europe (London and New York: Routledge, 1999); Brian L. McLaren, *Architecture and Tourism in Italian Colonial Libya: An Ambivalent Modernism* (Seattle: University of Washington Press, 2006); Joe Nasr and Mercedes Volait, eds., *Urbanism: Imported or Exported? Native Aspirations and Foreign Plans* (West Sussex: Wiley Academy, 2003); Panayiota Pyla, "Back to the Future: Doxiadis's Plans for Baghdad," *Journal of Planning History* 7:1 (February 2008): 3–19; Panayiota Pyla, "Hassan Fathy Revisited: Postwar Discourses of Science, Development, and Vernacular Architecture," *Journal of Architectural Education* 60:3 (February 2007): 28–39; Alona Nitzan-Shiftan, "Alternative Modernism: Erich Mendelsohn and the Tel Aviv Chug in Mandate Palestine," *Architectural History* 39 (1996): 147–180; Nasser Rabbat, "The Formation of the Neo-Mamluk Style in Modern Egypt," in Pollak, ed., *The Education of the Architect*; Paul Rabinow, "France in Morocco: Technocosmopolitanism and Middling Modernism," *Assemblage* 17 (April 1992): 52–57; Peter Rowe and Hashim Sarkis, eds., *Projecting Beirut: Episodes in the Construction and Reconstruction of a Modern City* (Munich, New York: Prestel, 1998); Hashim Sarkis, *Circa 1950: Lebanon in the Pictures and Plans of Constantinos Doxiades* (Beirut: Dar en-Nahar, 2003); Rafi Segal and Eyal Weizman, *Civilian Occupation: The Politics of Israeli Architecture* (New York: Verso, 2003); Maggie Toy, *Beyond the Revolution: The Architecture of Eastern Europe* (London: Academy Editions, New York: St. Martin's Press, 1996); Gwendolyn Wright, *Politics of Design in French Colonial Urbanism* (Chicago: University of Chicago Press, 1991).

15   In her introductory chapter, "Modernism on the Margins of Europe," Bozdoğan explains this in detail, underlining how imported ideas were intersected, justified, modified, and contested within local contexts in unique ways. Bozdoğan, *Modernism and Nation Building*, 6.

16   A comparative framework for the many "modernisms" in the context of the modern Middle East is offered in Isenstadt and Rizvi, eds., *Modernism and the Middle East,* and in Ergut and Ozkaya, eds., "Modern Architecture in the Middle East," which focuses on the architectural culture in this region to demonstrate the diversity of voices and complex social and aesthetic agendas that constitute architectural modernism, and searches for identity. For the multiplicity of postwar modernisms in other contexts, see Sarah Williams Goldhagen and Rejean Legault, eds., *Anxious Modernisms: Experimentation in Postwar Architectural Culture* (Cambridge, MA: MIT Press, 2000).

17   In discussing ways of reconceptualizing area studies, Arjun Appadurai refered to an idea of "process geographies" that views regions "not [as] permanent geographical facts" but rather as "initial contexts for themes," which can guide the study of cultural processes. Arjun Appadurai, "Grassroots Globalization and the Research Imagination," *Public Culture* 12:1 (Winter 2000): 1–19, quotation on 7.

DAMS, IRRIGATION, AND INFRASTRUCTURE

ASLIHAN DEMIRTAS

1

ROWING BOATS IN THE RESERVOIR: INFRASTRUCTURE AS TRANSPLANTED SEASCAPE

Imagine a landscape: flat land surrounded by mountains, in the midst of which stands a rocky hill, covered by a small town. Brown and ochre are the dominant colors. Brown comes from the infertile soil containing mostly limestone, ochre from the steppe, a semiarid grassland that is the predominant flora of the region. Rain and snow scarcely fall. The main water resources are three unstable and weak creeks. The described setting is Ankara at the time it became the capital of the new Turkish Republic in 1920, after the fall of the Ottoman Empire. It was a typical inland town with an arid climate, situated at the center of the Anatolian Peninsula.

Despite these natural geographical traits, the prominent newspapers of the 1930s often published articles and photographs that celebrated Ankara's "seas" and "shores" as "modern recreational spaces of the new capital."[1] Considering the arid, drought-ridden steppes of Ankara, the application of such wording sounds surreal. The peculiarity of these terms is revealed when one discovers that the "seas" are in fact man-made constructions of infrastructure: the reservoirs of the Atatürk Model Farm, the Çubuk Dam, and the Youth Park Lake, built between 1925 and 1943. The only three natural creeks in Ankara—İncesu, Çubuk, and Hatip Creeks—were fed into these three "grand projets," the new water bodies in the new capital.

While these sites were constructed as works of infrastructure, they were also designed to function as artificial nature and public recreational spaces. These novel landscapes operated as new public spaces synonymous with the modernization and development of the new Turkish Republic.

The Atatürk Model Farm and Forest, founded in 1925, was the most significant of the six Atatürk Farms in the country. President Kemal Atatürk was preoccupied with the correlation of nature and climate in determining the character of a society and its settlement patterns, as described in the writings of Jean-Jacques Rousseau. In his *Social Contract*, Rousseau establishes a direct link between the character of a nation, its form of government, and the fertility of the land:

> Freedom is not a fruit of every climate and it is not therefore within the capacity of every people... In every climate there are natural factors on the basis of which one can determine the form of government to which that climate leads... Mean and sterile places, where the product does not repay the labor, must remain uncultivated and deserted, or peopled only by savages... since no political society is possible [there]. Places where the surplus of product over labor is moderate or abundant are suited to free peoples.[2]

In Rousseauian terms, the new capital, Ankara, did not qualify as a land of free people—a sentiment shared by many foreigners who, for many years, refused to transfer their embassies from Istanbul to this remote city. The new capital was deemed inferior to the old seat of government in terms of its climate, nature, and geography. The steppe climate, arid and infertile, was criticized by the Istanbul governmental elite: "If even trees cannot grow, how would it be possible to raise men?"[3] The first priority in the construction of the new capital was to transform its nature to support a democratic government.

The transformation of Ankara's nature was therefore part of the project of creating a young and healthy nation. During the final years of the Ottoman Empire, the Europeans referred to it as the "Sick Man" of Europe, a characterization also adopted by the newly founded Turkish Republic in describing the former empire. A 1934 exhibition, "Economy Before and After Lausanne," held in Ankara relates the story of an Ottoman Empire slowly moving into poverty and collapse. One of the exhibition panels read: "The country regressed and shrank. The people became poor. The State lost its economical and political independence. The people who sacked the country also gave him this name: The SICK MAN. Was he really sick? The whole world replied yes. NO, said the leader [Atatürk]."[4] In this analogy, the remedy for sickness is agriculture; independence and development were equated with agriculture. Other panels read: "The Republic gave us wheat and our independence."[5] In this narration, where progress and cultivation is achieved through the redemption of the arid land, the trees and the fields stood for the physical and visual representation of a cultivated and civilized land and a developed nation liberated from backwardness. Agriculture was not only an act of freedom but also of legitimate possession:

There are two instruments of conquest in the world. One is the sword and the other, the plough.... [The] Plough is the device to progress nations in their lands, it is not like the sword. The more it is used the more powerful it becomes. The arm that uses the sword is apt to get exhausted but the one that uses the plough becomes the possessor of the soil. The sword and the plough. The former has always been defeated by the latter.[6]

In this intellectual climate the Atatürk Model Farm and Forest was founded, with the objective of promoting modern and scientific agriculture, and, more important, turning the brown landscape of Ankara into a green one.

The architectural components of the farm included the workers' and technicians' housing, a public bath, an agricultural tools factory, a zoo, a brewery, a dairy factory, and Atatürk's farm residence, which were commissioned to Ernst Egli, a consultant to the government and the reformer of Turkish architectural education. Similar to Rousseau, Egli was interested in the direct relation between nature/climate and architecture/urban planning. He wrote about the significance of "context," which is "the overall character of light, air, sun, wind, topography, terrain, water, vegetation, the harshness or mildness of nature."[7]

The water management system was an elaborate system of dykes, canals, dams, conduits, pumps, and reservoirs. The Marmara Pool and the Black Sea Pool are the two main reservoirs of this system situated on the highest grounds to enable gravity-flow irrigation. Yet rather than being designed as simple and efficient containers, the plans of pools exactly reproduce the contours of the seas for which they were named. The outlines of the seas were minutely copied to such a remarkable degree that even the islands, bays, and peninsulas were simulated and referred to by their real-life names such as "Gemlik Bay" and "Kapıdağ Peninsula." In the Black Sea reservoir, there is a connected but distinct pool called the "Azak Sea," the inner sea at the northern Black Sea to the east of Crimea.

These details make it harder to view these structures solely as hydraulic works. Clearly these pools were designed as sites of popular entertainment and public recreation, beyond their technical purposes of promoting scientific agriculture and forestry. Yet even though they were also designed as public pools, why were they modeled on the Marmara and the Black Seas, which surround Istanbul, and not the Aegean or the Mediterranean? In addition to their utilitarian and recreational function, there existed another layer of space both in the creation and experience of these structures, a "representational space." As formulated by Henri Lefebvre, representational space embodies "complex symbolisms, sometimes coded, sometimes not."[8] It is "directly lived through its associated images and symbols, and hence the space of 'inhabitants' and 'users'... It overlays physical space, making use of its objects."[9]

The Black Sea and the Marmara Sea pools embodied a representation of the geography of the former capital, Istanbul, with the inclusion of boat excursions, the inseparable leisure activity associated with the Bosporus. Festivities were almost always associated with water in the capital of the Ottoman Empire, not to mention the

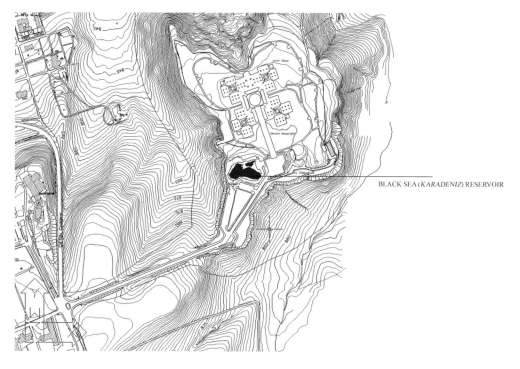

BLACK SEA (*KARADENIZ*) RESERVOIR

The Black Sea Reservoir Site Plan. Note that the shape of the reservoir replicates that of the Black Sea.

The Marmara Reservoir Site Plan. Similar to the Black Sea Reservoir, the Marmara Reservoir's plan replicates the shape of the sea for which it was named.

MARMARA RESERVOIR

overwhelming visual presence of water surrounding Istanbul. Especially beginning from the eighteenth century onward, life on the shores of the Bosporus and excursions on the water constituted an urban spectacle and became a marker of urban space and life.[10]

By transplanting "seas" in the middle of the Anatolian steppes, the pools set the stage for established rituals such as boating excursions, while also constituting a modern civic concept of public recreation and sports, implementing the radical agenda of the new regime to modernize everyday life. "New rituals or institutional configurations and new modes of social relations" were emerging in these new constructions of artificial nature.[11] Swimming was the newly popular recreative activity in the capital of modern Turkey—unthinkable within the territory and traditions of the Ottoman Empire.[12] The popular journals and newspapers of the time frequently published illustrated articles such as "Çiftlikte Yaz" (*Summer in the Farm*), showing women present in a public space—a novelty—and in swimsuits rather than veils.[13] These spaces, by definition and design, promoted the presence of women in public while also transforming women's physical representation.

Swimming also ideologically manifested youth and health. In her seminal work on early modern Turkish architecture, Sibel Bozdoğan states that Ankara was "the ultimate embodiment of youth and health, and these attributes found their more literal spatial expression in places of public recreation and collective sports where the regeneration of

A 1930s postcard with a view of the Marmara Reservoir. The island in the reservoir replicates an actual one located in the Marmara Sea.

A photograph of the Black Sea Reservoir published in *Ulus*, a popular newspaper of the time. The article accompanying the image is entitled "Summer in the {State} Farm," and it boasts of the citizens of Ankara relaxing in swimsuits on a hot summer day.

the body and in turn, of the nation was to take place."[14] "Moments of material practice," to use David Harvey's expression, "also instantiate and objectify human desires in the material world, not only through the reproduction of self and bodily being but also through modifications of surrounding environments encompassing everything from microtechnologies of the living and the workplace through to the built forms and created environments of cities, agrarian landscapes, and globally modified the ecosystems."[15]

The reservoirs transformed nature by supplying irrigation and thus "greenifying" an arid geography, and they also functioned as platforms for social transformations. They asked for a redefinition of a spatial experience, especially in terms of gender relationships. Giving way to new social practices, artificial nature (or the so-called beaches of Ankara) transformed the landscape of the capital and the bodies of its inhabitants.

THE BOSPORUS OF ANKARA: ÇUBUK DAM

The Çubuk Dam was constructed to regulate the waters of Çubuk Creek for Ankara's domestic, industrial, and agricultural consumption as well as for flood control. It was designed and built by a team of Turkish and German experts: Tahsin Ibrahim Bey, a graduate of the engineering school in Istanbul, Heiden Berger, a German expert in dam construction, and Walther Kunze of Karlsruhe University, who was appointed as technical consultant to the Turkish Waterworks General Directorate in 1931.[16]

Although the original project for the Çubuk Dam was a stone gravity structure in the style of its Ottoman precedents, here concrete replaced stone, as it was assumed to be more technically advanced and favored for its visually modern and progressive character.[17] Stone as a construction material and technique had associations with the Ottoman past, which had an advanced practice of waterworks, examples of which are the network of stone dams and aqueducts spreading from north of Istanbul into the walled city and finally feeding into an intricate system of distributions chambers, fountains, baths, and various other spaces that required water.[18] The Çubuk Dam was new and had to break away from the past. It was heralded as the first concrete dam in Turkey. Most of the material was imported from Germany, because concrete was not produced in Turkey at the time and therefore was expensive.

The dam had representational and symbolic significance beyond its utilitarian purpose as a reservoir: it was a showcase of the modern Kemalist regime.[19] Although most public dam projects demonstrated the power of the state over nature by their domineering presence, Çubuk Dam had a modest scale and program: it was not a hydroelectric plant but a simple reservoir.[20] The photographic album about the Çubuk Dam published by Nafia Işleri (Ministry of Public Works) contains mostly photographs framing the dam with a pastoral eye. The book is not focused on the technological aspects but rather celebrates the (artificial) natural setting created by the dam.[21] In most of the photographs, the huge body of the dam is often missing or obscured by foreground objects. These photographs emphasize the harmonious coexistence of the artificial with the natural. A writer mentions in an issue of *La Turquie Kemalist*— the propaganda journal of the Kemalist regime—that, "We will marvel at the beauty of the dam which not only provides the city with water but the populace with a beautiful outing spot."[22] The commentator chooses not to use words such as "power" or "grandeur," but "beauty." The enchantment with technology here is critically different from contemporary modernist tendencies of the 1930s in which technology becomes the means and the end. In the Çubuk Dam, technology is a means for recreating nature rather than a symbol of mastery over nature.

The dam, a pristine curved concrete wall, has several curious details: a landscaped park beneath and a restaurant-casino cantilevering over the tailwater. Designed with an elegant modernist aesthetic, the restaurant became a prime location for dining and mixed-gender entertainment—another new social practice in a model setting, part of the modernization project to transform society along Western lines. The artificial Baytın Island, located downstream from the restaurant, was connected to the shore

with a bridge and was used as a tea garden and a platform for dancing and concerts. An unusual detail in the design of the dam is the three water jets located in the tailwater across from the restaurant. As captured in a 1930s photograph, the jets shoot up water, transforming the tailwater of the dam into an urban spectacle in the spirit of ceremonial public fountains.

These social and aesthetic components remain outside the normative practices of infrastructure building: designing a restaurant overlooking the tailwater of a dam, embellishing the tailwater with water jets, including an island and a bridge in the master plan. The dam, like the reservoirs, was an outcome of a larger project to recreate an ideal nature for the new capital. Ideal nature implies more than "green" and "cultivated" in this context. It included boats, specifically, *kayık*s. Kayıks are very distinct in shape, just as the gondola is different from any other boat. As the gondola calls to mind Venice, the kayık alludes to Istanbul. As seen in images of the reservoirs and the dam, these water bodies were popular places for kayık excursions. Rowing boats in the Bosporus is an inseparable urban practice of Istanbul. Rowing boats in the reservoir, however, is a very subtle allusion to the Ottoman past from which the Kemalist revolution dissociated itself in every other way.

Opposite, top: A postcard from the 1930s showing the Çubuk Dam from the tailwater. The restaurant cantilevering over the water and a kayık are noteworthy in this photograph.

Opposite, bottom: A close-up view of the Baytın Island with a connecting bridge located in the Çubuk Dam. This island, shaded by trees, was used as a platform to organize parties and gatherings.

A postcard from the 1930s illustrating the Çubuk Dam with water jets in the tailwater.

Citizens of Ankara rowing boats in the Çubuk Dam tailwater. The water jets and the restaurant can be seen in the background.

According to a contemporary commentator: "It is very appropriate to call the dam 'the Bosporus of Ankara.' Smaller, less green and modest. Its length is only 7–8 kilometers. It is as wide as a medium-sized river. Tomorrow, the young trees will become a forest. They all bear the imprints of man's labor."[23] Despite its status as a monument of progress, the dam has other architectural components that allude to the Ottoman past. The cantilevered loggia attached to the arched body of the dam is a stripped replica of the Sultan Mahfili (Sultan's Pavilion), a major motif of Ottoman dams, such as Sultan Mahmud Dam in Istanbul, built in 1839. The dam's porticoes are detailed in the Ottoman revivalist nationalist style, which appropriated "decorative elements derived from classical Ottoman architecture."[24] Attached to the bottom of the grand curved wall of the dam, these porticoes give access to the drainage and distribution chambers, replicating the porticoes that typically marked the entrance to the distribution chambers of Ottoman dams. One portico also bears a commemorative inscription, a *kitabe,* dedicating the structure not to the sultan but to Atatürk, the capital, and the nation.

The evocation of Istanbul in the dam and the reservoirs points to the complexity of the symbolism in the making and experience of these spaces. Istanbul—cast in the republican discourse as a corrupt, imperial, cosmopolitan city, and the ideological other of nationalist, modern, and progressive Ankara—is an indirect yet dominant influence in the conception of these structures. The Çubuk Dam, while proving that the new regime can create its own nature and its modern spaces devoid of the Ottoman past, soothed the homesickness and nostalgia of the formerly Ottoman and recently Turkish citizens of Istanbul living in Ankara. This constructed nature, progressive in its making and appearance, was a transplanted Istanbul in the midst of the steppes. Even today, the neighborhood where the dam is located is still called Boğaziçi Mahallesi, meaning the Bosporus District. The ideal nature that was equated with the development of the country was a technologically (artificially) created space whose model was implicitly the nature of the former capital.

THE LAKE OF ANKARA: YOUTH PARK

The third major project that contributed to the redemption and greening of Ankara is a large artificial lake and park located in the midst of the city called the Youth Park, for which the waters of the Hatip Creek and part of the Çubuk Dam were diverted. It was initially conceived as part of German planner Herman Jansen's 1932 master plan of Ankara, on marshy land stretching between the railway station and the old city at the foot of the citadel.[25] The layout of the park included a large body of water around which recreation places such as playgrounds and tea gardens were arranged. However, the most interesting activities took place in the water; the water itself was the most celebrated part of the project. As newspapers stated, "water, Ankara's biggest yearning" was first poured into the "the dry-cracked breast of the steppe by the Çubuk Dam. But it [Çubuk Dam] is far."[26] Youth Park brought the water into the center of the new capital. In a special issue of *Public Works Journal* published in 1945, the following motivations are described for the conception of the lake: "When we decided to settle in the middle of the steppes, we became obliged to technically overcome the impossibilities of nature. Water was the scarcest gift of nature here... We had to work hard to create a lake, right at the center of the capital that would be a feast for the eyes and that could also distance us from the deprivations of the steppes."[27]

In addition to its visual and aesthetic function, the lake was also used for swimming, rowing, sailing, and ice-skating. On national holidays, swimming and rowing contests were organized as part of the celebration in the appropriately named Youth Park. The lake also contained "islands," one of which was a *kayıkhane*—a boathouse with a dock. Like the dam and the model farm, the Youth Park was one of the most popular legacies of republican Ankara, symbolizing the city's longing for the absent seashores while celebrating the technological reproduction of these shores, against all odds of nature, climate, and geography. Today, the pool remains empty and deserted.

The three projects—the Atatürk Model Farm, the Çubuk Dam, and the Youth Park Lake—are interesting precisely because they oscillate between categories and definitions that are typically in opposition. They do not lend themselves to a purely technical and utility-oriented interpretation: they are celebrations of both the technological object and artificial nature in terms of their aesthetic statements and functions. Although they are expressions of social engineering and state power, they also operate as places of popular empowerment, for they seek to transform everyday life as well. They are ambivalent in what they represent: modern and innovative spaces of a new nation, yet with allusions to the lost past and its capital.

These projects establish a point of reference for the more recent manifestations of hydraulic works in Turkey, conceived as a regional development plan. The most direct successor to the 1920s constructions is GAP, rooted in that era's quest for ideal nature and developed during the 1950s, a period identified with the first vast-scale development projects. GAP, devoid of the ambivalences and nuances of its 1920s and 1930s predecessors, constitutes an excellent example with which to elucidate the continuities and disparities between the post-World War I and post-World War II approaches in Turkey and to reveal how scale, levels of complexity in planning, and magnitudes of ambition affect the consequences of a built activity.

THE SEA OF THE SOUTHEAST ANATOLIA: GAP

With a geographical and chronological leap from the boats in Ankara to sailboats in the artificial lake of the Atatürk Dam in Urfa, we reach the largest and most celebrated part of today's Turkish hydraulic modernization. The $32-billion Southeastern Anatolia Project, a colossal regional development plan, consists of a vast system of hydroelectric plants and dams to regulate the waters of the Euphrates and the Tigris. The rivers originate in Eastern Turkey, traverse Syria and Iraq, respectively, and join the Gulf.

It would not be wrong to call the Atatürk Dam the offspring of the Çubuk Dam and subject it to an analysis of the differences and similarities of successive generations of hydraulic works undertaken as a means of modernization and development in Turkey. After the completion of the Çubuk Dam, the roots of what was to become GAP were planted with the establishment of the Directorate of Water Works in 1935. At the end of World War II and during the regime of the Democrat Party in 1954, the rather modest Directorate of Water Works was transformed into Devlet Su İşleri Genel Müdürlüğü, DSI—State Hydraulic Works General Directorate. With the foundation of this body, the entire country became the subject of a regional study and planning project. In the 1950s, the Democrat Party, upon coming to power, introduced liberal economy, contrary to the state-controlled economic model dominant since the foundation of the Turkish Republic. This shift was influenced by the Marshall Plan, a monetary aid package formulated by the United States at the end of World War II to rebuild the economies of Europe, including Turkey. This era in the new Turkish Republic is marked by investments being channeled mostly into agriculture—farmers and landowners constituted the base of the Democrat Party— and infrastructural projects, for the most part highways. Although improvement of the irrigation network was given priority, to support the development of the agricultural sector, the 1950s did not yield significant examples of artificial landscapes such as those from the 1930s. This was not due to the lack of investment in water infrastructure but, on the contrary, to a leap in scale in planning. With the newly founded DSI to cultivate the waters of the nation through a systematic approach, the 1950s can be characterized as the preparation period for a vast regional plan called GAP (Güneydoğu Anadolu Projesi), which incorporated the Euphrates and

Photograph of surfers and sailors in the Atatürk Dam Lake, taken during a choreographed performance for a national holiday celebration.

the Tigris Basins as its main resources. GAP, including the Atatürk Dam and its branches that reach into the southeast Anatolian landscapes, was born during the 1950s but would thrive during the 1980s, in the course of the second liberal economic episode in Turkey.

While the Çubuk Dam was executed "in a modest way,"[28] the Atatürk Dam was conceived as the epitome of an ambitious project of hydraulic and agricultural development. The official GAP website says: "Atatürk Dam Lake is the symbol of an important geographical change which opens up new horizons for the rich cultural heritage of the region. Extending over an area of 817 square kilometers, the lake is called 'sea' by local people."[29] The "sea" of southeast Anatolia—drought-ridden for centuries—is the conceptual continuation of the "seas" and "shores" of Ankara. It is the reiteration of an ideology of development that pursues an ideal nature, with a dramatic shift in scale and lacking most of the spatial complexities of the Çubuk Dam. GAP transforms the existing landscape, which for years has been identified with the ochre color of the local stone and the dry fields. This lexicon is now shifting to green, blue, and gray: green from the irrigated fields, and blue and gray from the huge lake and its tributaries that run through concrete canals and dikes. The natural vocabulary of the region is being replaced by what can be defined as the ideal modern landscape of the Turkish Republic.

Typical landscape vocabulary introduced by the GAP: gray concrete and blue waters.

Aerial photograph of the Atatürk Dam.

Compared with the images of Çubuk Dam, with its rowboats and picnicking public, the Atatürk Dam is a "megamachine," less concerned with public space and the modernization of everyday life than with the larger technical and ideological agenda of the nation-state.[30] The common daily kayık excursions in the Çubuk Dam, which required no permission, has turned into special-occasion choreographed sailboat performances in the state-sponsored festivities at the Atatürk Dam. The space the dam has produced is not part of the everyday lives of its inhabitants. When it is open to the public during these celebrations, the dam maintains an austere order; it is heavily guarded at all times. Unlike the public park or the tea garden and casino of Çubuk Dam, here the seats are in regular rows, and a ceremonial platform is prepared for official speeches. Held every year in early October or late September, the Water Sports Festivities recall the swimming and rowing contests held in the Youth Park. The posters for the event use a 1930s photograph of Atatürk with young swimmers. The Harvest Festivities also make use of a photo of Atatürk and his wife at the State Model Farm, a representation of a Turkey in the process of modernization by way of scientific agriculture—an ideal that GAP endorses at a colossal scale.

Unlike the Çubuk Dam, the Atatürk Dam is not a simple water reservoir: it is a hydroelectric power plant and water management center. It demonstrates how, with a massive scale and in the absence of a mitigating ambivalence, the modernist vision of mastering nature can become an oversimplified "high modernist" blueprint—a blueprint that disregards the complexity of nature and pays no heed to the fact that geography includes history, culture, and existing patterns of cultivation and settlement.

Evidence of this dominant and oversimplified attitude toward nature includes large inscriptions spread across the landscape. An inscription carved into the concrete wall in the Atatürk Dam reads, "How Proud I am to be a Turk!" The technological icon thus becomes a medium for the expression of national pride and power. Another inscription, located on the hills facing the main water channel where the water is forcefully released from the Atatürk Dam, reads: "We have pierced the mountains; we have pierced the epochs!", a quote from a speech by the prime minister of Turkey Süleyman Demirel, given in 1994. In addition to these assertions inscribed on the topography, the initials of the State Hydraulic Works, DSİ, are imprinted all over southeastern Anatolia like a brand name responsible for the production of the new landscape. They are narratives forged into the landscape that talk about progress and nationalism. Compared to the 1920s and 1930s infrastructural works, where the creation of a green and fertile landscape produced its own space with its own rituals, this new landscape does not materialize as a social space but rather reduces the landscape to a monologue of the state. With such an immense scale of intervention and the lack of intention to promote spatial and social practices, the outcome of GAP is a physical phenomenon with solely political, ecological, and economical outcomes.

Today, with its colossal scale, GAP creates complex problems in lieu of complex spaces. Given the massive interventions on the Euphrates and Tigris rivers, GAP creates ecological concerns in addition to international water rights conflicts. The two rivers have their sources in Turkey, and therefore the dams constitute a means of control

"Ne Mutlu Türk'üm Diyene" (How Proud I Am to Be a Turk), famous words of Atatürk inscribed onto the Atatürk Dam's concrete wall.

One of many inscriptions found in the artificial landscapes of the GAP, DSİ is the abbreviation for State Water Works Directorate.

over the flow of water to the downstream countries, Syria and Iraq. With water scarce in this region, its possession and control translates to political and economic power, as Stephen Kinzer points out: "The Tigris and Euphrates Rivers created the 'Fertile Crescent' where some of the first civilizations emerged. Today they are immensely important resources, politically as well as geographically. Through a system of dams in its southeastern provinces, Turkey controls their flow and is determined not to give up its control."[31]

On the other hand, the dams and the dam lakes created as constructed landscapes often obliterate the historical landscape. The priceless mosaics in Zeugma, a Roman archeological site discovered within the flood plain of a dam, were barely salvaged and stored in Gaziantep Museum before the site was flooded. In many flooded areas, large numbers of people get displaced. As a grand project of development, GAP is the physical product of a quantitative understanding, which defines development only as "growth in the income per person in [an] economically underdeveloped area."[32] This ideology considers nature and landscape as a resource to be harvested toward economic growth and state control. It has become increasingly less possible to talk about the human-scale sensitivities and spatial ingenuities, qualities that existed in the early Republican-era projects as a result of their relatively intimate scales. As the scales of the projects grew from ponds to megamachines, the resolution of the relationship between nature and its inhabitants became blurry—blurry enough to lose the details and the humility of the constructions that sought an *ideal nature* by bringing about a complex landscape and a complex space that embodied future, history, culture, agriculture, and aesthetics.

Notes

1 Yaşar Nabi Nayır, "Yazın Ankara," *Ulus*, May 31, 1938.

2 Jean-Jacques Rousseau, *The Social Contract* (London: Penguin Books, 1968), 125.

3 Falih Rıfkı Atay, *Çankaya* (İstanbul: Doğan Kardeş, 1969), 356. Journalist and writer Atay states the correlation of climate and human nature in his memoirs: "This (Ankara) is a plateau and on this high platform most rich civilizations have been born and prospered... Professor of Climatologie et Hydrologie Therapetique, Mr. Piery, in his oeuvre 'Traite de Climatologie Biologie et Medicale,' states that despite the fact that he considers the climate a steppe, he explains the abundance of the factors here that enable the establishment of a civilization: 'This climate is a unique school to train souls to endure difficulties. People here have adopted it as a moral to fight the rebelliousness of nature. They can adapt to the most hot and most cold weather. This climate develops the ability of initiatives and moral energy.'"

4 Illustrated in Burçak Evren, *20'li Yılların Bozkır Kasabası Ankara* (İstanbul: AD Kitapçılık AŞ, 1998), 63.

5 Ibid., 63.

6 From the speech given by Atatürk to the farmers of Adana on May 16, 1923, quoted in *Atatürk ve Tarım* (Ankara: Tarım ve Orman Bakanlığı-Ankara Ziraat Fakültesi, 1981), 19.

7 Ernst Egli, "Mimari Muhit" in *Türk Yurdu*, no-30-224 (1930): 32–33.

8 Lefebvre, *Production of Space* (Oxford and Cambridge, MA: Blackwell, 1991), 33.

9 Ibid., 39.

10 Celebrations were almost always associated with water in the capital of the Ottoman Empire, not to mention the overwhelming visual and material existence of water in Istanbul. Especially from the eighteenth century on, water became the marker of urban space and life. For extensive accounts on the importance of the Bosphorus, boat excursions, fountains, and their manifestation as urban spectacle, see Shirine Hamadeh, "The City's Pleasures: Architectural Sensibility in Eighteenth-Century Istanbul," Ph.D. dissertation, Cambridge, MIT, 1998, 39. Also see Tulay Artan, "Architecture as a Theatre of Life: Profile of the Eighteenth-Century Bosphorus," Ph.D. dissertation, Cambridge, MIT, 1989.

11 David Harvey, *Justice, Nature and Geographies of Difference* (Cambridge, MA: Blackwell, 1996), 105.

12 Uğur Tanyeli and Arzu Öztürkmen both state that prominent among the various symbolic spaces that represented the Early Republic were the beaches. They helped redefine the former public experiences in terms of gender relationships. Uğur Tanyeli, "Mekanlar, Projeler, Anlamları," in *Üç Kuşak Cumhuriyet* (İstanbul: Türk Tarih Vakfı Yayınları, 1998), 101-113, and Arzu Öztürkmen, "Cumhuriyetin Eğlenceleri," 69–71.

13 *Ulus*, "Çiftlikte Yaz," June 28, 1938.

14 Sibel Bozdoğan, *Modernism and Nation Building: Turkish Architectural Culture in the Early Republic* (Seattle: University of Washington Press, 2001), 75.

15 Harvey, Justice, Nature, and Geographies of Difference, 79.

16 Bedri Ölçer, *Çubuk I Barajı* (Ankara: DSİ Matbaası, 1971).

17 I use the word "assume" here, because material, stone or concrete, cannot solely determine the strength or the technological advancement of a dam. As is also acknowledged in the geological and engineering reports of Çubuk Dam itself, foundation conditions, the structure type, and many more criteria determine the material and shape. However, the shape of the dam, an arched concrete gravity structure, is considered to be structurally advanced.

18 For further information and visual reference, see Kazım Çeçen, *Sinan's Water Supply System in Istanbul* (İstanbul: İTÜ and İSKİ, 1991); *İstanbul Vakıf Sularından Üsküdar Suları* (İstanbul: İTÜ, 1991), and *İstanbul Vakıf Sularından Halkalı Suları* (İstanbul: İTÜ, 1992).

19 Bozdoğan, *Modernism and Nation Building*, 75.

20 There is, for example, the Dnieperostroi Dam in the USSR, built around the same time, and the Huaihe Water Management System of post-Revolutionary China in the 1950s. Another example is the TVA project, a system of dams on the Tennessee River built to provide hydroelectric power, flood control, and soil conservation.

21 *Çubuk Barajı* (Nafia İşleri Vekaleti Neşriyatı, no. 8, Devlet Basım Evi, 1939).

22 "Ankara-Istanbul," *La Turquie Kemaliste* (1941): 53.

23 *Ulus*, "Ankara'nın Boğaziçi'si," July 26,1937. Translation mine.

24 Bozdoğan, *Modernism and Nation Building*, 18.

25 Turning marshes into agricultural land or parks was a central trope in other modernization projects such as those of Italy under fascism. See Diane Yvonne Ghirardo, *Building New Communities: New Deal America and Fascist Italy* (Princeton, N.J.: Princeton University Press, 1989). The State Model farm was also located on marshlands.

26 Nafia İşleri Dergisi (1942): 2.

27 Ibid., p.3

28 Atatürk, in his famous 20 April 1934 speech, said that "While grand hydraulic projects are our ideals, today we can certainly say this: our first ideal

is to succeed in small-scale hydraulic works in a modest way."

29 GAP Southeastern Anatolia Project Regional Development Administration Website: www.gap.gov.tr (accessed March 2000).

30 A term introduced by Lewis Mumford as a "rigid, hierarchical social organization" in Lewis Mumford, *The Myth of the Machine* (New York: Harcourt, Brace, and World, 1967), 43. As examples of the megamachine, Mumford points to the Great Pyramid and the world wars. Both were enabled by the organization of vast numbers of men, creating a human machine with great precision.

31 For a short but intelligent account of water as power in southeast Anatolia, see Stephen Kinzer, "Where Kurds Seek a Land, Turks Want the Water," *New York Times,* "The World" section, Feb. 28, 1999.

32. Gustavo Esteva, "Development," in *The Development Dictionary* (New Jersey: Zed Books Ltd., 1992), 12.

NEYRAN TURAN

2

THE STRAIT, THE BEACH, AND THE HIGHWAY:
SHIFTING EDGES OF ISTANBUL

Twentieth-century Istanbul was the context for a constant dialogue between geography
and urbanism. Fueled by the city's ever-changing geopolitical positioning and urban
growth, this dialogue generated particular relationships between the city and its landscape and territory. Examining the urbanism of twentieth-century Istanbul from this
new perspective, I will focus in this chapter on particular episodes in the evolution of
Istanbul. As part of a larger investigation of the potential interaction between geography, politics, and urbanism, this essay proposes that elucidating underexplored interactions among qualities typically understood to be unrelated or external to Istanbul's
urbanism allows for an alternative reading of urban history, one that takes geographies,
territories, and infrastructures into account, rather than merely surveying edifices
(buildings and monuments, etc.) and their urban surroundings.

   I address here three spatial elements and their transformation: the strait, the
beach, and the highway. In the first section, the modernity project of the early years of
the Republic of Turkey in the 1930s and its relation to urban landscape and geography
is explored through the contemporaneous political condition of the Bosphorus Strait.
With reference to the *Boğaziçi* magazine published in the 1930s, a new sensibility toward
urban landscape is explored in relation to the national territoriality of the Bosphorus. In
the second section, beaches of the 1930s are examined as the ideal public spaces for the
conjunction of the modernity project of Turkey and issues of territoriality. The third section looks at 1950s Istanbul by examining how changing geopolitical conditions were

reflected in the recontouring of the edge of the city with new highways. As the "modern nation-building"[1] project and national territoriality of the 1930s transformed into "modernization," "development," and "modern city-building" projects in the 1950s, there was a shift from a territorial to an infrastructural understanding of urban landscape.

THE STRAIT AND BOĞAZİÇİ

In 1936, a monthly journal was launched in Istanbul. Titled *Boğaziçi*—"The Bosphorus" in Turkish—the publication was sponsored by Şirket-i Hayriye, the Ottoman Empire's first inner-city maritime transportation company, founded in the nineteenth century. Due to the diminishing population in Istanbul after World War I and the construction of a tramline along the Bosphorus route in the 1930s, the company had experienced a decline in the numbers of passengers using their ships; the company created *Boğaziçi* as part of a campaign to illustrate the beauty of the Bosphorus and attract Istanbul residents to settle in the area.[2]

With the growth of the Ottoman economy in the nineteenth century and migration from lost territories in Europe, the population of Istanbul had reached 1 million by the end of the nineteenth century, nearly tripling that of the early 1800s. By the 1920s, however, the population had diminished to about 500,000.[3] This decrease was related to many factors: the exodus of higher-income groups, including foreign departures during World War I; migrations from Istanbul to Anatolia in response to economic pressures stemming from the war; and the relocation of bureaucracy (including embassies and military officials) from Istanbul to Ankara, the new capital city of the Turkish Republic.[4] By the 1930s, although still the most populated city of the country (in 1935, the population of Izmir and Ankara were 171,000 and 123,000 respectively) and with a slightly increasing population rate, the effects of the decrease in the 1920s were still felt in the city.[5]

To promote settlement in the area, Şirket-i Hayriye and the contributing authors of *Boğaziçi* called on the government to build housing and infrastructure such as schools, sport clubs, and other facilities. It was also repeatedly announced in the journal that for people building new houses along the Bosphorus, construction materials would be transported free of charge. In addition, residents would receive a government tax waiver as well as a free pass for transportation, valid for three years.[6] Şirket-i Hayriye even bought land, announcing in the journal that it would be sold to Istanbul residents at no profit. The journal also featured architectural/urban projects undertaken by the company. For instance, the company announced that it would construct a primary school in Kandilli (a small town on the Anatolian side of the Bosphorus), designed by a "precious Turkish architect," and that it had already purchased land near the school for seven housing units.[7]

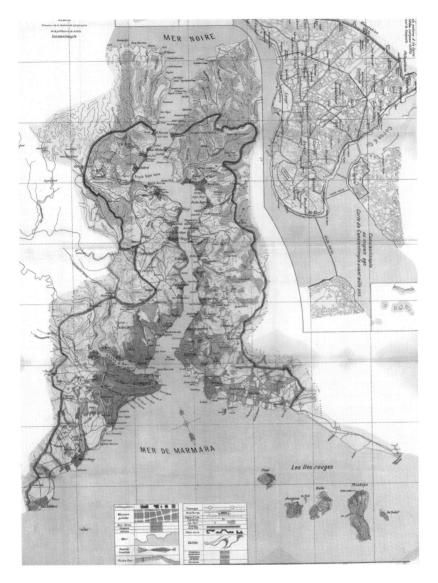

Istanbul and the Bosphorus in 1910. The urban fabric of the 1930s was not dissimilar
from that of the 1910s, where the population was mostly distributed among the
historical peninsula, Beyoğlu on the European side, Kadıköy and Üsküdar on the Asian
side, and the Bosphorus shoreline.

The journal can be regarded as a compilation of documents illustrating the reception of urban developments within the intellectual milieu of the time—that is, the era during which French architect/urban planner Henri Prost (1874–1959) started his work at the Planning Department of the Istanbul Municipality and Governorship and was appointed to develop a master plan for the city. The Early Republican government turned its attention to Istanbul in the mid-1930s, after an emphasis on the development of Ankara with the commissioning of German planner Herman Jansen (1896–1947) to prepare a city plan for the new capital.[8] In 1933, the government organized a limited competition to select an urban planner for Istanbul, inviting four planners to participate: Donald Alfred Agache (who had prepared the master plan of Rio de Janerio), Henri Prost (Chief of the Planning Bureau of Paris), H. Lambert, and Hermann Elgötz. Prost declined the invitation; Agache, Lambert, and Elgötz submitted their proposals the same year. The proposals shared common features such as recommendations for new urban transportation networks, the relocation of the port, functional zoning, and conservation of monuments.[9] Elgötz's proposal won the competition, but his plan was never implemented.[10]

An illustration by Cemal Nadir (Güler) in the *Boğaziçi* journal depicting the "old" versus the "new" Bosphorus. The illustration is titled "The Ones Thinking about the Bosphorus: 100 years ago." The documents sitting on the table of the "architect/engineer" says "Development Plan, Suspended Bridge."

In 1936, as *Boğaziçi* began publication, Henri Prost was invited once again to Istanbul (this time personally by President Mustafa Kemal Atatürk) to prepare the master plan for the city. Prost accepted the invitation, moved to Istanbul in 1936, and acted as the chief planner of Istanbul until 1950.[11] How was *Boğaziçi* related to these urban development plans as well as to the encouragement of citizens to settle in the Bosphorus? Perhaps more important, why is this a significant episode in the context of Istanbul in the 1930s?

Before elaborating on this question, a description of some of *Boğaziçi*'s content might be helpful. Based on the belief that the Bosphorus would be far easier, quicker, and cheaper to develop than the entire city of Istanbul, one author proposed that a "Bosphorus Development Bank" be established to invest in the area.[12] Because of the availability of vast land, it was argued that modest funding would be enough for the development of the Bosphorus, and that the capital of the proposed bank could easily be provided by the Real Estate Bank, Istanbul Municipality, Şirket-i Hayriye, the Government Estates Office, state banks, landowners in the area, and the "wealthy lovers" of the Bosphorus.[13] The desire for the development of the Bosphorus was complemented by various cartoons in the journal depicting the "new" Bosphorus as the landscape of modernity and development in contrast to the "old" Bosphorus, which connoted the idea of leisure and idleness.

In the same volume, other authors offered contradictory views concerning the coastal highway proposed by Prost along the northwestern bank of the Bosphorus.[14] In his essay, "The Bosphorus Tomorrow: The Bosphorus According to the Preliminary Plans of Urban Planner Prost," Burhan Morkaya, a noted writer of the time, celebrated Prost's plan for the Bosphorus and chided those "who portrayed the Bosphorus as an imagination, retreat and pleasure corner that belongs to the [Ottoman] Empire period and needs to be abandoned like an antique."[15] Praising the proposed 17-meter-wide coastal highway by Prost at the European (north) side of the Bosphorus, Morkaya suggested that the city would grow toward this new highway with houses with gardens, like the New Town (*Yenişehir*) of Ankara, in opposition to the "concrete bulk" of apartment buildings in inner Istanbul.[16] For Morkaya, the Bosphorus would not only provide a perfect setting for a true Garden City (as implemented in Ankara by Jansen), with its topography and picturesque views, but would also delineate the future growth of Istanbul: "Prost, who can clearly see the future and needs [of the city], has correctly understood that the direction of the city's expansion will be through the Bosphorus."[17]

Hüseyin Cahit Yalçın, also a well-known writer of the time, disagreed, criticizing the proposed coastal highways for giving an impression of "building a city from scratch." He wrote: "Are we are going to draw a chess board [gridiron on the Bosphorus] like an American city, which lacks any history and…masterpiece? Are we going to number our streets like newly born children whose parents are unknown?"[18]

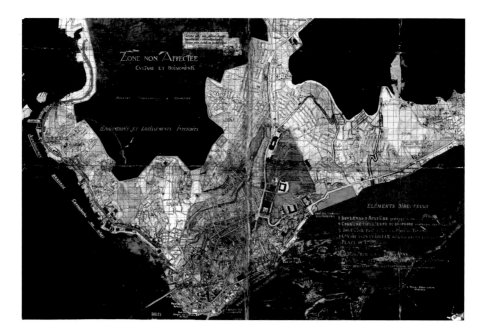

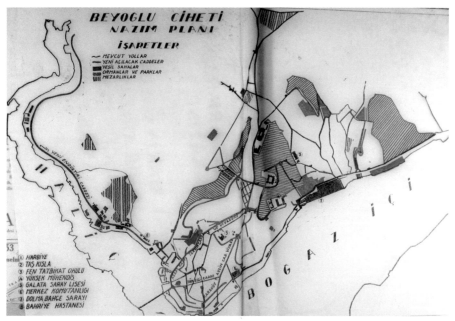

Top: 1937 Henri Prost plan showing Beyoğlu and the European side of the Bosphorus.

Bottom: Master plan of the European side of the Bosphorus from the Istanbul Municipality publication of 1939, illustrating the new roads to be constructed (in red).

Part of the caricature drawing by Cemal Nadir (Güler) from the *Boğaziçi* journal. The caricature compares the morning in the city (left) and at the Bosphorus (right).

The reaction against "concrete bulk" was understandable, especially if one considers the rise in apartment buildings during the 1930s in Istanbul.[19] More specifically, the Bosphorus was positioned as a counter to the apartment-building phenomenon in the "narrow and dark" city center: "With its unrivaled green hills, two sides of the Bosphorus are looking at each other with uncertainty. In contrast, the shapeless stone bulk is constantly rising at the narrow and dark center of the city."[20]

Despite disparate views on the Prost plan and the nature of urban developments in the city, one thing was certain: new development was desired on the "unrivaled hills" of the Bosphorus. More than a simple appreciation of visual pleasures in relation to the picturesque of the Bosphorus or a typical modernist reflection on the binary opposition of nature (garden city) versus city (artifact), this desire was ultimately linked to a much broader agenda.

BOSPHORUS, LANDSCAPE, GEOGRAPHY

Apart from illustrating the intellectual reception of urban developments, these examples provide a clear depiction of a different spatial sensibility that registered the city as landscape and geography. In addition to the majority of the articles in the journal that highlighted the picturesque aesthetic of the Bosphorus by focusing on its history, rich climatic zoning, and touristic potential, one could find articles written by bacteriologists pinpointing the positive health effects of the Bosphorus weather, suggesting a pseudo-scientific/modernist understanding of territory.[21]

In the journal, the sensibility toward the terrain was coupled with an appreciation of the population of the territory. Rather than proposing only new developments on the Bosphorus, the use of existing resources was promoted. For instance, Şirket-i Hayriye published an extensive booklet listing all vacant housing units along the Bosphorus (both rental and sale properties) that was distributed as an annual insert to *Boğaziçi*.[22] The booklet provided the name of the owner, the exact address, number of rooms, and monthly and yearly price of the unit.

Photomontages from the *Boğaziçi* journal. In the background, we see vistas from the Bosphorus.

Şirket-i Hayriye was a privately owned company, but the booklet was printed at the government-owned State Press, implying possible connections to government policies.[23] Because of the shrinking of the urban economy in Istanbul after World War I and during the early years of the Republic, economic concern was shared by local business circles and the central government. With the government's strong emphasis on building the new capital in Ankara, countervailing pressure was coming from business and trade circles in Istanbul.[24] Thus Şirket-i Hayriye's attempts could also be seen in the context of reactivating the urban economy rather than merely as commercial interest in stimulating more shipping business.

The new sensibility toward landscape and geography was also evidenced by the visual material featured in the journal. In photomontages, elements of a modern lifestyle (women, cars, and other images, mostly collected from European publications) were superimposed onto photographs of the Bosphorus. In relation to the political context of the time, these collages were in some ways similar yet also different from other visual representations of the "new" and "modern," which the "Kemalist woman" or modern cars typically connoted.[25] In this case, Istanbul did not seem to stand for an oppositional realm to the old but rather as a reframing landscape that facilitated various activities. The representational superimposition of these photomontages could be argued as a projection of a new vision onto Istanbul's geography, integrating the modern nation-building project of the new Republic with its new vision of the Bosphorus landscape.

THE STRAIT AND THE GEOPOLITICAL

Appearing in the December 1936 issue of *Boğaziçi*, an article written by Peyami Safa (1899–1961), a prominent Republican author of the time, helps to further contextualize the previously discussed sensibility on the Bosphorus landscape and geography as well its geopolitical association. Titled "The Defense of the Straits and the Bosphorus," Safa's article encouraged residents of Istanbul to settle in the Bosphorus area, as did other articles in the journal, but with a specific rationale.[26] Whereas other articles legitimized the support for settlement and a sense of local belonging with picturesque aesthetics, health, and recreation, Safa promoted the idea of "belonging" and "appropriation" with wider connotations such as the territorial belonging of the Bosphorus to Turkey.

Safa began his article with a reminder that other countries had always "burned with desire" to have the Bosphorus Strait. Later noting that the Bosphorus waterway, "flowing like a wine river," had even "intoxicated" Russians from a distance, Safa wrote:

> In the minds of various foreigners, the fact that Bosphorus is the symbol of Istanbul and Istanbul is the symbol of Turkey has not yet faded. This fact, whether meant by true or false intentions, should remind us of our various responsibilities: We should be aware of the fact that we can only resist foreign desires by embracing the Bosphorus. Not embracing the Bosphorus and not appropriating it suggests the idea that we do not deserve to live in its magnificent nature and inflates others' ambitions with great hope. **The defense of the Straits is possible with fortification, war and arming; but as for the defense of the Bosphorus, it can only be possible by embracing, appropriating, settling and living in it.** For many years now, although not facing any invasion of any sort, we have been constantly evacuating the Bosphorus...Why? The reason is not a lack of good taste. It is the sign of an unseen invasion that we are trying to escape, an invasion of negligence and desolation. The public cannot resist and do this all alone, nor can the Municipality, Şirket-i Hayriye, or the Government. There needs to be a common front for all of this. To save the Bosphorus, this front is viewed as an aesthetic contention for the sake of its beauty, but in reality it is nothing more than a front for the sake of national defense.[27]

Safa's assertion not only complicates our understanding of *Boğaziçi* and its call for settlement in the Bosphorus as merely a promotional enterprise aimed at producing business for the company's ships but also elucidates the (inter)national positioning of the Bosphorus Strait. It is not a coincidence that *Boğaziçi* was launched just three months after the signing of the Montreux Convention concerning the sovereignty of the Turkish Straits (Bosphorus and Dardanelles Straits).[28] The convention was an important treaty for Turkey that resolved a centuries-long territorial and maritime conflict. In ancient times, the Bosphorus Strait was an important route to control communication and trade between the Mediterranean and Black Seas; in the second century A.D., Aristides referred to the strait as the "Pontus [Black Sea] Key" to emphasize the control aspect of the gate that the residents of the ancient city could "lock" for various reasons.[29] With the conquest of the city in 1453 by the Ottoman Empire, the strait would become a space completely enclosed and controlled by the empire for about 300 years, or until the Russian-Turkish conflict that ended with a treaty in 1774, through which Russia gained power over the Black Sea and the privilege to pass merchant ships through the

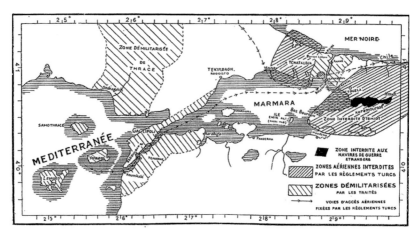

DÉTROITS
Zones démilitarisées, Zones interdites et Voies d'accès aériennes.

Demilitarization of the Turkish Straits (after World War I, before the Montreux Convention) as illustrated in the League of Nations Annual Straits Report of 1933.

straits. In the nineteenth century, the strait gained international importance mainly within the triangle of Britain, Russia, and the Ottoman Empire, a status that was intensified by Great Britain's control over the nearby waterways through the occupation of Cyprus and the Suez Canal.

The conflict remained unresolved until the defeat of the Ottoman Empire in World War I, after which the Zone of Straits was demilitarized and internationalized according to the Treaty of Sèvres of 1920. After the Turkish Independence War in 1924, the area was officially demilitarized by the Treaty of Lausanne, at which time control was appointed to the International Straits Commission under the auspices of the League of Nations. Demilitarization according to the Treaty of Lausanne covered both the land and territorial waters of the strait area. By the middle of the 1930s, concerned for its territorial sovereignty, Turkey called for a conference under the auspices of the League of Nations to review the Treaty of Lausanne, requesting acknowledgment of the sovereignty rights over the straits and the transfer of control to the Turkish government. The resulting conference that convened in Montreux, Switzerland, in 1936 produced the Montreux Convention for the Straits, still in force today. The convention gave Turkey sovereign rights over the straits to remilitarize it, and transferred control from the International Commission to the Turkish government while simultaneously declaring "complete freedom of passage and navigation" of the straits. Less than a month after the Montreux Convention was enacted, the Turkish government started modernizing the fortifications on the Bosphorus and the Dardanelles shores and extending them through military zones of defense.

BOĞAZİÇİ

Turkish flag and the Bosphorus as represented on the cover of *Boğaziçi* 14 (November 1937).

A comparison of the two Straits Annual Reports prepared before and after the Montreux Convention, one prepared by the International Straits Commission of the League of Nations and the other by the Turkish Government, in 1934 and 1938 respectively, would evidence the spatial consequences of the territorial changes that came with the convention, along with their repercussions on the Bosphorus landscape.[30] The League and Turkish reports included maps that portrayed the changes regarding control of the terrain, territorial waters, and airspaces, and specifically, the demilitarization of the Bosphorus territory (in the former) and remilitarization of it (in the latter).[31]

Boğaziçi's relation to the Montreux Convention and related territorial changes becomes more explicit in the first pages of the premiere issue of the journal in October 1936, which announced the recent decree about territorial changes along the Bosphorus, listing the areas that were transformed into "second-degree prohibited zones."[32] Giving a detailed description from military law, the announcement informed citizens that "according to the terms of this law,...other than foreigners, to accommodate, to travel, or to cultivate within this zone is free for all Turkish citizens."[33]

Although the strait was remilitarized by Turkey with the Montreux Convention, since the convention declared the passage as an international waterway within Turkish territory, international ships would still be using the waterway freely. Written only two months after the remilitarization of the straits, Safa's assertions clearly situate the promotion of settlement in the area and the appreciation of its geography in its political landscape.

"INTERNATIONAL" ISTANBUL

The Bosphorus had been an international strait since the eighteenth century; therefore the fin de siècle marked an unprecedented moment within the geopolitical history of Istanbul. With the weakening of the Ottoman Empire, discussions regarding the "extra-territorial" features of Istanbul and its condition as an "international right-of-way" would be pervasive.[34] Especially after the Ottomans lost World War I and no European power wanted others to gain control over the Bosphorus, the city's geopolitical role would be paradoxically intertwined with its "internationality."

A special issue of the *Architectural Review* in 1919, titled the "Peace Commemoration Number," presented a number of proposals for a future capital city for the League of

Nations.[35] Among articles in favor of Geneva, Brussels, and other cities, one written by a British parliament member was titled "Constantinople as the G.H.Q. of Peace." This piece opposed of the idea of Geneva as the League capital and instead proposed Istanbul as a perfect candidate.[36] Suggesting that "the headquarters city of the League of Nations will be looked upon as the Capital of the World" and that "Constantinople may...be associated with the world as a whole and with no particular sect of mankind,"[37] the argument was justified through the city's "extraterritorial" potential—the geopolitical role of the Bosphorus Strait. Written in the postwar climate and before the demilitarization of the Bosphorus by the League of Nations, the article advocated for the "internationalization" of Istanbul—the occupation and the administration of the city by an international commission. The author writes:

> No statesman can say to which nation Constantinople should be awarded. The strategical situation of the place is such that a strong power is made too strong by its ownership...For the home of the League we need a spot guarded as far as possible by the waters of the ocean—a fortress of freedom wherein no single nation can claim a right of influence...The first essentials of the Capital of the League are that it should be ex-territorial, international, and be endowed with the pomp and circumstance which are necessary in Peace as in War. Constantinople entirely fulfills these conditions. Nothing could be easier than to make it exterritorial and international. Its freehold must belong to the League. Constantinople would not be a State within a State. It would be a State by itself—the property of all. There is no other city that could be utilized in this manner.[38]

This very tension of "internationality" would elicit apprehension and ultimately a geographic understanding of the city-landscape after the remilitarization of the territory in the 1930s. The Bosphorus topography, with its changing heights and curves, allowed visibility of the appropriated national territory as international ships were navigating along the waterway in the 1930s; the "aesthetic" of the Bosphorus and the recurring call for settlement along the shores were related not only to international/territorial sovereignty relations over the sea but also to a complicated relationship between the aesthetic, the geographic, and the modern. This marked a new appreciation of the city as landscape— not merely monuments or buildings but geographies and territories as well.

LANDSCAPES OF VISIBILITY: THE STRAIT AND THE BEACH

Another episode occurring in Istanbul in the 1930s relates to the appreciation of the Bosphorus as a landscape of visibility, geopolitics, and modernity. As early as 1935, the Istanbul Festival based on sea sports on the Bosphorus began to be organized by the Istanbul municipality, and the construction of beach spaces and sea clubs increased dramatically.[39]

The beach is a space of contesting scales and boundaries. While involving the scale of the singular (body) with its direct engagement with nature (immersion and swimming), it also exposes an unconventional mode of public space. As with the photomontages in *Boğaziçi*, the pleasure gained by the view was both complicated and facilitated by the political imperatives of the time, in which the "Bosphorus as a landscape" served as a perfect intersection of national territoriality and the new vision of modern Turkish society. With the beach example, I would like to broaden the argument with not only representational but also bodily and social connotations. The immense increase in the number of beaches along the shores of Istanbul (sometimes with a state sponsorship) in the early years of the Republic was a reflection of the modern society-building project, increased sovereignty over the straits, and new ideas of public space. Here, in addition to its literal meaning, immersion also implies social and political engagement with the sea.

The beach, or immersion in water, is a phenomenon that began to appear in eighteenth-century England and France. Until then, the seashore was a great unknown that aroused horror. In the new aesthetic category of the sublime of the eighteenth century, the ocean was one of the foremost "astonishing" stimuli for the senses.[40] The first engagements with seawater began with a therapeutic objective: sudden immersion in cold water was believed "to cure the disorders of the soul." [41]

Almost simultaneous with the European sea-bathing machines, private sea-bathing (*deniz hamamı*) units started to appear along the Bosphorus as early as the eighteenth century. By 1867 there were sixty-two sea-bathing units along the shores of Istanbul.[42] Early beach life in Istanbul developed during the armistice years after World War I (1918–1922), when Russian refugees who had escaped the 1917 October Revolution settled in Istanbul. The first beach site of the city was created in the 1920s by the refugees in Florya.[43] After President Atatürk visited the site in 1935 and requested that a summer residence be built over the water on Florya Beach, this became an important recreation area. Architecturally, this summer residence is an important building in the history of the early Republican era of Turkey, since it is one of the "small but prominent samples of modernist-rationalist sensibility" of the time.[44] The building was designed by architect Seyfi Arkan (1904–1966), often considered to be "the first true Turkish modernist" architect, who interpreted a European aesthetic formal language in his work.[45] Arkan was selected for the project by Atatürk himself. The president used the residence from 1936 until his death in 1938, hosting international guests and spending days at the beach where he met with the public and sometimes even played soccer with his cabinet officers.[46] When crowds came to Florya to see how Atatürk "rested on the sands among other swimmers with burned skin,"[47] the beach became an unconventional site of social encounters.

Meeting with the public was not predetermined by the residence's location, but instead was a deliberate consideration that is argued to have affected the selection of this project by Arkan. Some historians note that after Atatürk examined the plans, he thanked Arkan for the appropriateness of the design for his own living and working

"Atatürk at the Florya Beach." Mansion construction is seen at the back.

style, and especially for the design's consideration of the beach and landscape around the mansion. Atatürk is reported to have said to Arkan, "I am very pleased to see that you studied me with my citizens."[48]

The other architect commissioned for this project was Martin Wagner (1885–1957), previously the chief city planner and councilor of Berlin in Weimar Germany.[49] Although Wagner was engaged to design the mansion, the beach environs, and a housing settlement in the area, Arkan's project was directly commissioned by Atatürk and immediately implemented.[50]

In parallel to Wagner's ongoing research and interest on city-countryside relationships (*Stadtlandschaft*) and the Garden City model, Wagner's project proposed a new housing development in the Florya environs, which included a Garden City (*Gardenstadt*) with detached houses and gardens, a school, a stadium, a resort city (*Wasserstadt)* by the waterfront, and a mansion for Atatürk.[51]

After losing the commission, Wagner intensely criticized Arkan's work as a "mishmash of Corbusier and Mies" in a letter written to Walter Gropius:[52]

Gropius, if you could only see here the sins committed by Corbusier and the Moderns by having trained fashion designers rather than architects, you would chase all your successors out of the temple....A young Talmi student of Poelzig [Seyfi Arkan], has now come here with the reputation of his master and is whipping out a sort of mishmash of Corbusier and Mies. In the bathing-resort of Florya,

Wagner's project for the Florya Beach and environs.

a suburb of Istanbul, we faced each other...In consequence, Seyfi designed a villa of Wansee [Wagner had designed a sea-bathing resort in Berlin-Wansee in 1928-30 with R. Ermisch that evoked the forms of a floating ship], and I, as a Berliner, went back to the function of the superb kiosks in Constantinople, and designed a real *maison de plaissarce* on the water....But before I had even finished my project, Seyfi could carry out his design...The worst part is that a "modern" building of this type pleases the people here because it has the appearance of being a "functional building" even it's actually far removed from its essential functions.[53]

While the preference for a modernist aesthetic seems not surprising for the recently established modern Republic, what merits further reflection is the dimension of the landscape—the preference for a modern public beach over a Garden City template as proposed by Wagner. Considering the extensive use of the Garden City model in the newly built areas in Ankara and concomitant local desires for turning the Bosphorus landscape to a Garden City (as discussed earlier via the authors of *Boğaziçi* journal), why was it not a plausible idea for Atatürk in Florya? Why would having a public beach next to his mansion be more crucial than a new Garden City?

An obvious answer would be a lack of resources for the development of Istanbul (a public beach being less expensive to fund than a new city) or a simple desire for modernist form. Another speculation could be made regarding the significance of the visibility of the modern man and women with their bathing suits in a modern pub-

Florya Beach after Arkan's mansion project was constructed.

lic space. Coinciding with the developments regarding the Montreux Convention, the visibility of dispersed beaches and public spaces along the Bosphorus territory might have been considered more important than a Garden City urban development at the outskirts of the city.[54]

Numerous beaches were built along the shores of Istanbul during the same period, some ordered directly by Atatürk.[55] After swimming was banned outside of designated beach or swimming areas in 1934, new beaches were created, some located at the edges of the city, some replacing the old public sea-bathing locations. Although built during the same years, each beach was different in terms of the entrepreneurship behind its creation and in its relation to the urban surroundings. For instance, Süreyya Beach was constructed by a former parliamentary representative who is considered to be a prominent—perhaps even the first—example of an "urban leader" in the early years of the Turkish Republic, and whose main goal was the modernization of the city.[56] Another entrepreneurial force behind the new beaches was Şirket-i Hayriye, which built beaches and organized special trips to the spots. The early beaches of Istanbul became recreation sites for the aristocracy. For instance, various forms of theater plays and musical recitals were held, and famous artists of the time would participate. The beach site evidently presented an unconventional but appealing social setting.

In the context of the modernity project of the early years of the Republic, various places for public recreation (parks, sport facilities, pleasure gardens, etc.) were built in Turkey (mostly in Ankara) in the 1930s. Associated with an image of youth and health, recreations were "school[s] for socializing people into modern citizens."[57] The relationship of sport-recreation and politics, concurrent with similar developments in Germany, Italy, and the Soviet Union (linked with Fascism, Nazism, and Socialism), was quite prominent in the early years of the Turkish Republic.[58] This relationship became visible especially with the agglomeration of bodies and their collective movements in mass gymnasiums.[59] However, although the beaches had connotations of sport and ideology, they can also be viewed as a different form of public space in terms of the social encounters and visibility they created. As noted by some historians, Atatürk "made speeches, but never in front of large crowds at organized rallies as Hitler and Mussolini... [h]e wanted to mold his people rather than mobilize and energize them in order to manipulate them."[60] The early beaches of Istanbul acted a perfect "molding" space for the modernity project of the early Republican Turkey.

Other modern recreational spaces of the time, such as Youth Park (Gençlik Parkı), Çubuklu Dam, Atatürk Model Farm and Forest (Atatürk Orman Çiftliği) in Ankara, and Taksim Park (Taksim Gezi Parkı) in Istanbul, were also prominent examples of places that served the "visibility" of the modernist subject, displaying new clothing styles, social attitudes, and recreational pleasures. For instance, Taksim Park, planned by Henri Prost in Istanbul, stands as the consummate public space of secularization and state policy regarding the visibility of modern Turkish women and youth.[61] What makes the early beaches of Istanbul unique, however, is the different social modalities and pleasures they provided. Rather than a planned and prescribed park, the beach presented an unstable form of public space that allowed unconventional encounters and social groupings. If the parks in the city (espaces libres) designed by Prost, such as Taksim Park, were points of publicness and visibility in the city, the beaches provided territorial points of publicness and visibility on the strait.[62]

As elaborated with the call for settlements along the Bosphorus in Boğaziçi, and the preference of dispersed public beaches, the development of Istanbul in the 1930s was strongly linked to the geopolitical positioning of the Bosphorus Strait. Contrary to the common depiction of Istanbul as a neglected or abandoned city in the early 1930s because of the relocation of the capital to Ankara, as a result of its geopolitical condition, Istanbul maintained an active role. This role engendered a specific sensibility regarding the Bosphorus landscape, one triggered by territorial visibilities on the waterway.

INFRASTRUCTURES OF VISIBILITY: THE HIGHWAY

After the territorial and national evolution of the Republican era (1923–1945), during which the nation-state's village- and industry-oriented spatialization, secular authoritarianism, nationalism, and isolationist economic policies dominated, Turkey turned toward economic policies based on models of development and modernization that would contribute to a more prominent regional role in the Cold War international order. Within the context of this bipolar world system, Turkey stayed on the capitalist side, as one of the first countries to join to the Bretton Woods system, followed by economic liberalization.[63]

In the years following 1945, the domestic affairs of the country remained complex. The transition to a multiparty political regime secured the victory of the populist democracy of the Democratic Party. The rapid increase in migration to the big cities, the formation of squatter housing (*gecekondus*), the increased ownership of motor vehicles, and inner-city industrialization all contributed to the incomparable speed of urbanization.[64] In this context, while recognizing that housing and urbanism were fundamental challenges, the prime minister and honorary mayor of Istanbul, Adnan Menderes (1899–1961), started an extensive development plan during the mid-1950s.[65] While the implementation of a new highway network system was a major component of his plan, the channeling of U.S. financial aid through this plan remained crucial for the populist political propaganda of the "little America" or "the welfare state." During a visit to the United States in the 1950s, Menderes promoted the "harmony and solidarity that prevailed among free nations" where "the Turkish nation has always felt profound admiration for the unstinting efforts exerted by the United States to safeguard freedom, justice and security in the world."[66]

On September 23, 1956, Menderes held a press conference to launch the urban development project for Istanbul and declared: "We will be re-conquering Istanbul and be rescuing her from the 1900s gaze...Istanbul will have an entirely new face and be made into a modern city."[67] Although some roads and highways had been constructed in Istanbul before the 1950s (including during the time of the previous mayor, Lütfü Kırdar), what made the operations under the directive of Menderes remarkable was their far more extensive scale.[68] The 1937–41 plans of Henri Prost, based mainly on circulation systems and public parks throughout the city, provided a foundation for the efforts of Menderes. In fact, a Revision Committee was established to evaluate Prost's plans after his departure in 1950. It prepared a report full of severe criticism for Prost,

Eisenhower's welcome to Ankara during his visit to Turkey in 1959. The quote on the poster reads: "You have won my heart, Eisenhower."

both for not basing his plans on contemporary documentation and research, and for the priority given to the beautification of the city rather than solving its essential problems, such as housing and transportation. Ironically, despite these criticisms, Prost's plans would still determine the routes of the majority of Menderes's highways.[69]

Between 1956 and 1960, following the main features of the Prost plans (but with major difference in the width of streets, as Prost's proposals were enlarged by a factor of two or three), and the slogan of "this city has a hunchback, let's straighten it," Istanbul would enter into a large-scale urban transformation, resulting in wide avenues cutting through the historical fabric of the city in a Haussmannian fashion. The development covered the old city as well as greater Istanbul and its territories. While Ordu, Yeniçeriler, Vatan, Millet, Eminönü-Unkapanı, and the Sirkeci-Florya highways were built within the limits of the old city, the Tersane, Necatibey, Meclis-i Mebusan, and Büyükdere highways, Barbaros Boulevard, the Bosphorus coastal roads, and the Edirne-Istanbul and Istanbul-Izmit highways were constructed within the greater Istanbul region.[70] Combining infrastructural monumentality with pragmatism, Istanbul would experience the most radical urban development in years.

Menderes was nicknamed as the "head architect of Istanbul," and the project group consisted of a team of Turkish and foreign architects, planners, bureaucrats, and engineers (with help from a consulting team of about fifty engineers from the U.S. Bureau of Public Roads). Because the implementation of the Menderes highway program lacked any systematic documentation, much information about its progress comes from popular magazines and daily newspapers, in addition to reports from the actors involved in the projects.[71] Among these, Istanbul Urban Development Bureau Director Ertuğrul Menteşe's report/article—published in *Arkitekt* (1955)—remains as an important primary source for the development plan.[72]

Stating that "making Istanbul a modern city can be likened to a gentle medical operation as it is far harder than creating a city from scratch like Ankara," Menteşe's report is helpful for understanding the territorial extent of the highways as well as the partial planning approach of the program.[73] As illustrated in the presentations of the highway program in the 1956 and the 1959 volumes of *Hayat* magazine, abundant aerial images in the media aimed to convey the scale of the intervention and its impact on the city.[74] These images were illustrative of the showcase quality of the construction, which valued publicity for the operations more than accurate and detailed documentation.

While the developmental promise of the highway infrastructures would resonate throughout Turkey during the 1950s, as the new highways were reconfiguring the territory via Marshall Aid, Istanbul would act as a showcase for these developments as Turkey's most important trade center. Istanbul was mentioned in the 1955 issue of the quarterly reports of the Marshall Plan prepared by the Turkish Ministry of Foreign Affairs, titled *The Marshall Plan in Turkey*.[75] In the report, it was noted that $80,000 was allocated to the General Directorate of Highways as direct aid for the engineering

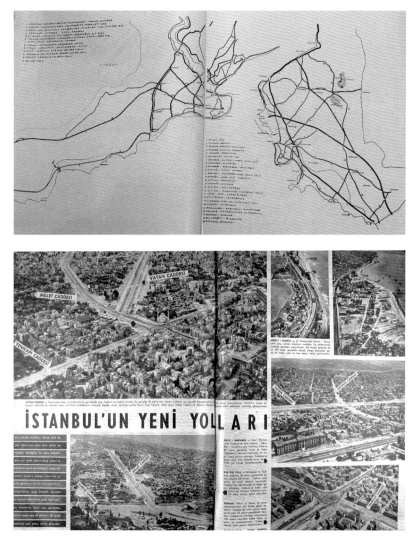

Top: New highways of Istanbul, as illustrated in Menteşe's report in *Arkitekt* (1955)
Bottom: Presented in the popular magazine *Hayat* (1958).

study of Istanbul traffic and the Bosphorus crossing.[76]Although the amount is modest compared to allocations for other Turkish infrastructure projects resulting from the Marshall Plan (in agriculture, industry, ports, etc.), it makes evident that the majority of funds for the Istanbul highways came from the Turkish Government.

The showcase quality of the Menderes highways can also be observed through the government publication titled "The Book of Istanbul" (*İstanbul'un Kitabı*), which promoted the accomplishments to the public, documenting the city modernization program:

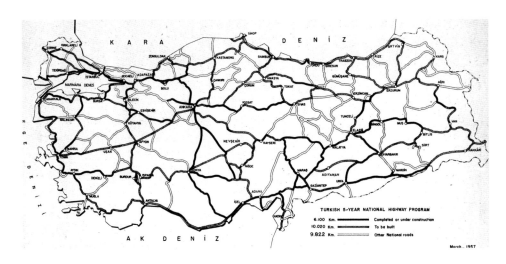

Turkish Five-Year Highway Program showing highways built and under construction,
prepared by the U.S. Federal Highways in 1957.

This book is prepared to inform the citizens about the past, present and future
of Istanbul...The preparer and writer of this book is not one or two people but is
Istanbul herself and her splendid development program...Istanbul is being con-
quered once again by the effort of Adnan Menderes. Fatih [Sultan Mehmet] had
acquired a victory against the Byzantine [Empire]. Now, Menderes has acquired a civilization victory against suffering, idleness, disorganization and vagabondism. That
is, Istanbul is taken on de novo with its highways, public squares, buildings, mosques
and historical artifacts, cultural and health facilities and with all other aspects.[77]

EDIRNE-ISTANBUL HIGHWAY: THE PERIPHERY AND THE "ENTRANCE TO THE CITY"

Apart from their massive effect on the city, the highways of Menderes triggered a specific type of interaction between geography and the city, that is, an infrastructural
understanding of the terrain with projections on the periphery. In that respect, the
Edirne-Istanbul Highway, running along the Marmara Sea hinterland and connecting
the new airport to the city center, would trigger discussions regarding the periphery of
the city and its connections to the outer world.

Standing as the first constructed highway within the Istanbul development program of the 1950s, the Edirne-Istanbul Highway replaced an existing 6-meter-wide road
previously referred to as the London Asphalt (*Londra Asfaltı*) which, according to the
presentation in *İstanbul'un Kitabı*, by then "suffer[ed] like a ripped apart reptile" next

to the "new, wide and oily" highway."[78] Having a width of 50 meters and connecting the city to the airport, the Edirne-Istanbul Highway entered the historical peninsula through the old city walls and connected to a major Haussmannian artery of Menderes (*Millet Caddesi*). Referring to the Edirne-Istanbul Highway and its important connection to the airport, Menderes declared:

> It is important to welcome those coming from Europe via a highway from…Yeşilköy airport and lead them to the city by a first-class road and prevent both friend and foe from entering the city through an area which resembles a backward-looking medieval town.[79]

The idea of the "entrance to the city" would resonate in terms of both the public reception of the highway in the popular media and the official U.S. Bureau of Public Roads reports on Turkey. For instance, in the final report prepared by the bureau on the highway development program in Turkey in 1959, a photograph of the Edirne-Istanbul Highway would be used as an illustration for the program's activities. Showing the city walls from a distance and illustrating the highway at a wider angle, the photograph's caption read: "Approaching the walls of Old Istanbul on the Road from the International Airport in Yeşilköy."[80]

The idea of an "entrance to the city" was important to the highway program for two reasons. First, by relating to the airport, the highway represented a geographical projection implying international connection and exhibitionism. Second, running in parallel and very close to the city limit in the east-west direction, the Edirne-Istanbul Highway was also emblematic of a new sensibility brought on by the peripheral highways of 1950s Istanbul. That is, while standing for attributes of "modernization" woven into populist development propaganda, a specific interpretation of infrastructure would reconfigure the peripheral landscape into a "modern city" and portray as it a recontouring edge of the city.

THE SIRKECI-FLORYA HIGHWAY AND THE BARBAROS BOULEVARD: PERIPHERY AS WATER, PERIPHERY AS NEW LANDSCAPE

Connection to the wider hinterland through a highway network was not an entirely new idea for twentieth-century Istanbul, as it had been proposed by previous master plans and reports of Herman Elgötz (1934), Martin Wagner (1936), and Henri Prost (1938 and 1941). For instance, Martin Wagner's regional plan, prepared when he was a consultant for the Istanbul Municipality in the 1930s, named the transportation system of the city and its connection to the hinterland as the major component in the implementation of a regional plan, while proposing three highway network systems: interior, military, and exterior, which would connect to London and Damascus.[81]

Top: Edirne-Istanbul Highway as illustrated in *Istanbul'un Kitabı*. The old Londra Asfaltı, which is referred to as suffering "like a ripped-apart reptile," is seen on the left.

Bottom: The highway after construction, seen next to the city walls as illustrated in a poster in *Hayat* magazine (1959). The caption of the poster reads: "Entrance to Istanbul."

In addition to the aspect of "connectivity" explored regarding the Edirne-Istanbul Highway, the recontouring of the edge was established by extending the highways out toward the water, establishing new views from the elevated topography, and projecting new towns. In this context, another highway that merits further attention is the 22- kilometer-long coastal Sirkeci-Florya Highway, constructed in 1957–59 along the shores of the Marmara Sea on the European side and renamed "Kennedy Highway" to commemorate U.S. President John F. Kennedy after 1963.[82]

Implementation of a highway along the southern border of the historical peninsula by the Marmara Sea followed the 1937 Prost plan, with major alterations. While not proposing an exact course for the road, Prost had suggested that the highway should trace inside the former Byzantine city walls (with a pedestrian road and public parks in front of the walls), and end before reaching Sarayburnu, proceeding as a pedestrian road/promenade path into an archeological park.[83]

Menderes's version of the Sirkeci-Florya Highway, however, was mostly based on the 1957 plan of Hans Högg—a German urban designer and Munich's former city architect, who was invited to Istanbul in the beginning of 1956 and officially commissioned to lead the urban reconstruction in 1957—where a tangent ring road would be constructed outside of the city walls on landfill. Although Högg's planning studies would later be criticized for serving to rationalize the Menderes operations "after they had been executed,"[84] because of Högg's proximity to central decision-making, his plans are particularly helpful in portraying the actual premises behind the highway design process.

In contrast to Prost's proposed highway inside the city walls, Högg's plan—aiming to lessen the traffic load within the historical peninsula—would propose that the highway ring outside of the city walls all the way to Sarayburnu, finally arriving at Sirkeci (instead of ending at Sarayburnu as Prost had proposed). Writing after the construction of the Sirkeci-Florya Highway and deploring the "unhygienic" situation of the older shoreline, Högg would argue that the Bosphorus view would have been blocked had the highway been built inside the walls, and that the new highway would not have views of the infinite waters.[85] Therefore, the tangent ring road was justified by Högg not only to alleviate heavy vehicular traffic within the historical peninsula and from outside the city walls but also to have a better view of the sea. Thus what makes the Sirkeci-Florya Highway significant is its emblematic projection on the city-periphery, in this instance, periphery understood as water.

Diagrams by Hans Högg comparing the interlocking traffic in and around the city core of Istanbul with the decentralized ring road along the city border.

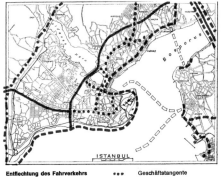

As noted, the highway was built along the southern border of the historical peninsula that had been enclosed by Byzantine city walls for centuries, and most of the walls were demolished during construction. Once surrounded by city walls, the historic peninsula was now surrounded by the modern highway, opening the city visually to its waters.[86] *İstanbul'un Kitabı* sheds further light on the contextualization of the Sirkeci-Florya Highway within Menderes's urban development program:

> Since the Byzantines, the coastline of Istanbul that is facing the Marmara [Sea] has been almost enclosed by the city walls and the worn-out squatter houses that surround the walls. This coastal shore of the Beautiful Marmara has been closed to Istanbulians not only for many years but also for many centuries. Being neglected across the board, Istanbul has turned its back on its coastal shores at many points. Taking on Istanbul's development, the Government has focused significantly on the highway that will reach up to Florya and, with a good course of action, has urgently taken positive steps.[87]

At this point, visibility of and from the highways became as significant as the constructions themselves. Compared to the 1930s, the visible territories of the Bosphorus Strait were replaced by the visible infrastructures delineated by the highways. Considering the well-known declaration of Menderes, in answer to a question about the possibility of developing a metro system in Istanbul ("he would not spend any money to the underground" as "his accomplishments should always be visible"[88]), infrastructural visibilities brought by the highways were their most important attribute for the Istanbul development program.

This prioritization becomes even more evident in the differences between the early beaches of the 1930s versus the beaches designed in the postwar era. The earlier beaches were strongly connected to the visibilities brought by the "modern nation-building" project and the Bosphorus Strait territory, while in the 1950s, the beach became part of the "modern city" project as well as its relationship to the highway infrastructures and other developments. For instance, for Ataköy Beach, the "modern" beach of Istanbul designed concurrent with the extension of the Sirkeci-Florya Highway and the Ataköy New City Project (located along the highway), Menderes was directly involved in the rapid design and funding for the beach construction; he even channeled the limited funding for housing projects to the beach.[89]

As exemplified with the Ataköy New City Project, reaching out to the periphery included a specific projection regarding new cities and modern housing projects that would emerge along the highway corridors. Reflecting the aspirations of an upper-middle-class population, the combination of the highways with "modern new cities" became the ultimate vision propelling modern Istanbul. While the peripheries had already become crowded with illegal squatters (*gecekondus*) by the mid-1950s, the highways and the new

Menderes in a discussion over the Ataköy New Town project model.
Next to him is Celal Bayar, the Turkish president.

housing developments would project a completely different image of the periphery, one that was occupied solely by modern housing for the upper-middle class. As ownership of a newly built apartment became the ultimate middle-class aim in 1960s Istanbul, the periphery would shape the development of the city in the years to come.[90]

A related document merits further attention in our discussion of highways and projected new cities on the periphery. A schematic plan prepared by Högg for urban development in Istanbul showed the new highways and projected new cities on the landscape. Depicting the existing fabric as black and the proposed highway and the new city developments as red, Högg's plan showed all major highways extending out from the city and connecting to the new cities that sat on the peripheral landscape: the New City Northwest (*Neustadt Nordwest*), the New City North (*Neustadt Nord*), and the New City East (*Neustadt Ost*), each of them strategically located with respect to the highways.

Barbaros Boulevard was another project implemented in conformity with Högg's proposal. The Boulevard started from the sea and reached out to the already built Levent New Town (the first Garden City of Istanbul) and the upper slopes of the Bosphorus via demolition of the existing fabric.[91] Since the location of Levent New Town was determined before the construction of the Boulevard, the highway's placement as well its actual route would reflect ideas presented in Högg's earlier plan (where highways would reach out to the new cities). Another factor influencing the final route of Barbaros Boulevard was its connection to the planned Bosphorus Bridge.[92]

EDGES REVISITED: CONCLUDING REMARKS

After the collapse of the Soviet Union in 1990, when its dependencies opened up their oil resources in the Caspian Sea to the world, the transportation of oil from the Turkish Straits gained importance. Because of conflicting interests in various pipeline projects and routes from the Caspian Sea to the Mediterranean, the Straits once again became an important strategic site.[93]

Just as the beauty and politics of the Bosphorus were described by Safa's article in *Boğaziçi* magazine in the 1930s, the intricate relationship between the political and the visual remains vital even today, albeit with altered political connotations. Oil tankers pass through the Bosphorus Strait every day, with the traffic increased tremendously compared to the 1930s, and the huge ships passing through the narrow strait can seem like a movie backdrop to the city.[94] The only time this stability has been distorted is when accidents have occurred—collisions, grounding, fire, or even ships ramming waterfront mansions by the sea. Although these accidents can be argued to be the only moments when the visual attachment is distorted, with those accidents the Bosphorus terrain transforms into a zone of risk, situated at the very heart of the city.[95]

Since the accidents highlighted the insecurity of the narrow waterway, tanker protests organized by governmental and nongovernmental organizations announce that the settlements near the waterway channel likely would be the ones most affected by

New highways and projected new cities as illustrated in Hans Högg's plan for Istanbul.

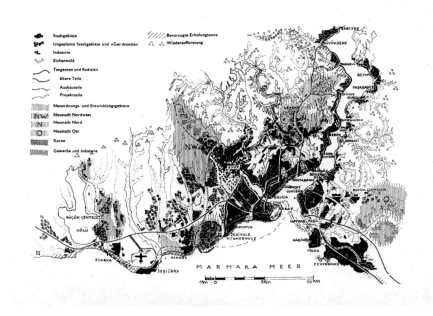

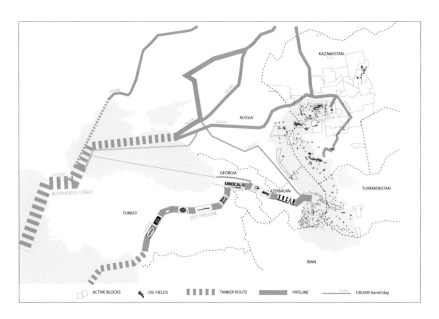

The Bosphorus Strait in its contemporary geopolitical context: Caspian oil, pipeline routes, and shipping routes. Line thicknesses indicate the amount of oil transported. As shown, the Bosphorus Strait and the BTC pipeline are the busiest spots in the region.

any accident. Turkey's apparent push to lower the volume of traffic passing through the straits by means of environmental and safety arguments, however, is not unrelated to the political calculations behind the government's promotion of the Baku-Tiflis-Ceyhan pipeline project.

Revisiting the discussions in *Boğaziçi* magazine and the promotion of development along the Bosphorus during the 1930s, we can see the changing geopolitical connotations of a given landscape and its relation to the city. While the "internationality" of the sea route made the Bosphorus Strait a "healthy environment" in the local imagination and highlighted its territoriality during the 1930s, by the late 1990s, the same international route would turn into a "liquid oil pipeline" and thus an "environmental risk zone" this time, highlighting its fragile ecology in the context of energy politics.

The aim of this chapter has been to highlight the active recontouring of the city edge particularly through interactions among landscape, urbanism, and geography. The conclusions that derive from the featured episodes portray two important lacunae in studying urban histories. First is the suggestion of a geographic appreciation in urban histories, one that would aim to depict wider connections, politics, and systems within which architecture and urbanism operate. Instead of seeing the totality of a city as a mere consequence of socioeconomic and administrative conditions, this appreciation portrays the city as it is molded by and projected onto its landscape and terrain. Second would be the possibility of an expanded and renewed understanding of the relationship between urban/architectural artifacts (buildings, monuments, city blocks, etc.) and their context. Rather than interpreting the idea of context as a passive backdrop of the immediate urban surroundings or merely an automatic sociopolitical consequence, the chapter portrays context as geographic: an active and synthetic framework that situates urban artifacts in their geopolitical, territorial, and infrastructural setting. This framework is important in terms of understanding histories as well as projecting new futures for urbanism.

Notes

1   "Nation building" refers to the political and cultural reforms made in Turkey to forge a modern, secular, and "Western" nation-state. See Sibel Bozdoğan and Reşat Kasaba, eds., *Re-thinking Modernity and National Identity in Turkey* (Seattle: University of Washington Press, 1997).

2   The founding of the Şirket-i Hayriye, as the first regular ferry services in Istanbul, should be seen as part of an ongoing infrastructure development in parallel to the urban legislative developments taking place within the nineteenth-century reformist Ottoman Tanzimat Era (1839–1876). Although the adoption of the first building codes and regulations date to 1796, Istanbul would witness most of its important legislative transformations—including the establishment of the first municipal organization, the formation of a road improvement commission, and the first plan or development policy of the city—in the nineteenth century. In addition to these legislations, Istanbul experienced a series of important infrastructure projects during the same era. In addition to the founding of Şirket-i Hayriye in 1851, the establishment of the first telegraph line, the illumination of some public buildings and the commencement of street illumination, and the construction of the first underground railway line would all take place in the last part of the nineteenth century. These developments can be traced in Zeynep Çelik, *Remaking of Istanbul* (Seattle: University of Washington Press, 1986). For an extensive history of Şirket-i Hayriye, see Murat Koraltürk, *Şirket-i Hayriye 1851–1945* (Istanbul: IDO, 2007). Also see Eser Tutel, *Şirket-i Hayriye* (Cağaloğlu, Istanbul: İletişim, 1994). For a water transportation history of Istanbul, see Mehmet Mazak, *Eski İstanbul'da Deniz Ulaşımı* (Istanbul, IDO, 1998).

3   The population of Istanbul was 356,653 in 1844; it reached 909,978 in 1914, and dropped to 500,000 in 1924. The population started to increase again after 1924 and reached 741,148 in 1935. Source: Zafer Toprak, "Tarihsel Nüfusbilim Açısından İstanbul'un Nüfusu ve Toplumsal Topoğrafyası," *Dünü ve Bugünüyle Toplum ve Ekonomi* 3 (1992), 120. Also see

Umid Meriç Yazan, "Bir Asır Boyunca İstanbul Şehrinin Nüfusunda Meydana Gelen Degişmelerin Tahlili 1840-1940," in *Tarih Boyunca İstanbul Semineri Bildiriri Kitabı* (Istanbul: Tarih Araştırma Merkezi, 1989), 59–84, and Zafer Toprak, "Cumhuriyet İstanbul'u," in *İstanbul'un Dört Çağı: İstanbul* Panelleri (Istanbul: YKY, 1996), 72–73. Also see Kemal H. Karpat, *Ottoman Population, 1830-1914: Demographic and Social Characteristics* (Madison, WI: University of Wisconsin Press, 1985). Detailed description of the shrinking population of the 1920s and the population dispersion of the time can also be observed in a report by Istanbul's Chamber of Industry and Trade: *Ticaret ve Sanayi Odasında Müteşekkil İktisat Komisyonu Raporu Tarafından Tanzim olunan Rapor* (Istanbul Ticaret ve Sanayi Odasi, 1924).

4   Istanbul was capital of the Ottoman Empire for five centuries. In transforming the country to a nation-state and establishing cities as the places of modernity, Ankara was chosen as the capital city of the newly founded Turkish Republic, rather than Istanbul. Some argue that this selection was the result of the search for a real modernization model for the nation-state; Ankara ultimately became the ground on which the Turkish modernist utopia set its first roots. See Ilhan Tekeli, "Türkiye'de Cumhuriyet Döneminde Kentsel Gelişme ve Kent Planlaması," in Yıldız Sey, *Bilanço'98: 75 Yılda Değişen Kent ve Mimarlık* (Istanbul: Tarih Vakfı Yayınları, 1998).

5   Umid Meriç Yazan, "Bir Asır Boyunca İstanbul Şehrinin Nüfusunda Meydana Gelen Degişmelerin Tahlili 1840–1940," 64.

6   Examples of such calls and announcements would be: "Şirket-i Hayriye'nin İstanbul Sayın Halkına Mühim İlanı: Boğaziçi'nde Yeniden Ev Yaptıranlara Kolaylık," *Boğaziçi* 9 (1937): 3–4; "Boğaziçi 'nde Bayındırlık Hareketi," *Boğaziçi* 3 (1936): 4–5; and Abidin Daver, "Boğazı İmar İçin," *Boğaziçi* 16 (1938): 5–6.

7   While Kandilli Primary School was constructed at Şirket-i Hayriye's initiation as announced, the housing project was never realized. A quote from the 1937 issue of the journal indicated that the mayor of Istanbul would consult Henri Prost for that project. In

his 1941 report explaining his plan for the Anatolian side of the Bosphorus, Prost said that the existing primary school in Kandilli was in an adequate situation but that the building lacked a playground/garden. Henri Prost, *Boğaziçi Anadolu Sahilinin 1/2000 Mikyaslı Nazım Planını Izah Eden Rapordur* (Istanbul: Istanbul Belediye Matbaası, 1941), 15–16.

8   Jansen prepared his first report for Ankara in 1927; and his master plan for the city was approved in 1929. For more on Jansen's plan for Ankara, see G. Tankut, "Jansen Planı: Uygulama Sorunları ve Cumhuriyet Bürokrasinin Kent Planlama Yaklaşımı," in Y. Yavuz, ed., *Tarih içinde Ankara* (Ankara: Ortadoğu Teknik Üniversitesi, 2001), 301–316. Also see Ilhan Tekeli and Tarık Okyay, "Case Study of a Relocated Capital: Ankara," in *Urban Planning Practice in Developing Countries*, ed. by John Taylor and David G. Williams (Oxford: Pergamon, 1982), 46–74.

9   For the proposals see: Alfred Agache, *Büyük Istanbul ve Imar Programı* (Istanbul Belediyesi, 1934); Herman Elgötz, *Istanbul Şehrinin Umumi Planı* (Istanbul: Ahmet Sait Matbaası, 1934); and Jacques Henri-Lambert, *Imar Raporu* (Istanbul: Milli Neşriyat Yurdu, 1933). For the detailed evaluation of the three projects by the competition jury, see "Istanbul Şehir Planı: Jürinin Ayırdığı Imar Komisyonunun Raporu," *Arkitekt* 1 (1935): 61–64.

10   Although it is unclear why the Elgötz plan was not implemented, Aron Angel, the Turkish architect who would later work with Prost as his assistant at the Urban Planning Bureau of the Istanbul Municipality, mentioned in an interview that it was Prost whom Atatürk actually wanted for the position. According to Angel, given Prost's previous experiences in Casablanca, Port of Algiers, and Rabat, Atatürk wanted someone who was experienced in working in a Muslim city and could bring the necessary radical yet practical vision, as he did with the urban plazas of Rabat. See the interview with Aron Angel: Burak Boysan, "Aron Angel ile Istanbul: Prost ve Planları Üzerine Söyleşi," 34," *Mimarlık* 285 (1999): 30–39.

11   For more on the work of Henri Prost, see Louis Hautecoeur, *L'Oeuvre de Henri Prost: Architecture et Urbanisme* (Paris: Academie d'Architecture, 1960). For Prost's work in Istanbul, see Cana Bilsel and Pierre Pinon, eds., *From the Imperial Capital to the Republican Modern City: Henri Prost's Planning of Istanbul 1936-1951* (Istanbul: Istanbul Research Institute, 2010). Also see I. Akpınar, "The Building of Istanbul after the Plan of Henri Prost 1937–1960: From Secularisation to Turkish Modernisation" (Ph.D. dissertation, University College London, 2003).

12   Abidin Daver, "Boğazı Imar Için," *Boğaziçi* 16 (1938): 1–2.

13   The article regarding the "Bosphorus Development Bank" was probably written after being informed of Prost's recent plan or notes on Istanbul. When this article was published in *Boğaziçi*, Prost had already finalized his master plan in 1937 and produced letters and notes, all of which were directed to government officials. The master plan reports and the majority of these letters were published by the municipal-

ity in 1937 and 1938. See Henri Prost, *Istanbul'un Nazım Planını Izah Eden Rapor* (Istanbul Belediyesi, October 15, 1937), and Henri Prost, *Istanbul Hakkında Notlar–1937* (Istanbul: Istanbul Belediye Matbaası, 1938).

14   The main features of Prost's 1937 master plan were proposals regarding new network of roads, functional zoning (industry, residential, and recreation), ports, parks, public promenades, and the preservation of the Bosphorus silhouette and the historic peninsula. The extensive plan for the Bosphorus shores were yet to be finalized in the 1940s; however, as early as the 1937 plan, Prost had already proposed a coastal highway extending toward the north of the Bosphorus as well as the removal of industries because of their negative impact on the aesthetics of the Bosphorus.

15   Burhan Cahit Morkaya, "Yarınki Boğaziçi: Şehir Mütehassısı Prost'un Avan Projelerine Göre Boğaziçi," *Boğaziçi* 16 (1938): 11–12.

16   Ibid. The New Town (*Yenişehir*) in Ankara was planned by Herman Jansen in 1928 according to the Garden City model. "Concrete bulk" connotes the reinforced concrete apartment buildings.

17   Ibid.

18   Hüseyin Cahit [Yalçın], "Boğaziçi'nin Imar ve Tezyini Etrafında Fikirler," *Boğaziçi* 18 (1938): 1–2. Yalçın's sentimental tone against the highway was similar to his writings appearing in other journals of the time regarding the "cubic house" phenomenon in the city center of Istanbul, such as houses built with associations to modernist architecture. For example, in another article Yalçın stated that "one would almost feel an irresistible desire to demolish all these apartment buildings and turn the land into arable fields." See Hüseyin Cahit [Yalçın], "Istanbul'u Kurtarmak Için," *Yedigün* 266 (12 April, 1938): 5.

19   According to an article titled "Istanbul'da Yapılar 1928–1934," in *Arkitekt* (1936), which compiled recent information from Istanbul Municipality Statistics, the amount of construction of villa-type houses was still approximately four times that of apartment buildings; however, as seen from the statistics, it is also apparent that the ratio was dropping every year. Also, one has to note that although not yet widespread in Istanbul, apartment buildings as Siedlung housing typology were prevalent throughout the Turkish cities that were built from scratch in Anatolia. Examples would be upper-middle-class housing for the new bureaucrats in Ankara, housing for industrial workers throughout Anatolia, and immigration housing. For more on the Siedlung model in Turkey in the early twentieth century, see Esra Akcan, "Modernity in Translation: Early Twentieth- Century German-Turkish Exchanges in Land Settlement and Residential Culture" (Ph.D. dissertation, Columbia University, 2005). For a further discussion on the "cubic house," see Sibel Bozdoğan, "Living Modern: The Cubic House in Early Republican Culture," *Tarihten Günümüze*

Konut ve Yerlesme = Housing and Settlement in Anatolia: A Historical Perspective (Istanbul: Türkiye Ekonomik ve Toplumsal Tarih Vakfı, 1996), 313–327.

20 Dr. Ali Rıdvan, "Bahçesiz Ev: Ciğersiz Adam," *Yedigün* 54 (21 March, 1934): 5.

21 Osman Şerafettin, "Boğaziçi'nin Güzel Havası ve Sıhhatimiz Üzerindeki Tesiri," *Boğaziçi* 4 (1937): 9–10.

22 See the two volumes: *Boğaziçi 'nde 1936 Senesi Zarfinda Kiraya Verilecek Ev, Yalı ve Köşkler Hakkında Bazı Malumati Havi Risaledir* (Istanbul State Press, 1936); *Boğaziçi 'nde 1937 Senesi Zarfinda Kiraya Verilecek Ev, Yalı ve Köşkler* (Istanbul State Press, 1937). Source: National Library Archives, Ankara.

23 Although a commercial entity, Şirket-i Hayriye had connections to the government and its policies through its shares and directors. For instance, when first founded in the Ottoman era, it was formed as a joint stock company in which 150 (of 1,500) shares belonged to the Ottoman Sultan Abdülmecid and his mother, with the rest divided among various pashas, governors, and businessmen. With minor adjustments, the administration of the company remained mostly unchanged throughout the Republican era, until the company was bought and nationalized by the government in 1945. During the time of the *Boğaziçi* publication (1936–1938), the director of the company was Necmettin Molla (Kocataş), a former Ottoman justice minister and also a former deputy member of the Turkish Republic Parliament.

24 See Murat Koraltürk, "Mütareke Sonrası Dönemde Nüfusun Azalması ve Kent Ekonomisine Yansımaları," *Toplumsal Tarih* 59 (October 1998): 38–42.

25 As one of the major symbols of the modernity project, the idealized figure of the Kemalist woman juxtaposed onto Istanbul images is often discussed as the visual construct of the new and the modern and as a declaration of the young and healthy Republic versus the city of sultans and imperial decline. Kemalist ideology refers to the doctrine of Mustafa Kemal Atatürk, the founder of the Turkish Republic in 1923. The era between 1923 until the early 1940s is referred to as the Republican/Kemalist era by most scholars (Atatürk died in 1938). For the role of women in the Kemalist project, see Sibel Bozdoğan, "Gendering the Modern," in *Modernism and Nation Building: Turkish Architectural Culture in the Early Republic* (Seattle; London: University of Washington Press, 2001), 80–87. Also see Z. Arat, "Turkish Women and the Republican Construction of Tradition," in F. M. Göçek and S. Balaghi, eds., *Reconstructing Gender in the Middle East* (New York: Columbia University Press, 1994), 57–78.

26 Peyami Safa, "Boğazların ve Boğaziçi 'nin Müdafaası" [The Defense of the Straits and the Bosphorus] *Boğaziçi* 3 (1936): 8. Safa's articles on modernity, technology, architecture, and social life appeared widely in the other magazines of the time.

27 Ibid., bold in original.

28 The Montreux Convention refers both to the Bosphorus (Istanbul) and Dardanelles (Çanakkale Straits) in Turkey. Here I will concentrate merely on the Bosphorus Strait. For more on the Turkish Straits and its geopolitical positioning, see Yüksel İnan, *Türk Boğazlarının Siyasal ve Hukuksal Rejimi* (Ankara: Turhan Kitabevi, 1995); Ismail Soysal, ed., *Turkish Straits: New Problems, New Solutions* (Istanbul: ISIS, 1999); and Nihan Ünlü, *The Legal Regime of the Turkish Straits* (The Hague; London; New York, Martinus Nijhoff Publishers, 2002). For the earlier significance of the strait as well as the Istanbul Port, see Wolfgang Muller-Wiener, *Bizans'tan Osmanli'ya Istanbul Limanı*, trans. Erol Özbek (Istanbul: Tarih Vakfı Yurt Yayınları, 1998).

29 G.V. Inciciyan, *Boğaziçi Sayfiyeleri*, trans. Kandilli Armenian Church Priest (Istanbul: Eren Yayıncılık, 2000), 41.

30 Both Annual Reports were prepared for the League of Nations in an attempt to circulate navigation regulations for sea and air passage over the straits as well as to provide an inventory for all the ships that had passed (with tonnages) through the straits within the preceding year. See Straits Commission, *Rapport de la Commision des Detroits a la Societe des Nations anne 1933* (Istanbul: Imprimeire Francause L. Mourkides, Luledji Hendek, 1934). Source: Republic of Turkey Prime Ministry General Directorate of State Archives, Ankara, Turkey, doc. no: 030.10.222.498.20, and Turkey Hariciye Vekâleti, *Rapport Annuel sur le Mouvement des Navires à Travers les Détroits et des Aéronefs Civils entre la Méditerranée et la Mer Noire* (Ankara, January 1938). Source: Harvard University Law School Library Archives.

31 The maps in the Annual Report from 1933, prepared by the International Straits Commission of the League of Nations, demarcate the actual limits of the demilitarized zones on both sides of the Bosphorus (stretching out to approximately 40 kilometers) and designate the air passage over the Bosphorus as unrestricted. In contrast, the maps of the 1938 report prepared by the Foreign Affairs Department show the limits of the first- degree Turkish military prohibited zones and airspaces, which cover the entire Bosphorus passage.

32 Two scholars have written about the journal *Boğaziçi*, so far all focusing on the transportation company owner, Şirket-i Hayriye. Both the study of Peyami Safa's article and speculation on the article's (and the journal's) historical link to the Montreux Convention are mine. See E. Nedret Işli, "İlk Osmanlı Anonim Sirketi: *Şirket-i Hayriye* ve İlginç Neşriyatı" *Arkitekt* 411 (1994): 58–63; see also Murat Koraltürk, "Bir Boğaziçi'li Boğaziçi Mecmuası," *Istanbul 39* (October 2001): 88–93.

33 "İstanbul Boğazı'nın İkinci Memnu Mıntıkaya Dahil Olan Yerleri" *Boğaziçi* 1 (October 1936): 6. For the announcement of the so-called territorial change at the official newspaper of Turkey, see "Çanakkale ve Karadeniz Bogazları'nın İkinci Menu Mıntıkalar Meyanına İthali Hakkında Tebliğidir" in *T.C. Resmi*

Gazete (September 24, 1936). The first-degree prohibited zone is a military zone designated for land areas that are adjacent to the second-degree prohibited zones (where entrance is limited to military officials and staff). The boundary for the second-degree prohibited zone is a line no less than 5 kilometers and no more than 10 kilometers (15 kilometers before 1981) from the first-degree prohibited zone. The range between the minimum and maximum lines is demarcated by the topography and visibility. See "Askeri Bolgeler ve Guvenlik Bolgeleri Kanunu," *Resmi Gazete*, 22 December, 1981, 73.

34 Examples of such discussions would be: Walter Robinson, *The Straits of the Dardanelles and the Bosphorus: The Right of Way under International Law* (London: W. Ridgway, 1878); Renée Pithon, *Karadeniz ve Boğazlar Meselesi*, trans. by Hüseyin Nuri (Istanbul: Kütüphane-i Askeri, 1909); Coleman Phillipson and Noel Buxton, *The Question of the Bosphorus and Dardanelles* (London: Stevens and Haynes, 1917).

35 *Architectural Review* (December 1919), "Peace Commemoration Number."

36 Major David Davies M.P., "Constantinople as the G.H.Q. of Peace," *Architectural Review* (December 1919): 146–150.

37 Ibid., 147, 148.

38 Ibid.

39 The Istanbul Festival lasted until 1939 and ceased because of World War II.

40 In Edmund Burke's writings, the ocean appears as the first example from nature that causes a feeling of terror: "The passion caused by the great sublime in nature, when those causes operate most powerfully, is Astonishment; and astonishment is that state of the soul in which all its motions are suspended, with some degree of horror. In this case mind is so entirely filled with its object, that it cannot entertain any other, nor by consequence reason on that object which employs it... Astonishment [...] is the effect of the sublime in its highest degree; the inferior effects are admiration, reverence and respect...A level of vast extent on land, is certainly no mean idea; the prospect of such a plain may be as extensive as a prospect of the ocean; but can it ever fill the mind with anything so great as the ocean itself? This is owing to several causes, but it is owing to none more than this, that the ocean is an object of no small terror. Indeed terror is in all cases whatsoever, either more openly or latently the ruling principle of the sublime." Edmund Burke, *A Philosophical Inquiry* (Oxford: Oxford University Press, 1998), 53–54. For history of sublime and its relation to aesthetics, see especially the chapter by Peter De Bolla, "The Discourse of the Sublime," in *The Discourse of the Sublime: History, Aesthetics& the Subject* (Oxford: Basil Blackwell, 1989). For a more general overview of the aesthetic sublime and its relation to the sea, see the chapter "Freshness of Wonder," in Alain Corbin, *The Lure of the Sea: The Discovery*

of the Seaside in the Western World 1750–1840 (Berkeley: University of California Press, 1994). For a history of spaces of swimming, see Thomas A. P. van Leeuwen, *The Springboard in the Pond: An Intimate History of the Swimming Pool*, ed. by H. Searing (Cambridge, MA: MIT Press, 1998).

41 Corbin, *The Lure of the Sea*.

42 Visual resources (engraving, photographs, etc.) offer documentation of the sea-bathing units on the shores of Istanbul in the nineteenth century; for the eighteenth century, however, this is rare. Burcak Evren cites a document from the Ottoman Archives (dated 1781) that notes a sea-bathing fountain on the shores of Istanbul. Another document he references, from 1847, indicates that the body that authorizes sea-bathing was the Royal Shipyard (*Tersane-i Amire*). In 1868–1870 the administration of the sea-bathing units was transferred to the municipality (*Şehremaneti*). In 1870, the municipality decided to construct twenty-one public sea-bathing units, and in 1875 official regulations for both private and public sea-bathing units were published (*Umumi Deniz Hamamları Hakkındaki Nizamname*). See Burçak Evren, *Istanbul'un Deniz Hamamları ve Plajları*, 11.

43 Mehmet Temel writes that 200 households of Russian refugees were accommodated on land in Florya in 1920. See Mehmet Temel, *Isgal Yıllarında Istanbul'un Sosyal Durumu* (Ankara: T.C. Kültür Bakanlığı Yayınları, 1998), 124. Also see Burçak Evren, "Florya Plajı," in *Istanbul Ansiklopedisi*; also see the part on refugees in Bilge Criss, *Istanbul Isgal Altında* (Istanbul: Iletisim, 1994), 51–56.

44 Afife Batur, "Florya Cumhurbaşkanlığı Köşkü," *Istanbul Ansiklopedisi*.

45 See Uğur Tanyeli, "Seyfi Arkan: Bir Direnme Öyküsü," *Arredamento Dekorasyon* 3 (March 1992): 88–95. Seyfi Arkan graduated from the Academy of Fine Arts (Istanbul) in 1927. Between 1930 and 1933, Arkan worked with German architect Hans Poelzig in Poelzig's architectural office in Berlin and also took master classes from him at the Prussian Academy of Arts in Berlin. In 1933, Arkan returned to Turkey and started giving urban design lectures at the Academy of Fine Arts. Florya Mansion was not the first task Arkan took on for the Turkish state. Arkan had designed the Foreign Affairs Minister's House, which was also his first commission in Turkey (Ankara, 1933–1934). Arkan's other important projects for the state would include: mansions for the Presidency Assistant and Internal Affairs Minister (Ankara, 1935–1936); Office for the Presidency General Secretary (Istanbul, 1935–1936); mansion for the Prime Minister and Guests (Ankara, 1935–1936).

46 Willy Sperco, *Yüzyıl Başında Istanbul*, trans. R. Koymen (Istanbul: Istanbul Kütüphanesi, 1989), 81.

47 Ibid.

48 Evren, *Istanbul'un Deniz Hamamları ve Plajları*, 52.

49 Wagner was appointed as a consultant to the Istanbul Municipality in 1935. Martin Wagner was also teaching courses on urbanism at the Academy of Fine Arts (Istanbul). He was an expert on the Weimar housing programs of the 1920s and was Bruno Taut's

colleague from the GEHAG cooperative housing program in Berlin. See the section on Wagner in Hasan Kuruyazıcı, "Osmanlı'dan Cumhuriyete Turkiye'de Alman Mimarlar," *Arkitekt* 4 (2002). Wagner stayed in Turkey until 1938, when he moved to the United States and was appointed to teach at the Harvard Graduate School of Design in Cambridge. For more on Wagner's émigré years, including Istanbul, see Bernd Nicolai, "'World-dynamite'—Martin Wagner's (Lost) Years on (E) migration: Intellectual Challenge and Professional Frustration in Architectural Modernism and Town-Planning between Berlin, Istanbul and Harvard," in *Arkitektur und Exil: Kulturtransfer und Architektonische Emigration von 1930 bis 1950*, ed. by B. Nicolai (Porta Alba: Trier, 2003), 145–155.

50 Although Martin Wagner was originally appointed at the Urban Development Directorate at the Municipality in 1935, he left the municipality in 1937 and started to work for the Head of Building and Reconstruction Works at the Ministry of Public Works in Ankara.

51 For Wagner's earlier writings on the new housing estate-city, see Martin Wagner, *Die neue Stadt im neuen Land* (Berlin: Karl Buchholz, 1934).

52 Re-quoted from Bernd Nicolai, "'World-dynamite'—Martin Wagner's (Lost) Years on (E) migration," 148–149.

53 Ibid. It is interesting to note that, five years later, when Wagner was teaching at the Harvard Graduate School of Design, he would write another harsh letter to Gropius (professor and chairman of the Department of Architecture, Harvard GSD) criticizing "the mistakes in imitating Corbusier and Mies," this time at the GSD. Martin Wagner, Letter to Gropius, September 8, 1940, Houghton Library, Harvard University, bMS Ger 208 [1681].

54 In his notes for the Florya beach in 1937, Prost stated the "irrelevance to construct a new settlement" in Florya and proposed the development of road infrastructures around the site so that it would increase land prices and subsidize the construction of new buildings in the area. Prost proposed a Youth Park to be constructed at the site, which would include treadmills, games, and gymnastic areas, and would serve as "a real gymnastic ground" for the city. Henri Prost, *Istanbul Hakkında Notlar–1937*, note 21.

55 For instance, the Beyazpark Beach (at the northern Bosphorus) was constructed by a direct order from Atatürk around 1936 (to replace the existing sea-bathing units).

56 Uğur Tanyeli, "Kentsel Değisimde Önderlik Sorunu ve Süreyya Paşa," *Istanbul* 3 (1992): 117–123.

57 Zeynep Uludağ, "Cumhuriyet Döneminde Rekreasyon ve Gençlik Parkı Örneği," *Bilanço'98: 75 Yılda Değişen Kent ve Mimarlık*. Bozdoğan also notes that "the idealized qualities of being 'young' and 'healthy' signified a state that had successfully broken ties with 'the old empire' or 'the sick man of Europe,' as the Ottoman Empire

was known in the nineteenth century." Bozdoğan, *Modernism and Nation Building*, 75.

58 For instance, see John M. Hoberman, *Sport and Political Ideology* (London: Heinemann, 1984).

59 The parades at the 19 May Stadium (1936) in Ankara (designed by the Italian architect Paolo Vietti Violi) would also be an example of this. As Hannah Arendt posited, the sheer size of the masses is the most important requisite for the functioning of totalitarianism. See Hannah Arendt, *The Origins of Totalitarianism* (New York: Meridian Books Inc., 1958). For more on the crowd as spectacle, see Susan Buck-Morss, *Dreamworld and Catastrophe: The Passing of Mass Utopia in East and West* (Cambridge, MA: MIT Press, 2000); on the spectacle of mass gymnastic displays, see Pert Roubal, "Politics of Gymnastics: Mass Gymnastic Displays under Communism in Central Eastern Europe," *Body and Society* 2 (June 2003): 1–25.

60 Feroz Ahmad, *Turkey: Quest for Identity* (Oxford: Oneworld, 2003), 152.

61 Ipek Yeda Akpınar, "Pay-ı Tahtı Sekülerleştirmek: 1937 Prost Planı," *Istanbul* 44 (January 2003): 20–25.

62 Taksim Park was part of a large-scale project (called "Park No. 2") proposed by Henri Prost in his 1937 plan. The Park No. 2 project was comprised of proposals for various recreational activities such as a large amphitheater, congress center, etc., most of which were built after the plan.

63 This loyalty to the capitalist system was assured by the United States' financial aid through the Marshall Plan; a clear alignment with the West resulted in sending Turkish troops to the Korean War, allowing U.S. air bases on its territory and, finally, a NATO membership for Turkey. For Turkey's role in Cold War politics, see George McGhee, *The U.S.-Turkish-NATO Middle East Connection: How the Truman Doctrine Contained the Soviets in the Middle East* (New York: St. Martin's Press, 1990). For U.S.-Turkey relations in this context, see George Harris, "Turkish-American Relations since the Truman Doctrine," in *Turkish-American Relations: Past, Present, and Future*, edited by Mustafa Aydın and Çağrı Erhan (London and New York: Routledge, 2004), 66–88.

64 In the early 1920s, the population of Istanbul was around 500,000; in 1950 it was 975,000, and in 1965 it reached 2,141,000.

65 Honorary mayorship was given to Menderes by the Istanbul Municipality in 1958.

66 Adnan Menderes, "Transcript of the interview with Prime Minister Adnan Menderes on 'The Leading Question,' the CBS Radio Network program origination in Washington, D.C., October 9, 1959," in Turkish Information Office, *Prime Minister Adnan Menderes in the United States, October 5–16, 1959* (New York: Turkish Information Office, [1959]).

67 *Cumhuriyet* (24 September 1956).

68 According to a government publication, the expenditure of the Istanbul municipality on highways and bridges increased by 334 percent during 1950–57 compared to spending in the period 1923–1949. The roads of Istanbul had started to emerge in the

nineteenth century as a corollary to Istanbul's increasing connection to the world economy and the related urban development and planning regulations that shaped the city form. The first attempts to modernize roads for car transportation in Istanbul date back to a law enacted in 1839, which classified roads as 20, 15, 12, and 10 meters wide, determined the height of buildings adjacent to roads, prohibited cul-de-sac construction, and required that the roads be built according to a "geometric" basis. Incessant fires in the city were the main instigators of urban planning and development in the nineteenth century. According to a publication by the Istanbul Municipality, at the beginning of 1939, the length of all Istanbul roads was 1,489 kilometers, and the total area was 12,200,000 square meters. Only about one third of this total were highways (including concrete, asphalt concrete, macadam, and block pavement); the rest was divided between rough cobblestone pavement and dirt roads. *Yenileşen Istanbul: 1939 Başından 1947 Sonuna Kadar Istanbulda Neler Yapıldı?* (Istanbul Belediye Matbaası, 1947), 15. For a detailed history of the development of roads and rail infrastructures during the Ottoman era and Republican Turkey, see Ilhan Tekeli and Selim Ilkin, *Cumhuriyetin Harcı: Modernitenin Altyapısını Oluştururken* (Istanbul: Istanbul Bilgi Universitesi Yayinlari, 2004).

69 For the report of the Revision Committee, see *Revizyon Komitesi Raporu* [prepared in 1951] (Istanbul Belediye Matbaasi, 1954), Istanbul Municipality Archives. Between 1951 and 1956, born out of the Revision Committee, the Istanbul Urban Development Plan Commission (*Istanbul Sehir Imar Plani Daimi Komisyonu*) was established, comprised of architects, planners, engineers, and bureaucrats. Prost's plan would remain as the only approved master plan of the city until the 1970s.

70 With the operations of Menderes, 7,289 buildings were demolished in three and a half years. Doğan Kuban, *Istanbul, an Urban History: Byzantion, Constantinopolis, Istanbul* (Istanbul: Economic and Social History Foundation of Turkey, 1996), 397. It was announced by the government that, for the Menderes highway construction between 1950 and 1957, about 335 million Turkish liras were spent on the condemnation of property—thirteen times the amount spent before (between 1923 and 1949). *Istanbul'un Kitabı* [The book of Istanbul] (Istanbul: Istanbul Vilayeti Neşriyat ve Turizm Müdürlügü, 1957), 127.

71 Menderes operations were already criticized at the time of their application as having no accurate plan. Question remains whether or not the actual plans were lost within the context of the political climate of the 1960s Turkey, or never existed in the first place.

72 Ertuğrul Menteşe, "Istanbul'un Imarı" [Urban development of Istanbul] *Arkitekt* 24 (1955): 27–35.

73 The only drawing that shows all of the highways is

a schematic one without topography, built fabric, or dimension. There are partial plans, models, and sketch drawings for specific sites.

74 *Hayat* was a magazine whose content and style was not similar to the 1950s American *Life* magazine, but its title translated as "Life" in Turkish.

75 On 12 March 1947, addressing a joint session of Congress, U.S. president Harry S. Truman requested $400 million in military and economic aid for Greece and Turkey. Of that, $300 million was military and economic aid for Greece and $100 million was military aid for Turkey. Of the $100 million allocated for Turkey, $5 million was targeted for highway purposes. Initially, priority was given to highways that were strategic in terms of transporting military forces and supplies to key defense locations—like the highway from the Iskenderun port to Kars and Erzurum, as well as the Edirne-Istanbul Highway in Thrace. Following a formal agreement signed by the Turkish Ministry of Public Works and the American Mission for Aid to Turkey, a group of twenty-five American highway engineers and a number of mechanics and equipment specialists from the U.S. Bureau of Public Roads arrived in Turkey in December 1947. Following the group's inspections and field-trip studies, a report was submitted to the Turkish Ministry of Public Works. Following the report, the plan to construct 23,000 kilometers of National Highways in nine years was approved by the Turkish Council of Ministers; and the General Directorate of Highways was founded, as recommended by the report, and began to work as an autonomous department in 1950. The General Directorate of Highways targeted the completion of the proposed highway network in nine years and aimed to have eleven field divisions "strategically placed" around the country.

76 Turkish Ministry of Foreign Affairs, Secretary-General's Office of the Organization for International Economic Cooperation, *Quarterly Report on the Marshall Plan in Turkey* 24, (1.7.1955–30.9.1955): 12. The amount and content of the Marshall Plan funding as well as the status on all of the projects implemented under the program (including highways, energy, industry, agriculture, mining, irrigation, and military) were all published in these quarterly reports by the Turkish General Secretary's Office of the Organization for International Economic Cooperation, in both English and Turkish. Accordingly, for each year, the accomplishments for the highways were reported under the Public Roads section. The first issue covers the years 1948–1949, and the last issue (number 47) covers the second quarter of 1962. According to the reports, the total amount provided by the United States to Turkey between the years of 1948 and 1960 for the construction of highways is around $40 million. The majority of these funds (around $36 million) were used between 1948 and 1955.

77 *Istanbul'un Kitabı* [The book of Istanbul], 1.

78 "Şimdi o dar yol, tertemiz geniş, gelişi gidişi ayrılmış, yepyeni, yağ gibi asfalt bir yolun eteklerinde,...parça parça kopmuş bir sürüngen gibi kıvranıp durmaktadır." *İstanbul'un Kitabı*, 12.

79 "Sayın Başvekil Basına Geniş İzahat Verdi ve İstanbul'un İmar ve Kalkınma Prensiplerini İzah Etti" [Dear prime minister, gave comprehensive explanations and explained the principles of the Istanbul planning and development], *İller ve Belediyeler Dergisi* 132 (October 1956): 645.

80 U.S. Bureau of Public Roads, *Final Report on Technical Assistance to the General Directorate of Highways of the Republic of Turkey* (Washington, D.C., 1959). U.S. Department of Transportation Library Archives.

81 Martin Wagner, "Istanbul Havalisinin Planı-Der Landesplan von Istanbul," [The regional plan for Istanbul] *Arkitekt* 1(1936), 301–306, 333–337.

82 Sirkce-Florya highway was initially proposed in the 1933 Elgötz plan in 1933. Elgötz, *İstanbul Şehrinin Umumi Planı*, 14–15.

83 Henri Prost, 1937 *Istanbul Master Plan*.

84 Tekeli, 12.

85 Hans Högg, "Die neue Uferfront am Marmara-Meer," [The new seafront by the Marmara Sea] in *Istanbul: Stadtorganismus und Stadterneuerung* (Ludwigsburg: Karawane-Verlag, 1967), 312.

86 The Sirkeci-Florya highway construction surrounding the city walls required 300,000 cubic meters of landfill; part of this amount was debris from the buildings demolished for the construction of the Hausmannian boulevards inside the city. The landfilling process was justified as financially more viable than property condemnation. It was announced in *İstanbul'un Kitabı* that it would cost 100 million Turkish liras if a condemnation was made for the construction of the Sirkeci-Florya highway, which passed in front of the city walls. Of the 22-kilometer-long construction, 12,600 meters (connecting Sirkeci to Baruthane) of this was constructed by the General Directorate of Highways; 2,400 meters by the Real Estate Credit Bank (connecting Baruthane to the Ayamama Bridge (*Ayamama Köprüsü*); and, the remaining 7,000 meters (connecting Ayamama to Florya) by the Istanbul Municipality. *İstanbul'un Kitabı*, 72.

87 *İstanbul'un Kitabı*, 69, 72.

88 *İstanbul Ansiklopedisi*, 368.

89 For the design and construction of the Ataköy Housing Project and its relation to the Ataköy Beach , based on the Real Estate Credit Bank's archives, see Murat Güvenç and Oguz Işık, *Emlak Bankası 1926–1998* (Istanbul: Emlak Bankası, 1999), 179–180.

90 [italics original] Keyder, "The Housing Market from Informal to Global," in *Istanbul: Between the Global and the Local*, 151.

91 See, "Levent Mahallesi," *Arkitekt* (1952). The Levent New Town was built by the Istanbul Municipality and the Real Estate Credit Bank in the late 1940s at the urban periphery and completed by 1957. It consisted of four sections. The first and fourth sections were designed by architect Rebii Gorbon and planner Kemal Ahmet Aru. The second and third parts were designed again by Aru.

92 Although the bridge would have to wait until the 1970s to be built, the Turkish government had already commissioned the American firm De Leuw, Cather & Company in 1956 to prepare a plan for the Bosphorus Bridge; the company report was submitted to the Turkish Government in May 1956. De Leuw, Cather & Company, Consulting Engineers, Chicago, *A Bosphorus Straits Bridge and Connecting Highway System, Istanbul, Turkey*, prepared for the General Directorate of Highways, Republic of Turkey (May 1956). Project no: 77-31-243-3-50057, International Cooperation Administration, United States of America, U.S. Department of Transportation Library Archives. The same company would prepare another updated report for the bridge in 1968. See De Leuw, Cather & Company, Consulting Engineers, Chicago, *Updating of the Bosphorus Bridge and Connecting Highways Feasibility Study*, prepared for the General Directorate of Highways, Republic of Turkey (October 1968). Also, for a criticism of these reports, see the report/commentary prepared by the Chamber of Architects: Mimarlar Odası Boğaz Köprüsü Komitesi, *Boğaz Köprüsü Üzerine Mimarlar Odası Görüşü* [Ankara], [197-].

93 See the chapter titled "Energy Conflict in the Caspian Sea Region," in Klare, *Resource Wars: The New Landscape of Global Conflict* (New York: Metropolitan Books, 2001).

94 In 1936, an average of seventeen ships passed through the Bosphorus per day, usually carrying grain and weighing no more than 13 tons. Today, however, the average number of ships per day is around 100, weighing around 200,000 tons and often carrying oil, gas, chemicals, nuclear waste, and other hazardous materials. Trade Environment Database, Mandala Project, American University, "Bosphorus Strait Regulation and Central Asian Oil," http://www.american.edu/ted/bosporus.htm.

95 Between 1953 and 1992, 110 accidents occurred in the Istanbul Strait; for the years 1982–1998, the number increased to 714. For the concept of accident in our contemporary era, see Paul Virilio, *Unknown Quantity* (London, New York: Thames and Hudson; [Paris]: Fondation Cartier pour l'art contemporain, 2003).

ELIZABETH BISHOP

3

CONTROL ROOM: VISIBLE AND CONCEALED
SPACES OF THE ASWAN HIGH DAM

Even the power plant with its turbines and generators is a man-made means to an end established by man.[1]

The idea for the Aswan Dam began to take shape at the end of World War II, when British hydraulic engineers proposed a flood-control and power-generation project that would incorporate the entire Nile River Valley, a "century storage" plan to eliminate differences between high- and low-flood levels over a 100-year period.[2] From the plan's beginnings, it had a crucial political dimension, as proposals for Nile regulation involved both the nation's territorial space and imperial and neo-imperial spaces elsewhere. A commentator asserted the inevitability of such a plan's extraterritoriality: "There is no doubt, the creation of a system of complete regulation of the Nile will require the establishment of control works in Ethiopia, Uganda, and the Sudan; their operation will need to be planned and regulated by a single Nile Valley authority."[3]

A high dam at Aswan, however, would accomplish "century storage" within Egypt's boundaries, and after the 1952 revolution in Egypt, the ruling Free Officers adopted it as exemplary of new forms of political belonging. This innovative structure, with a hyper-scaled reservoir for "dead" storage of upstream silt and sentiment, would control the Nile within Aswan-to-Alexandria borders.[4] A high dam—in addition to providing flood control—would produce electricity and, by extending perennial irrigation, increase cultivable land inside Egypt's borders by a third. This project became a showcase for the new government's transformation of the country. Preliminary project designs from December 1954 sketched an earth-filled structure with seven tunnels. A panel of international consultants suggested a construction site midway between the Nile inlets Khor Kundi and Khor Agorma, 6.5 kilometers upstream from Aswan.[5]

Foreign technicians' preference for a single reservoir was not without its regional effects. Leaders of recently independent Sudan claimed that the maximalization of water in Egypt imperiled upstream neighbors' sovereignty.[6] The mega-reservoir would flood Sudan's border town, Wadi Halfa, and displace its exchanges of goods and services to Egypt's border town, Aswan. At the same time that postcolonial Cairo renounced its British-supported claims over the Sudan, the oversized reservoir would redirect Aswan's trade and labor migration toward Cairo and the North.[7]

As this project strengthened Egypt's control at the expense of its neighbor's resources, the funds for the project remained unbounded. The Word Bank evidenced interest in underwriting similar interventions, proposing development assistance to Egypt as a "new nation." With the United Kingdom, United States, and Federal Republic of Germany providing money, international technicians specified project details.[8] Five engineers (Karl Terzaghi, I. G. Steele, Max Pruss, André Coyne, and Lorenz Straub) provided overlapping areas of expertise. However, support for the project was reterritorialized in July 1956, when the United States claimed that new military procurements strained Egypt's national budget and withdrew civilian assistance. In retaliation later that summer, Egypt's president seized foreign investors' assets—including the Suez Canal— to redirect their income to the transformation of the Nile landscape. Local financial responsibility was clarified the following October, when the USSR offered to fund the project out of respect for Egypt's national economic development goals.[9]

The Hydroproject Research Institute in Moscow, "Gidroproekt," established a final design for the project in 1958.[10] Gidroproekt, represented by the Soviet Ministry of Foreign Trade's "Technopromeksport" foreign trading company, submitted to the Egyptian clients blueprints for an earth-filled dam 1 kilometer long from its upstream bank to its downstream cutoff. Six tunnels channel Nile waters to a concealed power plant. This project was distinguished by small enhancements, such as moving the dam axis to eliminate water filters at the back of the dam. A first delegation of experts from the USSR arrived during the spring of 1959 and, as specified by the initial Technopromeksport contract, construction equipment and supplies of dynamite began to be delivered to the site during the last months of the year.

As equipment and materials were offloaded at local ports, Soviet and Arab authors emphasized how this development project would transform Egypt's sovereignty by means of a return to its past.[11] Some compared the development project's architectural modernity to its Pharaonic heritage:[12] "The hydroelectric stations' gigantic building's series of concrete columns somehow or another remind me of the ancient Abu Simbel temple, above these same waters on a high Nile bank a thousand years ago."[13] In this way, Soviet travel writers collapsed modern into ancient Egypt within the state's postcolonial borders. Texts in Arabic also collapsed distant historical periods within the space of the nation. In his novel *Person of the High Dam* (1967), Son'allah Ibrahim compares the dam to the Pyramids, and the minister responsible for it—Sidqi Sulayman—to a Pharaonic statue.

When the author joined Sulayman's living body to Egypt's stony antiquity, he was drawing attention to exchanges between a body and the landscape. *Person of the High Dam* begins with an epigraph by poet 'Abd al Rahman al Abnudi, who wanted to pour his body's fluids into the development intervention: "I feel that the arm of the high dam needs some of my blood."[14] The novelist's narrative experiments furthered this collapsing of development landscape and intimate embodiment. Literary critic Ceza Kassem-Draz compares *Person of the High Dam* with Son'allah's second text, *Star of August* (1976). Between this and his later novel, also set at the dam, the author alternated between opaque and transparent narratives. The earlier text is "opaque," according to Kassem-Draz, in that it mediates between the reader and the event. Scientific and technical documents are similarly "opaque" in that they emphasize their own mediation. The second novel is transparent: "[*Star of August*] is systematically stripped of all tropes and tends towards a type of innocent and neutral discourse which Roland Barthes has termed 'writing degree zero.'"[15] In "transparent" narratives, language effaces itself to allow the referent to emerge in total objectivity.

In this chapter, I will discuss gender, labor, and democracy from "opaque" and "transparent" narratives. The reservoir, tunnels, and control room exemplify what is visible and what is concealed in this development project and in state modernization more generally. The periodical press that described Soviet specialists' work alternated between "opaque" and "transparent" narratives for postcolonial citizenship. Equals under both Soviet and Egyptian law, men and women experienced administrative regulations differently. These regulations brought them into national modernity on the basis of their remunerated labor as well as their family status. The state, in effect, achieved modernist employment by delegating sovereign powers to families, thereby denying individual rights. Each of the following sections will begin with technical details from the project, to address gendered political belonging and assess the high dam as a first test for democracy in Egypt.

Aswan High Dam under construction, 1965

AFP collection/Getty Images

Because of the Nile's particularly steep banks, Gidroproekt technicians designated a narrow stretch as the right site for an artificial closing or "diversion" of the river. Modeled by Gidroproekt employees in Moscow, the dam would form a reservoir with a 146-cubic-kilometer capacity at an elevation of 180 meters at average flood levels. During high floods, the reservoir's capacity was to top off at a 164-cubic-kilometers capacity, at 183 meters. Workers built up and grouted the dam to 130 meters following Soviet specifications, with the 1964 flood as a strict deadline for the first stage of construction. Laborers excavated water-passing structures into the right bank, where temporary lower openings of the intake structure and tunnels allowed runoff to pass until 1964. According to initial calculations, the reservoir would then slowly fill to capacity sometime between 1975 and 1980. This required crowds of laborers with skills in handling and placing dynamite, operating heavy construction machinery, and keeping equipment in working order.

While in Aswan, a provincial city on the farthest southern border from Cairo, Soviet development specialists found assignments to the dam construction site to be much like their previous jobs. Project executives' responsibilities were similar to those at construction sites near the smaller cities of the Soviet Union. A.P. Aleksandrov, director of the Aswan project, contributed to the reconstruction of the Volga-Don canal after World War II, and Chief Expert I. V. Komzin had been head engineer of the Kuibishev dam.[16] Their living conditions at Aswan were also similar to those back home: housing was in short supply, consumer prices were rising, and the need for significant domestic labor between shifts at the construction site was challenging.[17] For newspaper readers back in the USSR, gender proved central to discussions of the Aswan development landscape. Russian-language papers explained that husbands and wives worked together at the construction project, and reported wedding and birth announcements from abroad to illustrate the normalcy of gender relations. Anna Karaseva and Anatoli Dunaev married,[18] children "quickly acclimated,"[19] Zakhariia Mohiedin (Egypt's minister of the interior) gave a piano and toys to a new school for specialists' children.[20]

Martin Heidegger offered a discussion of the landscape that serves as a metaphor for Soviet specialists' gendered labor contributions. In his essay, "The Question Concerning Technology" (1954), he distinguished the modern technical vision of landscapes as calculable resources from a traditional or artisanal appreciation of materials.[21] According to him, modern research (characterized by apparatus-dependent science and mathematization of the world) challenges the Earth to "reveal itself" in the form of resources for consumption—its rivers to providing extractable resources whose extent and yield could be mapped and calculated in advance.[22] The modern technical vision to which Heidegger referred did not view only landscapes as calculable resources; labor and skills were also attributes to be "given over." Individuals' labor could be "brought forth" in a way that could also be mathematized, calculated, and modeled.

The idea of "bringing forth" can be interpreted to mean "imposing on" as an unequal, unjust process. As Heidegger wrote, "For man becomes truly free only insofar as he belongs to the realm of destining and so becomes one who listens and learns, and not one who is simply constrained to obey."[23] Some of the secondary Soviet population centers such as those that sent specialists to Aswan were exposed to Heidegger's ideas about the domination of natural environments, as academics at provincial cities introduced Continental philosophy to state socialism.[24] The "realm of destining" and the realm of those "constrained to obey" can be unequal in global terms, such as a distinction between citizens of the global North and South. The disparity can also be framed in regional terms, such as Moscow's control over natural resources east of the Urals, or Sudanese resistance to Cairo's sovereignty over its southern border.

This "bringing forth" can also be conceptualized with regard to the gendered distribution of resources. As they discussed their work, Soviet engineers expressed ideas about technical domination over the natural world in terms that were gendered and sexualized. Such narratives combined political, economic, and reproductive orders, offering gendered images in place of technical accuracy.[25] When Euro-American journalists reported that construction at Aswan lagged behind expectations due to poor communication between the Egyptian High Dam Authority and the Soviet Ministry of Foreign Economic Ties, the Soviet daily press responded that such disruptions were no more than the minor disagreements normally encountered in the course of married life.[26] Soviet journalists extended the construction project as a metaphor for marriage, when they described the process of bringing male technical authority to the female Nile.[27] Similarly, Soviet workers on the construction site wrote "opaque" narratives in which they adopted the wisdom of the Egyptian countryside, comparing the Nile's flow and Egypt's economic productivity to female fecundity.

With references to marriage and reproductive fertility, texts about the dam draw attention to women's productive labor. Women contributed to Gidroproekt's design work and the "mathematization of the world." Although the research institute employed more men than women, women supplied remunerated labor to every level of its technical hierarchy. Personnel records list 35 women among the 318 Soviets assigned to the Aswan project's Moscow-based design tasks.[28] Sixteen or seventeen women worked as engineers, nine as senior engineers, five or six as senior technicians, two or three as technicians. One woman was a department head (nachal'nik otdeleniia), out of more than twenty male department heads or deputies.[29]

State-led transformation of natural landscapes "brought forth" women's productive labor differently from men's. Wendy Goldman states that Soviet industrial enterprises used women as a labor reservoir, temporarily mobilizing them into modernist employment.[30] According to Goldman, although women contributed to the USSR's industrial revolution, their skills did not transfer to highly remunerated employment in heavy industry. Likewise, while women contributed to apparatus-dependent science within the Soviet Union's borders, they found that their skills did not transfer abroad. Specialists whom Gidroproekt sent to Aswan were male (with two identified exceptions—V. I. Kalygina, likely an economist in the Chief Expert's Authority, and L. P. Karataeva, a senior engineer in both Moscow and Aswan).[31] It seems that development interventions allocated priority employment to men, thereby deskilling women. At Aswan, most Soviet women were restricted to civic, domestic, and sexual roles, their presence justified by marriage to employed specialists.

International development assistance masculinized technical interventions, as revealed by "opaque" narratives' reference to gender. Similar observations encompass other development landscapes in the region. Gidroproekt projects include the Mansour Eddahbi complex and the Moulay-Youssef complexes in Morocco; the Euphrates and Tishrin dams and the Al-Baas barrage in Syria; and the Kasseb project in Tunisia.[32] Although this discussion of the Aswan dam's reservoir as a metaphor for the "standing reserve" is exemplary, it indicates a set of effects visible on development landscapes elsewhere in the east and south Mediterranean.

THE TUNNELS

Six tunnels distinguished Gidroproekt's designs from those proposed by the board of international consultants. These displayed to best advantage the skills that Soviet specialists had developed on municipal subway construction projects. Construction of the Aswan tunnels began when upper and lower fissures were blasted into the sides of the canals in August 1961. Once engineers had penetrated the rock face, skilled workers on platforms excavated the tight upper tunnels, using 1.25-cubic-meter capacity excavators to lower muck into 5-ton dumptrucks. In the lower tunnels' comparatively wider spaces, workers drilled the rock floor with rotary-percussion rigs and used supersized 4.6-cubic-meter capacity excavators to dump muck into 25-ton trucks. All tunnels were then wedged with steel-framed panels, and from September 1962, laborers filled these reinforcing frames with wet concrete. Breaches at the original water level permitted temporary regulation of the Nile flow until the 1964 river diversion, while the upper openings were designed for long-term regulation.

In the Soviet Union, construction workers had just started to enjoy a form of economic stability. Employment in the industry was booming, and the percentage of salaried engineering-technical workers increased as the percentage of workers paid by the day decreased.[33] Due to recent wage reforms, paychecks that development advisors received before coming to Aswan had risen by 10 to 20 percent, practically eliminating differences between the highest and lowest pay grades.[34] From their own experiences, foreign specialists predicted that Egyptian employees would come to enjoy what they conceptualized as "dignity," explaining: "Nobody cleans shoes here. Every street hawker [lotoshnik] dreams of being a professional excavator operator or driver."[35]

During the frenzied first stage of construction in the tunnels, Egyptian workers and foreign specialists worked side-by-side. Although those who carried Soviet passports and those with local identity documents in their pockets were apparent equals on the job site, their laboring experiences differed. Development advisors complained to Technopromeksport about the low level of qualifications of local workers in order to exclude Egyptians from technical responsibility and premium remuneration. Soviet sources blamed British imperialism for the dearth of local technical specialists ("In Cairo, for example, there had been eight thousand lawyers, but only tens of engineers."[36])

Under imperialism, they claimed, public administration extended the rule of law over property at the expense of technologies to regularize labor. Hence postcolonial citizenship came to be institutionalized as technical difference, as pay grades and training programs distinguished foreigners from local workers.[37]

Project managers provided disability insurance and retirement benefits to attract Egyptian laborers to the site.[38] Insurance offered lifetime security for all workers at Aswan by guaranteeing their salaries in the event of on-the-job accidents. It also provided married men with forms of security that unmarried men of the same age cohort could not enjoy, since it promised to support their families in the event of death. When the state transferred benefits from productive labor to reproductive units, unmarried men were relegated to a second-class form of security. Presidential Decree 63 (1964) extended workers' benefits to all in public employment nationwide.[39]

Administrative regulations' "opaque" language hid the experience of danger. From the beginning of underground work in 1961 until the tunnels were flooded in 1964, all six were stifling places where from 100 to almost 3,000 men worked in multiple shifts. In 1963, the tunnel department had its highest number of local workers—2,946 Egyptians, with 335 foreign specialists.[40] Side-by-side, Soviet and local laborers placed dynamite, exploded charges, excavated rubble, and placed struts. Workers later described the work site's hazards: "It immediately became clear why all was in lilac-colored smoke. It was the emissions from hundreds of vehicles. The sharp scent of gasoline hit the nose, drew tears from the eyes. It was hard to breathe. It tickled the throat."[41] Wet drilling and curing concrete's noxious gases increased humidity in the tunnels until it approached 100 percent. Even management's progress reports confirmed that the air was contaminated "with dust and noxious fumes produced as a result of blasting operations and utilization of motor vehicles."[42]

Official documentation makes geological factors responsible for hazards. In the same way journalists naturalized gender difference, official reports justified the

"From the beginning of the underground work in 1961 until the tunnels were flooded in 1964, all six were stifling, hot places where from one hundred to almost three thousand men worked in multiple shifts." From *Materials for Final Engineering Report on the High Aswan Dam Project 2*, "Construction of Tunnels," 1969.

tunnels' minimal reinforcement: "In the course of driving the diversion tunnels the condition of rock, in general, offered adequate stability of the roof without any temporary strengthening except for a few areas crossing the main tectonic zone." Management's trust in nature put workers at risk when 200 cubic meters of rock collapsed in tunnels one and two.[43] The tight schedule that required the tunnels to be ready for use by 1964 increased the danger. The tunnel department recorded the highest number of accidents among all High Dam Authority departments. Six were fatal, 259 resulted in more than three days' loss of work, and 357 accidents necessitated a total of 1,405 days of lost work.[44]

Like management, Soviet specialists fell back on "nature" to explain the difference between their and their local colleagues' accident rates. Specifying skills needed at the construction site, foreign specialists emphasized the intuitive nature of their expertise. Soviet workers' memoirs refer to a "sixth sense" they brought to their work in Aswan. This risky job required a special touch: "Tunnel work—it's not just knowledge, stuff that you memorize, not just formulas—you have to have a personal feel for it! That old guy doesn't hear anything, he feels it . . .Excavating a canal [in the open], you can stand as many drilling rigs as you like. But inside the tunnel, it's narrow, you understand? Every man, every jackhammer has to stand exactly in the place where they ought to be. That's how it goes!"[45] Local hires apparently lacked such intuition, and the construction site marked their bodies; Egypt's census notes construction workers who lost the use of one or both eyes, their hearing, or their power of speech.[46]

THE CONTROL ROOM

The completed power station's external slice of modernist colonnade is modest in comparison with its internal view. Its machine hall—a lengthy, light-filled room finished in blues and grays—is bisected by a second-floor visitors' gallery, permitting a dramatic view of the twelve turbine covers, painted yellow. After the initial celebratory lights of the photographers' flashbulbs during the opening ceremony, however, few have paused in the visitors' gallery. Closed off from public access, the control room offers this chapter its concluding metaphor for postcolonial citizenship in Egypt. The turbine covers, in marking the location of hidden tunnels, conceal any view from the tunnels to the machine hall and the turbines that convey power generated below the floor to the electrical substations. The skylights prevent any view to the spillway, which is the most that Egyptians ever see of the high dam because national security priorities keep the public out of the control room. The only people within are two engineers who monitor a panel graphically depicting the upstream reservoir, tunnels, and downstream channel. Under parallel skylights, these technicians manipulate controls to regulate the turbines' productivity.

Like the misleading appearance of equality between foreign specialists and Egyptian workers, new laws seemed to make women the legal equals of men. The country's 1956 constitution (article 31) specified: "Egyptians are the same in the eyes of the law: they

Under parallel skylights, two technicians manipulate controls to regulate the
turbines' productivity.

[are] equal in rights and public duties. There [is] no discrimination among them on the
basis of sex, ethnic origin, language, religion, or creed." To make women's work equal to
men's, this new state drew on international standards. International Labor Organization
Convention 100 (1951) granted men and women equal remuneration for equal jobs,
and Convention 111 (1958) prohibited gender discrimination in employment. Both
regulations came into force in the Nile Valley during the 1960s. Law 16 (1964) established
women's right to work as a citizenship right.[47] As the law came into practice, public
institutions became leading sites for educated women's paid employment. Egypt's Law
14 (1964) guaranteed jobs in the state sector for all with secondary-school diplomas
and college degrees, regardless of gender. Presidential Decree 75 (1964) imposed a
year's public employment for engineering school graduates regardless of gender.
This technical service was comparable to men's military conscription.[48] In the 1971
constitution, article 13 defines work as a right, a duty, and an honor guaranteed by the
state. In this way, the state intervened to ensure women at every level of the technical
hierarchy equal access to the value of their labor.

Just as women contributed to the "standing reserve" of the USSR's industrial
revolution, Egyptian women's employment brought them into the "reservoir" of civic
belonging. And just as men's employment at Aswan earned benefits for their families,
women discovered that public employment provided benefits to them as mothers. Law
No. 197 (1959) gave female employees the right to a fully paid fifty-day maternity leave

three times throughout their careers.[49] Large employers were required to grant a year's unpaid leave (without loss of seniority) to new mothers and provide daycare for female workers with young children. Articles 10 and 11 of Egypt's 1971 constitution impose an obligation on the state to protect mothers and children as well as to reconcile women's duties toward their families with their work in society.

Egypt ratified International Labor Organization C98 (granting rights to organize and collective bargaining) in 1954, and C87 (assuring freedom of association) in 1957.[50] But even as the state confirmed workers' rights, administrative action removed labor organizations and women's groups from the ILO's line of sight.[51] The state absorbed independent labor unions and the feminist movement into the Arab Socialist Union.[52] By granting generous maternity benefits, the state satisfied women's needs as mothers at the expense of their needs as workers.[53]

Such a "state patriarchy" continues to restrict Egyptians' access to democracy. Webster's *Third International New Dictionary* provides seven definitions for democracy. One is "political, social, or economic equality: the absence or disavowal of hereditary or arbitrary class distinctions or privileges"; another is "a state of society characterized by tolerance toward minorities, freedom of expression, and respect for the essential dignity and worth of the human individual." Democracy is at the center of the predominantly Islamic Arab states' struggle for economic development and against imperialism. In a background paper to the first *Arab Human Development Report* (2002), respondents from the region were more likely to support the statement "Democracy is better than any other form of government" than were respondents from eight other country groups.[54] While the law provides for free expression, administrative regulations restrict Egyptians' discussions. The current constitution's fourth principle declares, "Freedom of thought, creativity, opinion, housing and property is a right." However, Emergency Law 162 (1958) empowers the president with censorship as well as the authority to confiscate and close newspapers on the grounds of public safety and national security: this law has been invokes as recently as late January 2013. Furthermore, the Ministry of Information owns or operates the broadcast media and a percentage of three newspapers, and the equivalent of a presidential decree is required to appoint an editor to a daily newspaper.

Lila Abu-Lughod writes about the impact of politics on Egyptian television since 1960, when Soviet and Egyptian development advisors were working toward the diversion of the Nile. Electricity from the high dam permitted television to be installed in almost every domestic and many public spaces.[55] Abu-Lughod places television at the center of concepts about Egypt as a developing nation moving toward progress and enlightenment.[56] While she follows paternalism/maternalism in current broadcast programming, cinematic film from the high dam era remains quite visible even now. The government's two nationwide television channels screen an hour and a half from Egypt's "golden era" of film each day, equivalent to the programming time they devote to current events. Such films keep fresh the postcolonial priority on citizens and their romantic partnerships, reinforcing gendered and sexualized ideals that characterized the first half of the 1960s. This "control room" provides a constant message that companionate marriage and reproduction are central to a Heideggerian concept of "coming-into-being" as citizens.

When Egyptian writer Son'allah Ibrahim was offered a literary award in 2003, he reached back to a Cartesian tradition of transparency to criticize President Hosni Mubarak's government, with reference to Egyptian state television: "We no longer have theater, cinema, or scientific research; we only have festivals, conventions and a box filled with lies."[57] Because of its wide visibility, some consider television indicative of governance in the Arab world. Egyptian filmmaker Jehane Noujaim chose *Control Room* as the title for her 2002 documentary on the independent satellite television channel Al Jazeera, based in Doha, Qatar. The film began with senior producer Samir Khader's statement: "The message of Al Jazeera is first of all educational, to educate the Arab masses on something called democracy, respect [for] the other opinion, free debate, no taboos . . .and to try by using all these things to shake up these ancient societies, to awaken them." Producer Deema Khatib explained in a scene excised from the final film, "We don't think, we just present the news and people think." These paired assertions suggest such a "control room" is an opaque narrative of rule.

Since the end of Mubarak's regime, the Supreme Council of the Armed Forces promised to amend the 1971 constitution to limit the president to two terms and make other changes regarding the executive branch. During the months and weeks leading up to elections to the legislature's lower chamber, individuals (according to Ibrahim Saif) campaigned for seats with the promise "that they would provide more transparency, less corruption, and a set of values and morals."[58] The number of Egyptian citizens who turned out to vote in the 19 March 2011 referendum on the constitutional amendments was unprecedented. Following the victories (first) of members of the Muslim Brotherhood's "Freedom and Justice" party to the legislature, and (later) of Muslim Brotherhood member Mohamed Morsi to the office of president, a second referendum on a draft constitution was set for 15 December of the following year. This time, however, hundreds of thousands of citizens marched on the Presidential Palace in protest. Resisting the opacity of the structure that gave rise to the draft document, they urged the president to postpone the referendum. On the basis of the small number of people who turned out for the 22 December 2013 vote, a National Salvation Front was formed (representing the secular opposition led by Mohamed ElBaradei and Hamdeen Sabahi) to call for suspension of this newly ratified constitution. As at Aswan, the tension between opaque and transparent narratives continues to accompany the uneven advance of democracy.

Notes

1   Martin Heidegger, "The Question Concerning Technology," *The Question Concerning Technology and Other Essays*, translated by William Lovitt (New York: Harper & Row, 1977), 5.

2   James Dougherty, "Aswan Decision in Perspective," *Political Science Quarterly* 74:1 (1959), 25, refers to *The Observer*, 22 July 1956, H.E. Hurst, *The Nile* (London: 1952), chapters 16 and 17, and M. Philips Price, 25 July 1956, *Parliamentary Debates*, Commons, Fifth Series, 1956, vol. 557, s. 96.

3   K. M. Barbour, "A New Approach to the Nile Waters Problem," *International Affairs* 33:3 (1957), 321.

4   Barbour, "A New Approach," 321; Dougherty, "Aswan Decision in Perspective," 22; see also Robert Rycroft and James Szyliowica, "Technological Dimension of Decision Making: The Case of the Aswan High Dam," *World Politics* 33:1 (1980), 42; see also "Short Account on the High Dam Project," UAR Ministry of Electric Power and High Aswan Dam, *Materials for the Final Engineering Report on the High Aswan Dam Project* 10 (1970), 8.

5   Taher Mohamed Abu Wafa', *Mashru'a Al Sadd al 'Ali* (Cairo: Ministry of the High Dam, 1967), 74, 375. I'm grateful to Yehia Wael Hafez for drawing these to my attention.

6   Dougherty, "Aswan Decision in Perspective," 22, 25. For high-modernist regimes and freedom of speech, assembly, and the press, see James Scott, *Seeing Like a State: How Certain Schemes to Improve the Human Condition Have Failed* (New Haven, CT: Yale University Press, 1998) 97–102; on development projects that transform inhabitants to oustees, then refugees, see Eftihia Voutira and Barbara Harrell-Bond, "'Successful' Refugee Settlement: Are Past Experiences Relevant?" in *Risks and Reconstruction: Experiences of Resettlers and Refugees*, Michael Cernea and Christopher McDowell, eds. (Washington, D.C.: World Bank, 2000), 59, 71; and on regional economic patterns that make populations vulnerable to forced and/or voluntary migration, see Seteney Shami, "Mobility, Modernity, and Misery: Population Displacement and Resettlement in the Middle East," in *Population Displacement and Resettlement: Development and Conflict in the Middle East,* Seteney Shami, ed. (New York: Center for Migration Studies, 1994), 3.

7   Speech, 26 July 1956, Alexandria, Egypt; law 285 of 1956 nationalized Suez Canal assets for the construction project; histories of the project include I. Beliaev, "Semnadtsat' Piramid Keopsa," *Sovremennyi Vostok* 11 (1959), 40; I. V. Komzin, "Gidroenergeticheskii Gigant v Afrike." *Sovremenyi Vostok* 11 (1960), 36; I. V. Komzin, *Zapiski Sovetskogo Energetika* (Moscow: Gospolitizdat, 1960), 91; "Novaia Sud'ba Drevnego Nila," *Sovremennyi*

Vostok 12 (1960), 23, 25; I. T. Novikov, "Ukroshchenie Nila: Beseda s Ministerom Stroitel'stva Elektrostantsii SSSR I. T. Novikovym" *Novoye Vremia* 6 (1960), 16; P. Beliaev, "Asuanskii God." *Novoye Vremia* 4 (1961), 14; "Reportazh iz Asuana," *Aziia I Afrika Segodnia* 12 (1962), 40; "Shag v Budushchee." *Kul'tura I Zhizn* 5 (1962), 35; P. Beliaev, "Asuan—Simvol Druzhby Narodov," *Vneshnaia Torgovlia* 11 (1962), 38. I'm grateful to June Farris for assistance with source notes.

8   For the high dam's design's debt to the U.S. Tennessee Valley Authority, see Timothy Mitchell, *Rule of Experts: Egypt, Techno-Politics, Modernity* (Berkeley: University of California, 2002), 45; and Scott, *Seeing Like a State*, 270; for competing concepts of Nile control, see Terje Tvedt, *River Nile in the Age of the British: Political Ecology and the Quest for Economic Power* (London: Tauris, 2004), 262–265; and for international funding for the high dam, see Diane Kunz, *Economic Diplomacy of the Suez Crisis* (Chapel Hill: N.C., 1991), 40.

9   Hashim Behbehani, *Soviet Union and Arab Nationalism, 1917–1966* (London: KPI, 1986); Adeed Dawisha, "Soviet Union in the Arab World," in *Soviet Union in the Middle East: Policies and Perspectives*, eds. Adeed Dawisha and Karen Dawisha (London: Holmes & Meier, 1982), 8–23; Theodore Friedgut, "The Domestic Image of Soviet Involvement," Research Paper No. 26 (Jerusalem: Hebrew University, Soviet and East European Research Centre, August 1977); Galia Golan, *Soviet Policies in the Middle East from World War Two to Gorbachev* (Cambridge: Cambridge, 1990); Esmail Hosseinzadeh, *Soviet Noncapitalist Development* (New York: Praeger, 1989); Franklyn Holzman, *Soviet-American Rivalry in the Middle East*, J. C. Hurewitz, ed. (New York: Praeger, 1969); George Lenczowski, *Soviet Advances in the Middle East* (Washington, D.C.: American Enterprise Institute for Public Policy Research, 1971); Walter Laquer, *Soviet Union and the Middle East* (New York: Praeger, 1959); Said el-Naggar, "Soviet and Other Sources of Aid," in *Foreign Aid to United Arab Republic* (1963); Oles Smolansky, "Moscow and the Suez Crisis, 1956: A Reappraisal," *Political Science Quarterly* 80:4 (1965), 581–605; P. J. Vatikiotis, "The Soviet Union and Egypt," in *The Soviet Union and the Middle East: The Post World War II Era*, Ivo Lederer and Wayne Vucinich, eds. (Stanford, CA: Hoover, 1974).

10   USSR Ministry of Foreign Affairs, "Soglasheniie ob Okazanii Soiuzom Sovetskikh Sotsialisticheskikh Respublik Ekonomicheskoi I Tekhnicheskoi Pomoshchi Ob'"edinennoi Arabskoi Respublike v Stroitel'stve Pervoi Ochredi Vysotnoi Asuanskoi Plotiny," 27 December 1958, *SSSR I Arabskie Strany 1917–1960 gg.* (Moscow: Gospolitizdat, 1961), 683–688; Technopromeksport, Sadd-el-Ali Supreme Committee; Contract no. 059 of 8 September 1959, "On Rendering

Technical Assistance in Construction of the First State of the Aswan High Dam,"Ministerstvo Vneshnikh Ekonomicheskikh Sviazei (henceforth MVES), fond 365, op. 6, ed. khr 865. See also G. I. Sukharev, "Kak Bylo Organizovano Stroitel'stvo," in *Podvig Na Nile* (Moscow: Politicheskoi Literatury, 1970), 160–171; and N. S. Khrushchev et al., *Asuan—Simvol Sovetsko-Arabskoi Druzhby* (Moscow: Politizdat, 1964).

11 I. Beliaev, "Semnadtsat' Pyramid Kheopsa," *Sovremenyi Vostok* 11 (1959), 42; Sukharev, "Asuan," 39-59; I. V. Komzin, *Svet Asuana* (Moscow, Molodaia Gvardiia, 1964), 5-6; *Zapiski*, 102; V. Galaktionov, "Plotina Asuana," *Novyi Mir* 2 (1961), 173, 176; I. Beliaev, "Shag v Budushchee," 35; P. Beliaev, "Na Stroitel'stve Asuanskoi Plotiny," *Novoye Vremia* 33 (1962), 26.

12 MVES, f. 365, op. 2, ed. khr. 2359, 3; G. Gerasimov, "Egipet i Nil," *Novoe Vremia* 52 (1957), 28; I. Beliaev, "Semnadtsat' Pyramid Kheopsa," 39; Komzin, *Zapiski*, 91; "Novaia Sud'ba," 23, 25; Novikov, "Ukroshchenie Nila," 16; Beliaev, "Asuanskii God," 15; V. Galaktionov, "Plotina Asuana," 172; N. A. Dlin, "Nil I Asuanskaia Plotina," *Priroda* 8 (1962), 76; Beliaev, "Reportazh," 41; P. Beliaev, "Asuan—Simvol," 41; I. V. Komzin, "Bol'shaia Plotina na Nile," *Druzhba Narodov* 5 (1963), 231; Aleksandra Gorobova, *A S Dvukh Storon—Pustynia: Ocherki* (Moscow: Sovietskii Pisatel', 1970), 9.

13 Boris Ivanov, *40 Vekov I 4 Goda* (Moscow: Sovetskaia Rossiia, 1966), 102.

14 For an alternate reading of al Abnudi that emphasizes his affiliation with Egypt's folk tradition over his affiliation with Egypt's technical modernity, see Lila Abu-Lughod, *Dramas of Nationhood: The Politics of Television in Egypt* (Cairo: American University in Cairo Press, 2005), 72.

15 Céza Kassem-Draz, "Opaque and Transparent Discourse: A Contrastive Analysis of the *Star of August* and *The Man of the High Dam* by Son' Allah Ibrahim," *Alif: Journal of Comparative Poetics* 2 (1982), 44. Reference is to Roland Barthes, *Writing Degree Zero and Elements of Semiology* (Boston: Beacon, 1970).

16 Aswan personnel directed construction projects that drew on a reservoir of convicted persons' labor. A.P. Aleksandrov was director of the Lower Don labor camp which was organized on 4 August 1952; by 1 September 1952, it commanded the labor of 37,679 prisoners; see M. V. Smirnov, *Sistema Ispravitel'no-Trudovykh Lagerei v SSSR 1923–1960: Spravochnik* (Moscow: Zven'ia, 1998): 336; see also the third edition of the *Bol'shaia Sovetskaia Entsiklopedia* (Moskva: Sovetskaia entsiklopedia, 1970) I, 412. I. F. Komzin, a general-major of engineering-technical services in the police, was chief engineer at Kuibyshevgirdrostroi MVD SSSR from the summer of 1951, reporting to the Moscow operations group, according to MVD no. 00106 of 03.03.1951; see Smirnov, 124; also I. Komzin: "Volga na Beregy Nila" and "Asuan u Rechki Skhodni" in *Svet Asuana*, 31-37 and 120-138; "Kuibyshevskaia Gidroelektrostantsiia na Reke Volge," *Pravda*, 4 September 1950; "God Napriazhennogo Truda," *Komsomol'skaia Pravda* and "Plan Velikoi Stroiki v Deitstvii" *Pravda*, both 21 August 1951; "Velikaia Pobeda Sovetskogo Naroda," *Komsomol'skaia Pravda* 27 July 1952; "Dva Goda Velikikh Rabot," *Bakinskii Rabochii* and "S Chest'iu Vypolnim Zadanie Rodiny," *Pravda*, both 21 August 1952; "Vesti v Stroi Kuibyshevskiu Gidroelektrostantsii v 1955 Godu," *Pravda*, 21 August 1955; "Schast'e Stroitelia," *Trud*, 14 November 1957. While Heidegger dwells on the violence of wresting value from resources, alternate perspectives draw attention to administrative regulations that exclude individuals and their labor's value from the law's protections; see, for example, Giorgio Agamben, *Homo Sacer: Sovereign Power and Bare Life* (Stanford, CA: Stanford University Press, 1998).

17 The annual report for 1961 records 122 specialists with 95 family members including 29 children; see Tsentralnogo gosudarstvennogo arkhiva narodnogo khoziaistva SSSR (henceforth TsGANKh), fond 9572, op. 1, ed. khr. 1588, p. 58. As of 1 September 1961, there were 274 specialists in Aswan (TsGANKh, fond 9572, op. 1, ed. khr 1927, l. 25); as of 10 November 1961, 547 specialists, 163 wives, and 117 children (TsGANKh, fond 9572, op. 1, ed. khr. 1927, l. 96). *Materials for the Final Engineering Report on the High Aswan Dam Project* 10 identifies the number of laborers at 12,000, with 175 engineers on technical staff and 660 Soviet specialists; dependents are not mentioned (Aswan, 1970), 96.

18 Komzin, "Bol'shaia Plotina," 233.

19 A. Agar'shev, "Granit Asuana, Po Sledam Sovetskogo Diploma" in *Komsomol'skaia Pravda*, 9 January 1970.

20 Komzin, "Bol'shaia Plotina," 233. See also Sukharev, "Russkii Dom," 79-96.

21 "Die Frage nach der Technik," "The Question Concerning Technology" was first given as a lecture on 18 November 1955 as part of the Bavarian Academy of Fine Arts lecture series "The Arts in the Technological Age," published in the Academy's yearbook, volume III, edited by Colemens Graf Podewils (Munich: R. Oldenbourg, 1954), 70; republished in *Vorträge und Aufsätze* (Pfullingen: Günther Neske, 1954); subsequently republished in *Die Technik un de Kehre* (Pfullingen: Günther Neske, 1962).

22 See Zoë Sofia, "Container Technologies," *Hypatia* 15:2 (2000), 195. Two others who have coaxed feminist readings from Heidegger include Leslie Paul Thiele, "Heidegger on Freedom: Political not Metaphysical,"

American Political Science Review 88:2 (1994); and Stephen White, "Heidegger and the Difficulties of a Postmodern Ethics and Politics," *Political Theory* 18:1 (1990), 80–103. For Heidegger's significance for postcolonial studies, see Achille Mbembe, "Necropolitics," *Public Culture* 15:1 (2003), 11–14; and to critical Cold War studies, see Timothy Brennan, "The Cuts of Language: The East/West of North/South," *Public Culture* 13:1 (2001), 39–63.

23 Heidegger, "The Question Concerning Technology," 25.

24 "Toward a Criticism of Martin Heidegger's Ontology" was published in the bulletin of the Kurgan pedagogical institute, G. I. Patent, "K Kritike Ontologii Martina Khaideggera," *Uchenyyi Zapiskii (Kurganskii Pedagogicheskii Institut)* 5 (1963); the following year, "Understanding 'Nihilism' and 'Nothing' in M. Heidegger's Existentialism and Anticommunism" appeared among the higher schools of philosophical sciences' scientific reports; I. S. Narskii, "Poniatiia 'Nigilizma' I 'Nichto' v Ekzistentsializme M. Khaideggera I Antikommunizm," *Nauchnyi Doklady Vyssh. Shkoly. Filosofskogo Nauki* 3 (1964).

25 Anne McClintock, *Imperial Leather: Race, Gender, and Sexuality in the Colonial Context* (London: Routledge, 1995), 1–4.

26 Beliaev, "Reportazh," 40, 41. See also Iu. Zviagin, "Asuanskii Orekh," *Novoye Vremia* 5 (1960), 9–11.

27 Gerasimov, G. "Egipet I Nil," *Novoe Vremia* 52 (1957), 28, Komzin, *Zapiski*, 86, 91; P. Beliaev, "Asuan—Simvol Druzhby," 38; Galaktionov, "Plotina Asuana," 182–183; P. Beliaev, "Na Stroitel'stve," 26.

28 For Soviet specialists assigned to the high dam project, see Komzin, *Zapiski*, 100–103; "Novaia Sud'ba," 24; Galaktionov, 186, 188, 190; Komzin, "Bol'shaia plotina," 225; Nikolaev, *Opalennyi Pal'me*, 26.

29 TsGANKh, f. 9572, op. 1, ed. khr. 1927, TsGANTD, fond R-109, op. 1-6, ed. khr. 493.

30 See chapter 7 in Wendy Goldman, *Women at the Gates: Gender and Industry in Stalin's Russia* (Cambridge: Cambridge University Press, 2002).

31 Kalygina: TsGANKh, f. 9572, op. 1, ed. khr. 1927, l. 27; Karataeva: TsGANTD, fond R-109, op. 1-6, ed. khr. 493, l. 15.

32 *Gidroproekt Za Rubezhom/Hydroproject Association Abroad* (Moscow: Vneshtorgizdat, 1991), 1.

33 S. Joseph Cerniglia, "Wages in the USSR, 1950–1966: Construction," Department of Commerce, Bureau of the Census, Foreign Demographic Analysis Division, *International Population Reports Series* P-95, no. 63 (October 1967).

34 Rachel Golden, æRecent Trends in Soviet Personal Income and Consumption,æ Joint Economic Committee, U.S. Congress, *Dimensions of Soviet Economic Power*, Eighty-seventh Congress, second session, 1962; see also Walter Galenson, "Soviet Wage

Reform," *Proceedings* of the thirteenth annual meeting of the Industrial Relations Research Association, December 1960.

35 Ivanov, 56. See also Evgeniii Vorob'ev, "Dobrye Liudi iz Asuana," *Novoye Vremia* 34 (1964), 26_27.

36 Ivanov, 56, 60. See also Sukharev, "Rasgovor po Dusham," 144–151.

37 Sukharev, "Est' Arabskie Gidrostroiteli," 97–108. See also MVES, f. 365, op. 2, ed. khr. 2368, l. 37; 2400, ll. 16, 18; 2435, ll. 26, 38, 65, 66; 2436; l. 15; 2529, l. 29; 2704, ll. 33, 42. Compare such assertions with the *1960 Census of Population,* which lists Arab and foreign men and women who were "architects, engineers and surveyors," including 17,176 male and 92 female Egyptians; 49 male "other Arabs," 22 male Syrians, 14 male Sudanese, 12 male Palestinians, along with 188 male Italians, 215 male and 10 female Greeks; table 28, p. 88.

38 Sadd el Aali Authority, [71].

39 I'm grateful to Yehia Wael Hafez for this observation.

40 "Personnel and Their Welfare Facilities at the Construction Site," UAR Ministry of Electric Power and High Aswan Dam, *Materials for the Final Engineering Report on the High Aswan Dam Project*, 10 (1970), table 12, p. 98; table 16, p. 105.

41 Ivanov, 53.

42 Official reports state, "provision of an efficient ventilating system [was] of an utmost importance." UAR Ministry of Electric Power and High Aswan Dam, *Materials for the Final Engineering Report on the High Aswan Dam Project*, 2 (1969), 93, "Ventilation and Dewatering."

43 Ibid.), 11, "Brief Characteristics of Structures and Geology of Rocks."

44 Ibid., 11, "Organization of Labour and Safety Engineering."

45 Nikolaev, 46.

46 1960 Census of Population, table 44, 299.

47 As of 20–21 November 1960, Egyptian women's highest economic activity rates were in the 15–19 and 20-24-year-old age brackets (8.6 percent and 7.3 percent, respectively). Most women were employed in manufacturing industries and what are described as "community, social, and personal services" (including remunerated sales workers and clerical workers) (tables 1 and 2A); ILO (Geneva), *Yearbook of Labor Statistics: Retrospective Edition on Population Censuses, 1945–1989.*

48 *Al Jarida al Rasmiya*, 22 March 1964.

49 For gender in Egypt's planned economy, see Judith Tucker, "Egyptian Women in the Work Force," *MERIP* 50 (1976), 9.

50 Joel Beinin, "Labor, Capital and the State in Nasserist Egypt, 1952–1961," *International Journal of Middle East Studies*, 21:1 (1989), 74; Ellis Goldberg,

"The Foundations of State-Labor Relations in Contemporary Egypt," *Comparative Politics* 24:2 (1992), 151.

51 Margot Badran, "Competing Agenda: Feminists, Islam, and the State in Nineteenth- and Twentieth-Century Egypt," in Deniz Kandiyoti, ed., *Women, Islam, and the State* (Philadelphia: Temple University, 1991), 217.

52 Salma Botman, "Women's Participation in Radical Egyptian Politics, 1930–1952," in Magida Salman et al., eds., *Women in the Middle East* (London: Zed, 1987), 1–25.

53 Margot Badran, *Feminists, Islam, and Nation: Gender and the Making of Modern Egypt* (Princeton: Princeton, 1995), 205; see also Deniz Kandiyoti's chapter on gender in political analysis, "Contemporary Feminist Scholarship and Middle East Studies," in *Gendering the Middle East: Emerging Perspectives*, ed. Deniz Kandiyoti (London: Tauris, 1996), 3–4.

54 United Nations Development Program, Arab Fund for Economic and Social Development, *Arab Human Development Report 2003; Building a Knowledge Society*, p. 19.

55 For television's spread throughout Egypt due to electrification and labor migrants' wages, see Lila Abu-Lughod, "The Objects of Soap Opera: Egyptian Television and the Cultural Products of Modernity," in *The Anthropology of Media: A Reader*, Kelly Askey and Richard Wilk, eds. (London: Blackwell, 2002), 376.

56 Abu-Lughod, *Dramas*, 86.

57 Hassan Saber, "Brotherhood Running the Country Like a Supermarket; Son'allah Ibrahim," *Aswat Masriya*, 17 January 2013.

58 Roula Khalaf, "Arab World: Underfunded Renaissance," *Financial Times*, 10 February 2013.

URBAN TRANSFORMATIONS

ELENI BASTÉA AND
VILMA HASTAOGLOU-MARTINIDIS

4

MODERNIZATION AND ITS DISCONTENTS

IN POST-1950s THESSALONIKI:

URBAN CHANGE AND URBAN NARRATIVES

Urban historians have long associated modernizing a city with the modernization of people's mentalities. In reviewing the planning of Paris under Baron Haussmann (1853–70), the art historian T.J. Clark asserted: "Part of Haussmann's purpose was to give modernity a shape, and he seemed at the time to have a measure of success in doing so: he built a set of forms in which the city appeared to be visible, even intelligible: Paris, to repeat the formula, was becoming a spectacle."[1] Nevertheless, Clark and others considered Haussmann's project incomplete and unsuccessful, as it met with constant opposition by the citizens.[2] Reviewing the same period through a different lens, the cultural historian Marshall Berman focused on the work of the poet and critic Baudelaire, who, according to Berman, "shows us something that no other writer sees so well: how the modernization of the city at once inspires and enforces the modernization of its citizens' souls."[3]

Does urban change, indeed, affect inhabitants' daily patterns and their mental picture of the city? Is it possible to examine how new architecture and planning affect the people? Can the modernization of a city cause the modernization of the citizens' souls? We will examine these questions by focusing on Thessaloniki, Greece. After a review of the city's earlier history, we will focus on the major urban projects and the relevant urban literature since the 1950s. Our aim is to gauge the support for and resistance to urban changes, as reflected in the literature. Although literary depictions of a city do not necessarily represent mainstream public opinion, they do open a window onto people's private thoughts. We believe that our research reveals an image of the city that is at once familiar to locals and illuminating to urban planners and historians.

Furthermore, by examining the image of the city through the eyes of writers, we are obliquely addressing the following broader questions: Do changes in the architecture and planning of a city enter into people's consciousness? In short, do architecture and planning matter?

THESSALONIKI BEFORE THE 1950S: AN URBAN AND LITERARY OVERVIEW

Located on the major routes linking Europe with the Orient, Thessaloniki has had a continuous urban presence for more than twenty-three centuries. Founded around 315 BCE, the city became an important commercial, administrative, and cultural center, passing successively through Hellenistic, Roman, Byzantine, and Ottoman periods. Each period left its particular imprint on the city's architecture and urbanism. A large community of Spanish Jews was established in the city at the end of the fifteenth century, further enriching its cosmopolitan character. Thessaloniki was incorporated into the Greek state in 1912. As the second-largest city in Greece, it has continued to enjoy steady growth.[4]

At the turn of the twentieth century, Thessaloniki was a multiethnic city with a population of 150,000. Its medieval framework, with dense and irregular streets, clearly defined urban clusters, and introverted neighborhoods, survived and supported the city's demographic and social physiognomy. As the Ottoman Empire instituted westernizing reforms (Tanzimat, from 1839 to 1876), Thessaloniki underwent gradual modernization from 1869 onward. Its sea walls were demolished, allowing the city to expand toward the sea, where a modern quay was developed. Thessaloniki's occidental character was enhanced by a new rail link with Europe and Istanbul, newly organized port facilities, a modern central business district, and the construction of new residential areas outside of its traditional nucleus. These changes sharpened the city's socioeconomic stratification, but did not alter drastically its overall urban character.

In 1912, the Greek army succeeded in capturing Thessaloniki and the surrounding regions from the Ottomans, incorporating them into the Greek state. According to the 1913 census compiled by the new Greek administration, there were 157,889 inhabitants, of whom 61,439 (38.91 percent) were Jews, 45,867 (29.05 percent) were Muslims, and 39,956 (23.31 percent) were Orthodox Christians.[5] There were also French, English, and Italian inhabitants. Thessaloniki's residential and civic/religious sectors reflected the city's multiethnic population. While the city had enjoyed a central commercial role under Ottoman rule, comparable to that of Izmir or Alexandria, after its incorporation into the Greek state it was downgraded to a provincial center. Between 1855 and 1930, Greek literary production in Thessaloniki remained rather slight.[6] Athens served as the undisputed capital of the Greek novel until at least the 1920s.[7]

In 1917, a major fire destroyed 128 hectares (316 acres) of the tightly built historic center. The fire dealt a major blow to the prominent Jewish community, destroying three-quarters of its neighborhoods and leaving 70,000 people homeless.[8] Immediately after the fire, the Greek government redesigned the downtown according to the latest methods of modern town planning. The Ministry of Communications (the government department responsible for town planning) set up an International Commission for the New Plan of Thessaloniki, headed by French architect Ernest Hébrard.

Hébrard's plan, which followed Beaux-Arts principles, radically reshaped the urban space along European lines. Thessaloniki was to be transformed into a national urban center of monumental scale. The proposed regular blocks and broad boulevards reflected planning principles of the preceding decades, evident in Haussmann's designs for Paris, the City Beautiful movement in the United States, and contemporary colonial designs around the world. Ancient, Byzantine, and Ottoman historic buildings became focal points of the composition, projected against a neo-Byzantine architectural background. Traces of the old city's layout were swept away, except for the Upper Town, which was preserved due to its picturesque qualities. Hébrard's plan also echoed the rigorous grid pattern of Hellenistic Thessaloniki, but articulated it with major diagonal avenues for the accommodation of modern traffic. This drastic urban undertaking was intended to cement the Greek presence in the city and signal a new national beginning. Under Hébrard's direction, the commission completely redesigned the downtown area, introducing a central north-south civic axis, Aristotelous Avenue, linking the Upper Town with the sea. The redesign of the historic center, along with future extensions, was intended to accommodate a predicted population of 350,000 (as opposed to the existing 170,000), covering an area of 2,400 hectares (5,930 acres). The inward-focused character of the late Ottoman city gave place to a modern, open arrangement that introduced the apartment block, the use of reinforced concrete, and the freehold land system.

The freehold land system (or "horizontal landownership," as the term is described in Greek) allowed the ownership of individual apartments in a multistory building and the corresponding ownership of a percentage of the original building lot. Before the

The urban fabric of Thessaloniki before the 1917 fire (left) and after the new plan of 1918 (right).

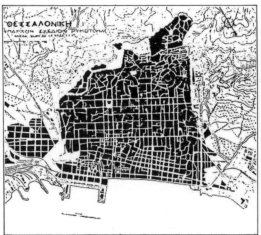

introduction of the freehold system, the owner of a lot was by law also the owner of the building on it. Co-ownership was not permitted within the same building. The freehold system was introduced for the first time in Thessaloniki's post-fire rebuilding. Later, it made possible the accommodation of the Asia Minor refugees of 1922–23 and the post-1950s internal migration. It liberated real estate properties from chronic ownership disputes and encouraged the redevelopment of urban centers and the construction of higher-density apartment buildings in Thessaloniki.[9]

The implementation of Hébrard's design proceeded slowly, frequently adjusted to accommodate property rights, increased speculative activity, and the sharp economic divisions that resulted after the fire. Although the newly designed center featured smaller squares and plots than those in the original plan, it signaled the radical modernization of urban structure and form for the intramural city. The new plan eliminated the old spatial patterns, erased the territorial basis of the ethnic-religious communities, and replaced them with a homogenized city fabric that was stratified according to social and economic criteria. Although new ownership of the historical center included many of its former residents, the numerous poorer inhabitants were forced out of the center. Traditional activities and old business sites were replaced with a modern urban center that included financial, commercial, and civic districts. The extraordinary political and military events that followed World War I, however, spelled the suspension of most planning activities and the drastic adjustment of the Hébrard plan.

Between 1919 and 1922, the Greek army led an expansionist campaign in Asia Minor, aiming to incorporate Izmir and its surrounding areas into the Greek state. After

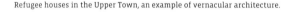

Refugee houses in the Upper Town, an example of vernacular architecture.

the defeat of the Greek army, Greece and Turkey signed the Treaty of Lausanne (1923), which stipulated the compulsory exchange of minority populations between the two countries. More than 1.2 million Christian Greeks from Asia Minor migrated to Greece, and 355,000 Muslim Turks from Greece migrated to Turkey. At the time, Greece had fewer than 5 million inhabitants. From the start, Thessaloniki was the main pole of attraction for the urban refugees: 117,000 settled in the city between 1920 and 1928, while approximately 25,000 Muslims left with the forced exchange. These dramatic changes placed extraordinary pressures on the physical resources of the city and strained the finances of the city and the state. To control these changes, the public sector stepped in to approve all levels of planning, from the allocation of refugee settlements to the urban design and building of dwellings.[10]

Given the urgency and speed of these extensive building efforts, planning was reduced to the most rudimentary level. As evidenced by the 1923 decree "On the rural settlement of refugees," every settlement was to be "planned in a rough manner and divided into building blocks."[11] New buildings had only the minimum essentials, and almost no social amenities, such as parks or public squares. By 1930, the refugees had founded more than fifty settlements on the city's outskirts. These settlements, together with the camps for the Jewish victims of the 1917 fire, formed the "outcast city." They formed a ring of ghettoized districts, contrasting with the air of urbanity of the historic center.

The implementation of the new city plan, designed by Hébrard's team, was now restricted to the historic city center. Housing projects for the refugees bore no resemblance to Hébrard's elaborate design. Instead, they followed plain and uniform grid patterns and simple building codes and construction techniques, without regard to each site's special conditions or the cultural background of each refugee community. Even the city center was negatively affected by the strained economic resources. The construction of civic buildings was abandoned due to lack of funds, while the building blocks of the city bazaars were subdivided to accommodate small shopkeepers. Nevertheless, the city center emanated an air of vibrant economic activity that did not extend to the refugee developments.

In an expedient and haphazard manner, Thessaloniki underwent an unprecedented expansion in all directions, covering a surface area of more than 1,500 hectares (3,706 acres) by 1928 and 2,000 hectares (4,942 acres) by 1940. Although the influx of refugees helped transform Thessaloniki into a regional industrial metropolis, the complete neglect of the cultural particularities of the different refugee groups accelerated its transformation from a communal to a socially stratified city. Throughout the city's twentieth-century development, the historic center managed to retain some of its earlier character. This historic core overlaps with the Ottoman historic residential and commercial center, stretching north–south from the Upper Town to the Thermaic Gulf (or Gulf of Thessaloniki), and east–west from the White Tower to Vardari Square and the city's port. Modern architecture was restricted to the city center, with multistory apartment buildings becoming the new form of bourgeois housing. In contrast to the center's modern urban eclecticism, working-class housing on the city's outskirts was modest and semi-rural in appearance.

THE LITERARY RESPONSE

How did literature respond to the radical urban transformations following the 1917 fire and the influx of refugees? As the literary historian Peter Mackridge pointed out, after the incorporation of Thessaloniki into the Greek state in 1912, the nation-building project included the creation of literature that featured the expanded territories.[12] While the architects reshaped Thessaloniki into a modern Greek city, the writers were expected to compose new literary landscapes about Greek Thessaloniki.

The School of Thessaloniki was the first major modern Greek literary movement. It flourished between 1930 and 1940 and represented the work of a fairly close-knit group of writers. They produced the modernist literary journal *Makedonikes Imeres* [Macedonian Days] (1932–39) and published mainly works of experimental prose. Despite its name, the School of Thessaloniki became known for its lack of place specificity and recognizable social and historical settings. Ignoring not only the nationalist propaganda but also the city's historical past, the writers described an introverted and troubled relationship to their environment, reflecting a private sense of loss and rootlessness. Most of the members of the School of Thessaloniki focused on the search for self and the cultivation of one's inner world, as articulated in the long interior monologues and their experimental novels. For example, Petros Spandonidis, in a poem titled "Saloniki! Saloniki!" (*Macedonian Days*, September 1932), describes the city as "chaos city." The speaker, as a citizen of "chaos city," has chaos within himself as well.[13] We believe that these writers, most of them newcomers to Thessaloniki, avoided specific discussions of the city in part because they did not yet possess a personal and deep familiarity with it. Moreover, their focus on the interior world and experimental prose reflected their engagement with a broader, contemporary European modernist movement that favored these themes.

THESSALONIKI SINCE THE 1950s: URBAN DEVELOPMENT AND LITERARY NARRATIVES

Planning Changes and the Destruction of Neighborhoods

All architectural and planning activity in the city came to a halt with the outbreak of World War II. Greece endured a brutal German occupation (1941–44) and a violent Civil War (1946–49).[14] In 1943 Thessaloniki witnessed the mass expulsion of virtually the entire Jewish community (50,000 people) to the German camps, where most died—a loss of a population that had been a major component of the city's character for centuries.

Beginning in the 1950s, the population measured over 300,000. In an attempt to revive the local economy and reduce the growing housing problem, the government decided to mobilize private capital. The notorious increase in the building coefficients in 1956 and 1960 permitted an extensive exploitation of building plots (much denser in Thessaloniki than in other Greek cities) and triggered feverish building activity throughout the 1960s and 1970s. At the same time, the great wave of internal migra-

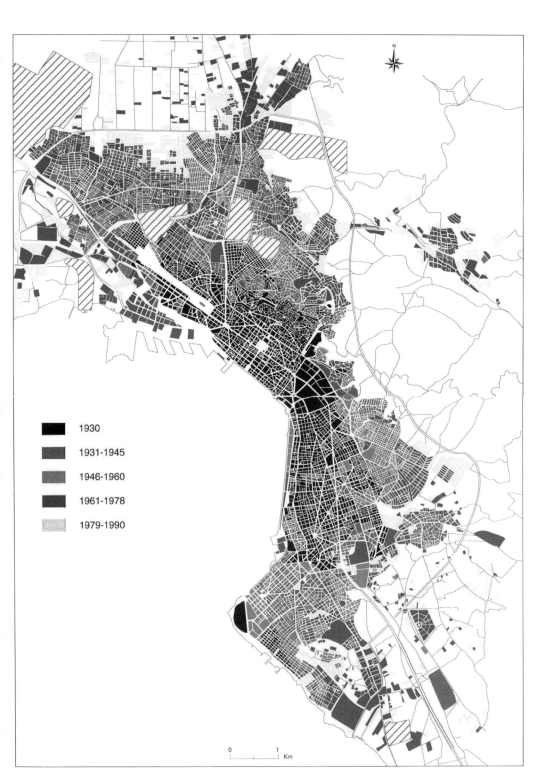

Urban growth from 1930 to 1990.

Legend:
- 1930
- 1931-1945
- 1946-1960
- 1961-1978
- 1979-1990

tion increased both the population and the size of the city, creating squatter settlements on the western periphery. The city increased in population and density too, with 557,000 inhabitants by 1971 and 706,000 by 1981.

Most urban literature since the 1950s has focused on the physical destruction of the built environment. Writers who had come into adulthood during the interwar years dwelled on the loss of the historic parts of the city and of its medieval and Ottoman street pattern, most of which had been obliterated in the 1917 fire. Their emphasis on the city's physical destruction may also reflect a symbolic reference to the Greek military catastrophe in Asia Minor and the subsequent loss of the Greek presence there.[15]

Some writers recorded the process of change and the disappearance of the old city with a naturalist's curiosity. Others illustrated urban change using dramatic and apocalyptic visions. Nikos Gabriil Pentzikis (1908–93) was the only member of the School of Thessaloniki to describe the city in detail, through the eyes of a narrator who favored long walks. In his collection of essays titled *Mitera Thessaloniki* [Mother Thessaloniki] (1970), he wrote: "For years now they have been working on widening the road. Workers go up to the old houses and demolish them. At first, the wooden skeleton of the roof is laid bare. The roof tiles are removed. The houses are left without a hat. Then starts the lowering of the walls. [. . .] The interior is revealed [. . . .]"[16] Vassilis Vassilikos (born in 1934 and best known for his political novel *Z*) recorded primarily the changes in the historic center and the Upper Town, focusing on the demolition of old houses as they entered into an uneven battle with new apartment buildings. Through vivid and even violent metaphors, he depicted the little houses falling under the ammunition of advancing engineering offices, victims of heavy building artillery.[17]

Most writers also criticized the destruction of the urban and social fabric of the city's old neighborhoods. Unlike Baudelaire's celebration of modernity, noted at the beginning of this chapter, most Greek writers bemoaned the advent of modernity in Thessaloniki because it ushered in menacing, tall, anonymous, and unarticulated apartment buildings that destroyed the earlier neighborhoods and turned the streets into dark and narrow passages. Often they described the disappearance of a neighborhood through the eyes of the returning protagonist. For example, the main character in one of Vassilikos's novels returns to Thessaloniki after years abroad and becomes devastated to discover the disappearance of his neighborhood, and with it, "of many narrow roads, where he had planted his agonies, his heart palpitations, in short, his whole adolescence."[18] More often, the narrator reflects on his childhood memories, as Sakis Papadimitriou (b. 1940) remarked in one of his essays (1960–73):

> All these years in this quiet neighborhood I had almost no complaint. Of course, it was not some suburb with trees, green and openness, nevertheless, our house had its own little courtyard and next to us were other single houses or two-story houses. The apartment buildings were approaching in a threatening manner, two or three narrow streets further down. Eventually they would reach us, blocking the air, building up the courtyards, pulpifying the green. But for now, we still had a lot of time ahead of us.[19]

Street in the Upper Town in 1900.

While demolition crews uncovered the private houses and the lives taking place inside them, something about the mystery of the old city and perhaps the mystery of the narrators' own childhoods suddenly came into sharp focus, and then was lost forever.

Frequently the demolition of traditional buildings became a metaphor for the destruction of traditional neighborhood ties, as expressed in the following prose poem by Dinos Christianopoulos (b. 1931), published in 1986:

The Death of the Neighborhood

At night, the son of the neighbor woman, [who lived] across from me, was waiting for me at the door. "Tonight my mother passed away," he told me, his eyes filled with tears. For a while we both remained silent; at that point, there were no appropriate words. "I thought of letting our neighbors know of the funeral, but aside from Mrs. Despoina and you, no one else of the old timers is left. My mother, who saw all her neighbors off, will now pass on alone."

"Our neighborhood, too, died with her," I thought, feeling a tightness in my heart.[20]

Opposite: The death of the neighborhood: From the original historic fabric, only monuments survived the process of urban modernization. All houses have been replaced by multistory apartment buildings. Visible in this aerial photograph are the Alaca Imaret mosque in the foreground, a multidome mosque set in a square; the Yeni Hamam baths, with one dome, mostly visible; and the large basilica church of Hagios Demetrios, near the Yeni Hamam.

Above: Popular landmarks: The church of Hagia Sophia and the "red building," across Hagia Sophia Square, dwarfed by the taller apartment buildings surrounding it.

Despite the city's continuous physical expansion, most authors described a circum-
scribed area, one that focused on the historic center and on the same major landmarks.
These landmarks included not only historic buildings and sites but also commercial
establishments, new streets and squares, the seafront, and the sea itself, the Thermaic
Gulf. The White Tower continued to be the city's most recognizable symbol, a popular
meeting spot and point of orientation. The city's numerous Byzantine churches, especially Hagia Sophia, continued to act as points of reference, along with the Red Building
across from Hagia Sophia, with its ground-floor café, the foreign-language bookstore
on Tsimiski Street, the basement of the (original) Fokas department store, the Modiano
Market, and the Bravo coffee store. Narrators found themselves on Egnatia Street,
remarking on its cheap merchandise, and on the shopping street Ermou, aptly named
for the god of commerce, Hermes. See, for example, Yorgos Ioannou's reference in
Refugee Capital (1984), published when the author had moved to Athens permanently:
"Whether I arrive in Salonica by train, or in my imagination, I head straight up the Via
Egnatia, naturally, toward the tall building where I lived for twenty-five years..."[21]

There is some inconsistency in descriptions of the city's transformations. Modern
planning is supposed to produce an open city, legible to newcomers and old-timers
alike. Thessaloniki's new plan, ordered according to geometric and transportation axes,
transformed it from an inward-focused city, legible only to its own people through a
complex system of symbols and references, to a public city that was supposed to be
legible to everyone. In the process, writers maintained, the city lost its distinctive interi-
ority and its particular relationship with its inhabitants. This purported break with the
past was not always supported, however, by the literature we reviewed.

We found that most writers counterbalanced the effects of new planning by creating their own maps of Thessaloniki, organized around daily walks, shopping, and visits
to cafés. The image of the city that continued to emerge from these narratives is not
the open, modern city of the planners but rather the private city of its longtime inhabitants. In fact, as writers conveyed their own intimacy with Thessaloniki, even when they
did not live there permanently, they assumed that their readers experienced the same
familiarity. Consider, for example, the reference to a romantic date, described in one of
the short stories by M. Karagatsis (1908–60): "At six in the evening. I will be there in my
car in the narrow street behind the church of Hagia Sophia."[22] The reader is expected to
know the approximate if not precise spot of the meeting. The anti-development criticism regarding the destruction of the neighborhood notwithstanding, literary references to places—be they churches, cafés, or corner dairies—continued to appear in
the literature about Thessaloniki. This leads us to conclude that despite the drastic
planning changes, the literary city remained legible, and, for the most part, familiar
to its residents.

Another example of the writers' continued intimacy with their city is the persistence
of Thessaloniki as a *locus eroticus*. In the 1970s, the sites of this literary image focused
primarily around Vardari Square (near the train station), the undeveloped suburbs of
Karabournaki by the sea, in the suburb of Panorama in the hills, and in the unbuilt lots

throughout the city. The following undated prose poem by Christianopoulos reveals the narrator's search for intimate encounters among the city's familiar landmarks:

Saturday Night
From Vardari to the Fountain
And from the [White] Tower to Dioikitiriou Square,
I look for you in all the sidewalks of love for hire,
I have been by all the construction sites looking for you. . .[23]

Metaphorically, illicit love took place outside the newly planned city center, or in unde-veloped parts of the city. But as the population continued to expand, these earlier spaces of escape disappeared under the homogenizing effects of growth and develop-ment.[24]

Most of the well-known works on Thessaloniki were written by male authors, rep-resenting a decidedly masculine view of the city that offers sites for trysts (homosexual and heterosexual), exploration, and refuge. In many of these works, the female image represented a lover or a mother, both objects of desire and memory. Although there were female authors writing in Thessaloniki in the 1950s to 1980s, their sphere of activ-ity remained more limited, focusing often on the personal rather than the public urban experience.[25] The novel *Fear* (1998), written in English by the Greek-born Irini Spanidou, who lives and writes in the United States, referred to the exclusion of women in the traditional city:

"You and I should talk," he said.
He took her to a café, a dreary large-scale place with pale green oil-painted walls, a gray-and-black mosaic floor, and bright bare light bulbs hanging on black cords. There was a scattering of customers—two old men playing checkers, four men playing cards, a group of merchant marines drinking ouzo, and a solitary drunk.

There were no women. He always took her places where no women went: the barber, his tailor, men's cafés—places where he should be going alone but need-ed company.[26]

FROM HOME TO APARTMENT: MASS CONSTRUCTION, EVIL DEVELOPERS, AND PROVINCIAL NEWCOMERS

Thessaloniki continued to grow in a largely ad hoc manner, with more than ninety plan-ning extension decrees enacted between 1921 and 1979. The expedient and utilitarian land development adopted for the refugee resettlement presaged the extensive exploi-tation of building sites in the postwar years. Sudden industrial growth and major public works, accompanied by a dying agrarian economy, brought an influx of new residents during the 1950s and 1960s who came primarily from the countryside. Small houses gave way to multistory apartment buildings, which altered both the scale and the density of the city, destroying the earlier harmonious relationship between the city and its natural environment. Apartment ownership became the vehicle not only of urban development but also of urban assimilation. Throughout most of the city, modern architectural styles coexisted with the utilitarian design of the standard apartment block.

Most private home ownership was developed by small-scale contractors through the institution of *antiparochi*, a contractor-financed building arrangement that returned a percentage of the new development to the original landowner. Most new apartment buildings throughout Greece were financed through *antiparochi*. Building in Thessaloniki, however, was controlled by especially development-friendly building codes between 1956 and 1969. Throughout the consequent building frenzy, the state failed to undertake and safeguard the parallel development of adequate infrastructure for a functional and beautiful urban environment.[27] Multistory apartment buildings displaced the modest post-1950s housing construction in the city center and covered most of the open spaces. As building codes changed to allow still higher density, additional floors were added to existing low-rise structures. Private apartment ownership and exhaustive private development, at the expense of most other planning considerations, have governed most planning and design decisions to the present day.

Although the effects of unchecked urbanization can be seen throughout the country, they are especially apparent in Thessaloniki, where the homogeneous built fabric mirrors also its mostly homogeneous (Greek) population, contrasting with the celebrated multi-ethnic and visually distinctive city of the early twentieth century. Given the centralization of governmental, financial, and political institutions in Athens, Thessaloniki, like most other provincial Greek capitals, has been left to survive by its own devices.

As the city changed, writers bemoaned the loss not only of its earlier character but also of its earlier way of life. Postwar authors associated urban change with the advent of modernity, which they resisted and criticized. In one of his novels, Vassilis Vasilikos likened apartment buildings to prisons and apartments to prison cells. In another novel, the protagonist, alienated by the dominant political and social conditions, compared his situation to that of a deserted traditional single-family house, surrounded by identical apartment buildings with dirty light wells and no psychological escape.[28] (At the time, the apartment buildings lacked fire escapes as well.)

Although all of these changes were primarily the result of government legislation, most writers did not direct their anger toward the state. Contractors and predatory developers became the villains in many stories, as they exploited *antiparochi* and destroyed the city forever. Yorgos Ioannou (1927–85), one of the most poignant raconteurs of Thessaloniki, who appeared on the literary scene in the 1960s, described the situation in one of his short stories (1972–73): "The house had already been surrendered to a gang of developers and in its place was erected an apartment building, among the most hideous ones. Now they are getting ready to demolish it, these ridiculous people. Who knows what their cunning brains have conceived for the next business plan?"[29]

Perhaps these contractors were reviled precisely because they were "of the people," as they often came from the working class, but profited from the city's loss of character. In one of the novels by Nikos Bakolas (1927–99), contractors were compared to the black marketeers who profited from their compatriots during the German occupation.[30]

In the 1950s and 1960s, there were only two notable exceptions to the ubiquitous apartment building developments: the flight of many higher-income residents to the hills of Panorama, an exclusive Thessaloniki suburb, and the appearance of the "villa" typology, an expensive, often modernist single-family dwelling surrounded by a large garden. Yet even these villas succumbed to wholesale apartmentization of the 1970s.

The city's new planning and architecture intensified its social and economic stratification. Escaping to the city of the past became the defense mechanism for some of the writers, who did not recognize the new city, with its newcomers from the villages and the hinterland. In the literature from the 1960s and 1970s, we noticed a recurring distinction between the longtime urban residents of the city and the provincial newcomers, who became either excited or alienated by city life. Many of the writers dwelled especially on the inability and unwillingness of these newcomers to become integrated in the city's fabric, just as the earlier refugees from Turkey remained apart from the local population for at least one generation. In a story by Tilemachos Alaveras (1926–2007), published in 1976, the narrator observes that domestic refugees "from all of Northern Greece, from New Orestiada, to Tsotyli came and perched in the developers' matchboxes."[31] This distinction between old residents and newcomers was also subtly implied in the following newspaper chronicle by Ioannou, published in 1978: "In the wide streets stroll the people from the provinces on Sundays—in the morning, especially, and in the early afternoon. Of course, the locals stroll, too, but they are a lot fewer."[32] We believe that part of the criticism of the urban changes in Thessaloniki was the result of latent discrimination toward the newer residents.

In his essay collection *Mother Thessaloniki*, Pentzikis reflected on change through the eyes of an older woman:

> Already the street has been widened in parts and buses go by, full of the population that has increased. The little lady in the poor little house across the street does not recognize her neighborhood any more. "Where did all the mansions go" she reflects, looking out of the narrow window of her house [...] The only child of the wealthy home owner, who was planning to get married in that house some day, expired with the demolition of his house. Elsewhere, they destroyed altogether sixty imposing elm trees.[33]

It is not only the physical change that was recorded here. More deeply, the narrator describes the disappearance of the old, stable social order. Nostalgia was also laced with a conservative and selective reimagining of the past.

Nevertheless, not all literary references were negative. Some of the characters in the work of Vassilikos and Ioannou remark that although the demolitions and higher-density new building destroyed old neighborhoods, they did succeed in revealing and showcasing the city's Byzantine physiognomy, as many of the Byzantine landmarks became focal points of the new designs. These two authors also acknowledged that from the point of view of the poorer residents, moving into apartment buildings signaled an improvement of their living conditions. Ioannou underscored that for the first time, many of the refugees were able to move into their own apartments, after suffering through long periods of temporary, makeshift, and crowded housing. Some of the characters of Vassilikos, more cosmopolitan and often returning to Thessaloniki after long absences abroad, acknowledge the overall improvements in the city, even at the cost of the old neighborhoods.[34]

CONTEMPORARY PLANNING: PROTECTING THE PAST, ACCOMMODATING THE PRESENT

At the urban scale, Thessaloniki's historic identity was enriched by three major archeological discoveries. Since 1962, excavations for the foundation of a new court building in the upper part of Hébrard's civic axis uncovered the magnificent Forum Romanum. Meanwhile, ongoing excavations begun in 1945 in the eastern section of the historic nucleus (Navarinou Square) have unearthed the Palace and parts of the Hippodrome of the remarkable complex of Galerius Maximianus (reg 305–311). Furthermore, since 1990 a large part of the Hellenistic and Roman city has been uncovered at the northwest section of the center (Dioikitiriou Square). Also, for the first time a concurrent policy of conservation was applied, listing all of the city's Ottoman monuments.[35] Important as these discoveries were from an archeological point of view, they do not feature prominently in the city's literature.

Writers acknowledged the presence of the major squares and sites in their work, not only because of their urban significance but also because of their historical importance, from the Roman and early Christian periods to the German occupation and the expulsion of the Jews.[36] It was not only the personal memories that marked the topographies of their novels but also the memories of recent political events. Several works made references to the political assassination of Grigoris Lambrakis in 1963 near the intersection of Ermou and Venizelou Streets; this event became the subject of the book Z (1967) and the French-language political film of that name (1969). In a short story by Sakis Serefas (b. 1960), published in 1996, the narrator remarked: "My girlfriend was standing on the point where Lambrakis was killed right next to the commemorative sculpture."[37] Once again, a writer recorded the city's intimate history and topography from a local's point of view.

Beginning in the 1970s, the city initiated efforts to protect and enhance the Upper Town's architectural heritage. Until then, one could stroll along narrow streets and gaze at modest single-family houses from the nineteenth and early twentieth centuries. Since 1978, however, the intramural area of Upper Town has been transformed through a preservation and redevelopment project that allowed the construction of neo-vernacular two- or three-story apartment buildings, akin to the New Urbanism architecture in North America. In Thessaloniki's Upper Town, the ancient city walls, together with a limited number of the original buildings, acted as a picturesque backdrop for the housing of middle-income residents.

The Upper Town, with its traditional urban quarters and strong presence of refugee and Jewish residents, played a central role in the city's literary image. In a short story by Dimitris Miggas (b. 1951), published in 2003, the narrator seeks to escape from the present as he routinely climbs up to the Upper Town. Listing a string of streets and bus routes, he aims to fix the city in his memory unchanged: "It was raining again yesterday. I went up to the Walls by bus and then went down on foot. Akropoleos, Dimitriou Poliorkitou, Tsinari, Athonos, Theophilou, and Akropoleos again."[38] We find a similar stringing of place names in the works of Vassilikos, Ioannou, and Bakolas. As the literary critic Triantafyllos Kotopoulos remarked, they represent a broken, partial depiction of

Historic layering: the Roman Forum (left) and the Galerius complex (right).

The landscape of Modernism: the International Fair Grounds, the museums, and the lower part of the historic center.

the city, rather like the tesserae of a large mosaic of a broken image, a multifocal narrative of many heroes.[39]

In Vassilikos's novel *Thymata eirinis* [Victims of Peace] (1956) the protagonist brings tour groups to the Upper Town. By always following a strict, predetermined itinerary around the central sites, he is able to describe the city's historical continuity. But in his story "To phyllo" [The Page] (1994), the narrator wanders around the narrow and labyrinthine passages of Upper Town, which reflect his isolation and tangled human relations.[40] Thus in some cases, the Upper Town has been depicted as safely retaining the characters' youthful memories, while at other times it is shown in the throes of change and destruction.

A unified policy of major public works aimed to shape the city's modern character. Examples of modern architecture endowed this regional capital with distinctive public buildings, including the Thessaloniki University campus, the International Fairgrounds, and the Archaeological Museum. Both the establishment of the university and the fair-grounds signaled the progressive intellectual and commercial forces that have shaped northern Greece.[41]

Unalloyed modernism was first ushered into the city with the design of the Thessaloniki University complex, originally proposed by Hébrard (1919 and 1928) and later developed by Nikolaos Mitsakis (1939). The master plan for the Thessaloniki University campus was completed in 1950 by Vassilios D. Kyriazopoulos. Several prominent architects designed the individual buildings, which are part of a freestanding arrangement in a loosely articulated master plan.[42] Despite its central location and its significance as a site of modernist designs, the university campus remains outside of most city inhabitants' daily experience.[43]

The Thessaloniki International Fair, another modernist planning venture, has been embraced by a broad spectrum of the population. As an institution, the Fair began in 1926 on the Military Esplanade, moving to its present location in 1939. Its informal layout is punctuated by several exhibition pavilions, both permanent and temporary, with the most important structures completed between 1960 and 1975.[44] The Fair's populist organization, combining a variety of industrial exhibits with old-style amusement park entertainment, created an open environment for the promotion of modern architecture. For most visitors, the Fair offers one of the few opportunities to experience modern and avant-garde buildings. The significance of the Fair in people's lives is evident in the many commemorative family photographs that record annual visits. Most other new buildings in the city are still modest and utilitarian, while public amenities like parks and squares remain sparse.

Of all the new planning projects, the International Fair is the only modern site that is frequently mentioned in the literature we reviewed.[45] In the following undated poem, Christianopoulos captured the contrast between the urban resident, who yearns to escape the crowds, and his lover from the village, who revels in the Fair's opportunities for cheap amusement:

At the Fair

I met you at the Fair, amongst the lights,
amongst the crowd, very tight,
and immediately I suggested we go to some deserted area.

But you had come from the village for entertainment;
we had to get on the bumper cars,
buy ice cream, go into the House of Horrors,
I had to treat you to a sandwich and dark beer,
buy you a lighter as a souvenir.

I didn't realize that you were fed up with deserted areas.[46]

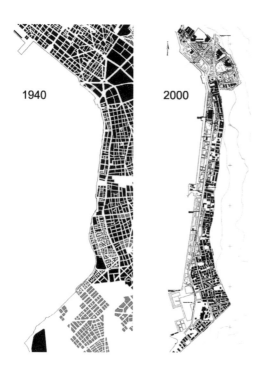

1940   2000

One of the major large-scale projects was the modernization and extension of the harbor, begun in 1953 and completed in 1973. The new quay (promenade by the sea) was created at the southeast seafront, extending from the White Tower to the Kalamaria boundary line. The development of the seafront became one of the city's most prominent architectural modernist projects. It changed the whole face of the city as seen from the sea and permitted the gradual replacement of the villas once lining the shore with the present row of free-standing massive apartment blocks. Moreover, there was a considerable effort to develop an appropriate eclectic or modern architectural vocabulary for the new apartment buildings that lined the newly expanded quay. Despite the straitjacket nature of individual lot development, the city's new waterfront as a whole presented an appropriate and successful modern design. The project also produced a 2-kilometer-long quay, with a 150-meter-wide strip of public space serving as a favorite promenade. In most literature, the seafront represents a central place of escape, entertainment, solitary reflection, and identification with the city.[47] While Pentzikis underscores the picturesque view of the sea from the city, Alaveras reveals the city's more recent problems with the polluting of the Thermaic Gulf.[48]

Opposite: The creation of the modern seafront on the southeastern shore.

The Aristotelous civic axis in the 1980s.

The development of Aristotelous Avenue gave the city its most important urban complex. It is bordered by symmetrical neo-Byzantine arcades, with prescribed building façades, terminating in an expansive square with a view of the Thermaic Gulf. This imposing north-south axis, one of the hallmarks of Hébrard's design, appeared in the work of some authors, including Vasilikos and Bakolas.[49]

In general, writers placed their characters in the city center when the story called for action and in the Upper Town when the story called for reflection, escape, or return to an earlier time. Given the relatively recent experiences of the German occupation and civil war, and considering the city's working-class roots, many stories hinge on political action, with their protagonists crisscrossing the city as they carry out special assignments. According to Kotopoulos, the sites of the city itself became the protagonists in some of the novels by Alavera and Ioannou, who depicted the city in exhaustive detail.[50]

CONTROL OF URBAN GROWTH AND THE ENHANCEMENT OF THE CITY'S HERITAGE SINCE THE 1980s

The first substantive attempt to control urban development was manifested in the Thessaloniki Master Plan (TMP), approved in 1985.[51] The aims of the TMP included highlighting the city's historical profile and enhancing the city center. It introduced measures to protect the archeological and historical sites and made possible the adoption of additional special measures and restrictions regarding land uses and traffic circulation. Furthermore, it proposed upgrading and linking the major historical sites and axes of special significance with a number of archeological walks. These included: to the east, from the White Tower up to Eptapyrgion; in the center, from Aristotelous Square up to Vlatadon Monastery; and to the west, from Vardari tower up into the Upper Town. In addition, the TMP proposed the qualitative upgrading of the city's traditional districts, including the Upper Town and the old commercial center.

According to the 1991 census, Thessaloniki's population was more or less stable at 750,000, though the city continues to spread over the surrounding area, particularly toward the southeast, with homes and businesses lining the major provincial roads. Considerable residential development has been registered in the last fifteen to twenty years toward the east, particularly toward Panorama and Thermi, where middle- and high-income residents have recently settled after abandoning the congested fabric of the lower city. To the west, where low-income districts have grown since the early twentieth century, the division of the land into ever smaller plots, combined with high building coefficients and lack of organized planning, have resulted in unattractive urban districts, lacking infrastructure and public spaces.

From 1992 to 1994, the European Union (sixteenth Directorate) sponsored a pilot plan for the revival of the city's historic commercial center that helped to upgrade and enhance the city's old markets, such as the harbor market (*Ladadika*) and the bazaars. The plan also funded the restoration of the Roman Forum. In 1994, a large part of the intramural city, coinciding more or less with the area destroyed by the fire of 1917, was declared a historical site. In 1997, on the occasion of Thessaloniki's designation as the

Cultural Capital of Europe, numerous projects and architectural competitions were promoted, including proposals for pedestrian areas, squares, archeological excavations, and redevelopment, originating in the planning framework previously described. Most prominent has been the integration of the historic part of the harbor into the city's cultural life. Other important projects included the restoration of the Galerius complex, restoration and landscaping of major Byzantine sites such as the powerful Eptapyrgion Fortress, and restoration of Ottoman monuments such as the Bezesten (Market), the Alaca Imaret (mosque), the Yeni Cami (mosque), and the Bey Hamam and the Pazar Hamam (Ottoman baths). Other planning projects included the recovery of the fin-de-siècle cosmopolitan physiognomy of the city, with the renovation of more than thirty buildings—private mansions, public buildings, manufacturing premises, and religious buildings, renovated to host new uses.[52] Thus in a belated manner, contemporary urban planning has attempted to recapture and reconstruct the lost image of early twentieth-century Thessaloniki, an image preserved and cultivated by the city's writers.

The enhancement of the old harbor with the surviving harbor market.

Despite these recent and ambitious planning efforts, Thessaloniki retains its popular identity as the "refugee capital" and "mother of the poor," now home to a new influx of economic migrants from the former Eastern bloc. The newest arrivals established themselves primarily in the upper part of the historic center, north of Egnatia Street, and in the northwest extensions of the city—that is, in areas that have received migrants to the city since the late nineteenth century.

CONCLUSION: LITERARY MEMORY AND URBAN CHANGE

Unlike newspaper accounts, which offer an ongoing commentary on contemporary political and urban changes, literature often dwells in the past. Poets and writers often reflect on earlier periods, as the past enjoys a firmer hold on the consciousness of both the writers and their readers. Current research on autobiographical memory concurs that only "few vivid memories are reported after early adulthood," resulting in "few new formative experiences occur[ring] after early childhood."[53] Most individuals, when asked to recount their past, give a very detailed account of their childhood, up to about age twelve. After that, their stories tend to trail off, and long periods of time pass in a cursory manner. "When I think of Buenos Aires, I think of the Buenos Aires I knew as a child: the low houses, the patios, the porches, the cisterns with turtles in them, the grated windows. That Buenos Aires was all of Buenos Aires," reflected the Argentine author Jorge Luis Borges.[54] Not only are most memories related to childhood, but memory itself seems to improve, not decay, with time. Encoded childhood memory appears more resistant to forgetting as time passes.[55] Notice, for example, how the author Sakis Papadimitriou described the changes in the Thessaloniki of his childhood in an essay collection (1960–73):

> The imposing new boulevard. All the houses that used to be by the sea retreated by about one hundred meters and in front of them, later, will be planted apartment buildings. And now I think of how we used to plunge into the sea from the courtyards, or go on a boat ride while our family watched us from one of the balconies. Everything was so close, squeezed tightly, gathered together. As I go by the boulevard by car now, I see the half-demolished single houses, as when we used to go out in the little boat; in a short while, none of the houses will be left. They are counterfeiting our memories, stealing our childhood images.[56]

One of Ioannou's narrators acknowledged the disappearance of the picturesque city of his childhood, the "old," "moldy," "burnt-smelling," "enchanting" city of around 1940. In another story, the narrator recommended better protection and preservation of certain old buildings. Demolishing these buildings betrayed the ignorance of those who control the city's future. Along the same lines, the narrator of another story underscores that the city's plan was drawn by "people who neither know us nor feel for us."[57] One of the characters of Alaveras reflects with melancholy that his nephews walk on the same roads, which, however, follow different planning trends. "The city's color has been altered." The neighborhood "is now defined by more multi-story buildings, and from two and three rows of parked cars."[58] Evocative as these comments are, they do leave open the question of *knowing* a city. How can planners come to know a city? How can newcomers come to know it? Should urban planning acknowledge the sites of specific historical events?

Several prominent themes emerge from the literature on Thessaloniki: nostalgia and sadness, anger, death, loss of recognition and identity, and illicit sex. Usually writers relied on their own memory to describe the destruction of old neighborhoods and the construction of new buildings. As a whole, literature has also waged a direct or indirect critique of various modernization projects. Although some of the writers embraced urban change, most criticized it, longing for the city of their childhood. Nevertheless, we cannot assign the statements or actions of narrators to the writers themselves. In fact, like the majority of the city's inhabitants, most writers lived in the new, poorly constructed, anonymous apartment buildings and only saw the few surviving old buildings in their walks. Nevertheless, they often chose to locate their narratives in the narrow parts of the city that had escaped demolition and rebuilding.

Writers did not criticize urban change only because it disrupted their childhood memories. Surrounded by buildings dating from the 1960s and later, the personal dislocation of the narrators became a metaphor for the dislocation, disorientation, and alienation of the modern inhabitant. Criticism of urban development often reflected criticism of modernization itself. Nevertheless, we believe that overall the Greek people oscillated in their position—at times identifying with the writers who held on to a world of the past, while at other times becoming seduced by the siren songs of progress and better life, as promised by small-time developers, architects, and the media.

More broadly, urban literature on Thessaloniki mirrored contemporary international literary tropes and themes. Although some writers around the world embraced life in the modern urban environment, others used literature for refuge and escape, making it possible to tolerate the modern city. The writers we reviewed may have criticized the lack of dreaming spaces in the modern city, yet they accepted the inevitability of that city and continued to reside in it.

Notes

We would like to thank Pani Pyla, Carol Krinsky, and the anonymous readers for their comments and suggestions. We received valuable bibliographic advice on literature from our colleagues Yiorgos Anagnostou, Christopher Bakken, Tina Godhi, Edmund Keeley, Helen Kolias, Vassilis Lambropoulos, Peter Mackridge, and Sakis Serefas. All translations from the Greek are by Eleni Bastéa.

1   T.J. Clark, *The Painting of Modern Life: Paris in the Art of Manet and His Followers* (Princeton: Princeton University Press, 1984), 66.

2   Ibid., 68–69.

3   Marshall Berman, *All That Is Solid Melts Into Air: The Experience of Modernity* (New York: Penguin Books, 1988), 147.

4   For an excellent and comprehensive review of Thessaloniki's history since 1430, see Mark Mazower, *Salonica: City of Ghosts, Christians, Muslims, and Jews, 1430–1950* (London: HarperCollins, 2004). For a review of Thessaloniki's planning history, see Vilma Hastaoglou-Martinidis, "A Mediterranean City in Transition: Thessaloniki between the Two Wars," in *Facta Universitatis*, Series: Architecture and Civil Engineering, vol. 1, no. 4, 1997, 493–507. In Greek, see Vassilis Dimitriadis, *Topographia tis Thessalonikis kata tin epochi tis Tourkokratias 1430–1912* [Topography of Thessaloniki under Turkish Rule 1430–1912] (Thessaloniki: Society for Macedonian Studies, 1983).

5   Dimitriadis, *Topography*, 463–464; Hastaoglou-Martinidis, "A Mediterranean City in Transition," 502, and Eleni Bastéa, "Storied Cities: Literary Memories

of Thessaloniki and Istanbul," in Eleni Bastéa, ed., *Memory and Architecture* (Albuquerque: University of New Mexico Press, 2004), 191–210.

6   Triantaphyllos I. Kotopoulos, *I Thessaloniki sto ergo ton Thessalonikeon pezographon* [Thessaloniki in the Work of Thessalonikan Prose Writers] (Thessaloniki: Kodikas, 2006), 43–44.

7   Lizy Tsirimokou, *Logotechnia tis polis* [Literature of the City] (Athens: Lotos, 1988), 15, cited in Kotopoulos, *Thessaloniki*, 15.

8   See C. Papastathis, "A Memoir on the Fire in Thessaloniki in 1917 and the Relief Victims," *Makedonika*, vol. 18, 1978 (in Greek), cited in Hastaoglou-Martinidis, "A Mediterranean City in Transition," 495. See also Alexandra Yerolympos, *The Replanning of Thessaloniki after the Fire of 1917* (in Greek, with summaries in English and French) (Thessaloniki: Municipality of Thessaloniki, 1985), 220.

9   The Property Law of 1929 established the freehold land system as the only system of land holding on a national scale. Based on the freehold system, all apartment owners in an apartment building today are co-proprietors of the lot and possess a percentage of the lot that is equivalent to the surface area of their apartment. No one knows or can know where exactly this portion is located. The complicated land ownership patterns that arose from this system make it nearly impossible to tear down and rebuild apartment buildings to better specifications and building codes. As a result, the city is now hostage to the system that allowed it to grow and provide apartment ownership to the majority of its population. On the freehold land system, see Manolis Marmaras, *I astiki polykatoikia tis mesopolemikis Athinas* [The urban apartment building of interwar Athens] (Athens: Politistiko Technologiko Idryma ETVA, 1991), especially 23–32.

10 This large-scale approach to urban design, unparalleled in Greek planning history, was backed by uniform legislation and made possible only after the reform of the Constitution in 1927 (article 119), permitting the establishment of urban refugee settlements. See Hastaoglou-Martinidis, "A Mediterranean City in Transition," 499 and 507, note 22.

11 Refugee settlements, haphazardly built on the city's outskirts, were outside the jurisdiction of the Ministry of Communications. Instead, the settlements fell under the jurisdiction of the Ministry of Social Welfare, a department lacking any city planning competence. See Nicos Kalogirou, "La croissance de la banlieu de Thessalonique. Les nouveaux caractères de l'espace urbaine" (in Greek with French summary), in *I Thessaloniki meta to 1912* [Thessaloniki after 1912] Conference Proceedings, 1–3 Nov. 1985 (Thessaloniki: Municipality of Thessaloniki, 1986), 488.

12 Peter Mackridge, "Cultivating New Lands: The Consolidation of Territorial Gains in Greek Macedonia through Literature, 1912–1940," in Peter Mackridge and Eleni Yannakakis, eds., *Ourselves and Others: The Development of a Greek Macedonian Cultural Identity Since 1912* (Oxford: Berg, 1997), 175–186.

13 Mackridge, "Cultivating New Lands," 180.

14 On the history of Greece, see Richard Clogg, *A Concise History of Greece* (Cambridge: Cambridge University Press, 2002).

15 Kotopoulos, *Thessaloniki*, 55–56.

16 Nikos Gabriil Pentzikis, *Mitera Thessaloniki* [Mother Thessaloniki] (Athens: Kedros, 1970), 13.

17 Kotopoulos, *Thessaloniki*, 110.

18 Vassilis Vassilikos, *O Evropaios kai i oraia tou yper-peran* [The European and the Beauty from the World Beyond] (Athens: Livanis, 1999), 159, cited in Kotopoulos, *Thessaloniki*, 110.

19 Sakis Papadimitriou, *Peza 1960–73* [Prose 1960–73] (Thessaloniki: Diagonios, 1980), 73, cited in Satrazanis, *La ville de Thessalonique dans la prose locale (1935–1985)* (Thessaloniki: Municipality of Thessaloniki, 1996), 230–231.

20 Dinos Christianopoulos, *Peza poiimata* [Prose Poems], fourth edition (Thessaloniki: Ianos, 2004), 38.

21 Yorgos Ioannou, *Refugee Capital*, translated by Fred A. Reed (Athens: Kedros, 1997). First published in Greek in 1984.

22 M. Karagatsis, *O Yiougerman kai ta sterna tou* [Yugerman and his last hours] (Athens: Estia, 2000), v. 2, 152, originally published in 1941 and cited in Sakis Serefas, ed., *Mia poli sti logotechnia: Thessaloniki* [A City in Literature: Thessaloniki], second edition (Athens: Metaichmio, 2006), 29.

23 Dinos Christianopoulos, *Poiimata* [Poems], fourth edition (Athens: Ianos, 2004), 66.

24 See, for example, the poems "Vardari [1977]" and "Karabournaki [not dated; 1978?]" by Christianopoulos in *Prose Poems*, 9, 17.

25 See, for example, the work of Zoe Karelli, Nina Kokkalidou-Nahmia, and of the authors included in the following anthologies: *I Thessaloniki ton Siggrafeon: 20 Diigimata gia ti Thessaloniki* [Writers' Thessaloniki: Twenty Short Stories about Thessaloniki] (Thessaloniki: Ianos, 1996); and Serefas, *A City in Literature: Thessaloniki*.

26 Irini Spanidou, *Fear* (New York: Alfred A. Knopf, 1998), 99.

27 Between 1965 and 1969, an Urban Development Study for Thessaloniki attempted to rein in urban development and proposed planned urban growth, yet it remained unimplemented. See Aleka Yerolympos and Vilma Hastaoglou, "Katastrophes kai metaplaseis: I gennisi tis sygchronis polis" ["Catastrophes and Remolding: The Genesis of a Contemporary City"], *Themata Chorou + Technon*, no. 23, 1992, 17–26.

28 See V. Vassilikos, *Den metanoiono gia ta dakrya pou echysa gia sena* [I Do Not Regret the Tears I Shed for You] (Athens: Nea Synora, 1996) and N. Bakolas,

Katapatisi [Violation] (Athens: Kedros, 1990), cited in Kotopoulos, *Thessaloniki*, 114.

29 Yorgos Ioannou, "Stou Kemal to spiti" ["In the house of Kemal"], short story included in the collection, Yorgos Ioannou, *I moni klironomia* [The Only Inheritance] (Athens: Kedros, 1974, 1982), 56. Also cited in Serefas, *A City in Literature: Thessaloniki*, 131.

30 Nikos Bakolas, *I megali plateia* [The Great Square] (Athens: Kedros, 1987), 86, cited in Kotopoulos, *Thessaloniki*, 114.

31 Tilemachos Alaveras, "Amixia" ["Separation"], short story included in the collection *Ap' aformi* [On occasion] (Thessaloniki: Nea Poreia, 1976), cited in Kotopoulos, *Thessaloniki*, 116.

32 Yorgos Ioannou, "Oi megaloi dromoi" ["The large streets"], *Kathimerini* newspaper column, 1978, reprinted in Yorgos Ioannou, *Eflekti chora* [Flammable Country] (Athens: Kedros, 1986), 9, cited in Satrazanis, *La ville de Thessalonique dans la prose locale*, 107.

33 Pentzikis, *Mother Thessaloniki*, 15.

34 See Kotopoulos, *Thessaloniki*, 116–121.

35 The Directorate of Byzantine and Post-Byzantine Monuments was established in 1938. The Directorate of Modern Monuments–that is, buildings dating after 1830–was established in 1979.

36 Kotopoulos, *Thessaloniki*, 138–141.

37 Sakis Serefas, "Telika bouti itan" ["At the end, it was a thigh"], short story included in the collection *To spiti ypodechetai* [The House Receives] (Athens: Kedros, 1996), 63, cited in Serefas, *A City in Literature: Thessaloniki*, 40.

38 Dimitris Miggas, *Tis Thessalonikis monacha* [Only for Salonica], (Athens: Metaichmio, 2003), 61.

39 Kotopoulos, *Thessaloniki*, 92.

40 Ibid., 105.

41 On the cultural and political significance of the university and the International Fair, see also Peter Mackridge, "Cultivating New Lands: The Consolidation of Territorial Gains in Greek Macedonia through Literature, 1912–1940," in Mackridge and Yannakakis, eds. *Ourselves and Others*, 176.

42 Nicos S. Kalogirou, *Post-War Architecture and Town Planning in Thessaloniki* (in Greek and English) (Athens: Barbounakis, no date), 9–17.

43 Novels and essays that make references to the university include those whose protagonists are students or faculty there. See Kotopoulos, *Thessaloniki*, 265–267.

44 Kalogirou, *Post-War Architecture and Town Planning in Thessaloniki*, 17.

45 Kotopoulos, *Thessaloniki*, 263–265.

46 Christianopoulos, *Poems*, 88.

47 Kotopoulos, *Thessaloniki*, pp. 182–190. See also the slim poetry volume by Zoe Karelli, *gia ti thalassa* [For the Sea] (Athens: Roes, 1988).

48 Kotopoulos, *Thessaloniki*, 190, 193.

49 Ibid., 123–124.

50 Ibid., 81, 92, 103–104, 106.

51 Law 1561, *Government Gazette* A-148/6.9.1985, and the General Urban Plan for Thessaloniki, approved early in 1993, *Government Gazette* A- 420/27.4.1993.

52 On the strategic plan of Thessaloniki, see *Thessaloniki in the Twenty-first Century: Growth, Environment, Culture. Contribution Towards the Development of the Strategic Plan* (in Greek), Organisation for the Master Plan of Thessaloniki, Greek Ministry of Planning, Research team: A. Yerolympos, K. Kafkoula, N. Papamichos (chair), V. Hastaoglou, K. Chadjimichalis, 1994–1995. On the planning events on the occasion of Thessaloniki, Cultural Capital of Europe, 1997, see Vilma Hastaoglou-Martinidis, "Looking Towards the Past, Looking Towards the Future. Urban Design Projects for 'Thessaloniki 1997' Cultural Capital of Europe." Paper presented at the Hellenic Studies Conference *Modern Greece and its Monuments*, Whitney Humanities Center, Yale University, April 5–6, 2002.

53 John A. Robinson and Leslie R. Taylor, "Autobiographical Memory and Self-Narratives: A Tale of Two Stories," in *Autobiographical Memory: Theoretical and Applied Perspectives*, Charles P. Thompson et al., eds. (Mahwah, N.J.: Lawrence Erlbaum Associates, 1998), 125–126.

54 Jorge Luis Borges, "Blindness," in Jorge Luis Borges, *Seven Nights*, translated by Eliot Weinberger, 1980, cited in Phillip Lopate, *The Art of the Personal Essay, An Anthology from the Classical Era to the Present* (New York: Anchor Books, Doubleday, 1994), 379.

55 Daniel L. Schacter, *Searching for Memory: The Brain, the Mind, and the Past* (New York: Basic Books, 1996), 72–97 and passim.

56 Papadimitriou, *Prose*, 76, cited in Satrazanis, *La ville de Thessalonique dans la prose locale*, 232.

57 Yorgos Ioannou, "Seich Sou" [Seich Sou] and "Apographi zimion" [Inventory of Damages] in the essay collection *To diko mas aima* [Our Own Blood] (Athens: Kedros, 1980), 147, 222, and Yorgos Ioannou, "Tsirides" [Screams] in *I sarkofagos* [The Sarcophagus], 1971, 107, all cited in Kotopoulos, *Thessaloniki*, 107–110.

58 Tilemachos Alaveras, "Arta Kor" [in Greek], short story included in the collection *Ap' aformi* [On Occasion], 104, cited in Kotopoulos, *Thessaloniki*, 108.

SIBEL BOZDOĞAN

5

RESIDENTIAL ARCHITECTURE AND URBAN
LANDSCAPE IN İSTANBUL SINCE 1950

As a "European Capital of Culture" that celebrated its "world city" status officially in 2010, İstanbul continues to offer a fascinating case study through which to observe the impacts of modernization and globalization on the urban landscape. Dramatic chang-es to the city's physical fabric since the 1950s replicate many of the patterns and pro-cesses that one may find in other post-imperial (and/or postcolonial) cities in peripheral geographies. Yet these patterns and processes unfold in ways that highlight the unique historical, cultural, political, and geographical circumstances of a complex metropolis whose comprehensive analysis cannot possibly be accomplished within the confines of this essay. What follows is an unsystematic overview of how paradigmatic residen-tial typologies have emerged and proliferated in the last fifty years, shaping İstanbul's urban image and reflecting deep divisions of class and culture within Turkish society.

While acknowledging the unprecedented political and cultural shifts since the 1980s, this discussion takes issue with analyses that treat post-1980 Turkey as a radically new (postmodern) era and instead highlights continuities (as well as ruptures) with the social and economic dynamics of modernization since World War II. Above all, İstanbul offers compelling testimony to the demise of traditional "modernization theory" as articulated by social scientists in the 1950s and early 1960s (Daniel Lerner, Cyril Black, Bernard Lewis) in favor of more nuanced recent theorizations of "alternative," "hybrid," or "other" modernities (Arjun Appadurai, Dilip Gaonkar).[1] Simply put, earlier modern-ization theorists postulated a universal, linear developmental path from tradition to modernity that all societies were expected go through, becoming more urban, more literate, more technologically savvy, more secular, more enterprising, and more "western" along the way. In the 1950s and early 1960s, Turkey was heralded by social scientists as a success story, demonstrating the validity of this theory.[2] More recently, however, we have been compelled to abandon the tradition/modernity binary opposition that is central to this theory and instead conclude with a profound ambiguity: societies such as Turkey have surely modernized and changed dramatically, but they have done so in their own ways and not in keeping with the predictions of modernization theory. Most have become less secular and less "western" as they have become more urban, more enterprising, and more technologically savvy. This does not, however, lessen the importance of modernization as a framework of analysis: it only marks a new stage in which new actors produce new forms of modernity. Here Dilip Gaonkar's distinction between cultural and societal modernity, and their perceived divergence in the contemporary scene (in contrast to modernization theory's prediction regarding their convergence), comes in handy.[3] Today, while preoccupations with identity, Islam, and nationalism are surely rampant in Turkey as elsewhere in peripheral geographies, the hunger for the latest technologies and commodities of western societies and the diffusion of a global capitalist consumption culture across all social classes are also overwhelming. Modernization is alive and well, and there is no better evidence of that than urban form.

Residential architectures, which constitute the more anonymous texture of İstanbul's urban form (in contrast with monuments and landmarks), by their nature offer the best index to this still unfolding and complex history of Turkish modernization since World War II. The first phase of that history gave İstanbul its urban apartment boom of the 1950s and 1960s as well as its first shantytowns (*gecekondu*), which emerged around the same time, offering early evidence of the problems, contradictions, and exclusions of modernization theory's smooth developmental models. These two residential typologies dominated İstanbul's macro form for about three decades until the 1980s, when new institutional, organizational, and technological changes began transforming housing production in Turkey, introducing new scales, new typologies, and a new urban aesthetic. Today, although medium-rise, reinforced-concrete frame apartment buildings dating back to the postwar decades still constitute the overwhelming residential fabric of the older neighborhoods of the city, newer residential construction is expanding the metropolitan boundaries in unprecedented ways. It is an expansion that entails new construction both at the upper end of the social spectrum (luxury gated communities, residence towers, and suburban villas) and at the lower end (a new generation of mediocre high-rise apartments on the urban fringes). The following is a broad outline of these developments along the two distinct phases mentioned: 1950 to 1980, and 1980 to the present.

1950–1980: URBAN APARTMENTS AND SHANTYTOWNS

With the election victory of the Democrat Party on May 14, 1950, the early republican period came to a decisive end in Turkey. Abandoning the secular authoritarianism, statist economic policies, and nationalist isolationism of the previous two decades, the DP

regime promoted populist democracy, private enterprise, and a more ambitious regional role for Turkey in a sharply divided Cold War world. Joining NATO in 1952, Turkey
received generous packages of development aid and technical assistance from the
United States to modernize agriculture, industries, and transportation networks. After
two decades of relative insignificance with respect to the capital city Ankara, İstanbul
was revitalized as the site of DP's spectacular urban modernization schemes under
the personal directive of Prime Minister Adnan Menderes. Benefiting from the relative
prosperity of the 1950s (largely due to the specific conditions of the Korean War, the
boom in agricultural exports, and favorable foreign exchange rates), the Menderes government undertook extensive demolitions, opened major arteries, and sponsored land-
mark buildings representing postwar modernism, such as the canonic Hilton Hotel of
1952–1955. Most significantly for its urban consequences, İstanbul became the center
of attraction for massive waves of migration from rural Anatolia, and its population
surpassed the 1 million mark in 1950 (up from 691,000 in 1927), making the provision of
urban housing a pressing problem in ways that it never was during the early republic.
Before the 1950s, a limited amount of new housing was produced in İstanbul, in the form
of individual villas or small apartments on small lots, with a single property owner who
would typically belong to the bureaucratic, professional, or military elite of the early
republic. After the 1950s, the need for large quantities of housing for a mass market of
anonymous users ushered in an entirely new phase in the urban history of İstanbul, as
well as all other major Turkish cities.[4] Thereafter, the meaning of "dwelling" changed
from an object of individual use to a commodity to be produced and exchanged within
capitalist market relations—a historical shift that has in turn informed both the architectural qualities and the urban impact of residential construction.

Beginning in the 1950s and continuing throughout this period, medium-rise (five to
seven stories, two or three units per floor), reinforced-concrete frame apartment buildings on small urban lots became the generic residential typology in İstanbul and other
Turkish cities. Formidable constraints such as shortage of urban land, speculative rise
of land values, and a general lack of capital for housing construction largely account
for the proliferation of this generic type as the preferred response to Turkey's growing
urban housing problem.[5] In conjunction with these constraints, three new developments made the apartment boom possible and pervasive. The first is the emergence
of a new actor in the housing market: the small entrepreneur/contractor (the so-called
yap-satçı in Turkish, literally a "builder-seller"). The absence of direct government investment in housing construction and the limited capacity of housing cooperatives to cope
with the magnitude of the demand created an incentive for these small contractors to
enter the market. The second factor, which made residential construction a potentially
profitable investment for these contractors, was the concomitant development of a
domestic construction industry. The state policy of import substitution (*ithal ikamesi*),
which Turkey adopted as its main national development strategy after 1960, supplied
the market with domestic alternatives for most building materials such as cement,
glass, tiles, pipes, and iron reinforcement, thus reducing dependence on expensive
imported building materials.

Generic dense residential fabric of urban apartments in Harem, Asian side of the Bosporus in İstanbul

The third and perhaps most decisive factor has been the "condominium or flat ownership" legislation (*kat mülkiyeti kanunu*), debated throughout the 1950s and finally approved in 1965, allowing investors the property rights to individual units within a multi-unit apartment building. Thus flat ownership has made it possible for multiple small investors to pool their resources into a housing cooperative or the hands of a small contractor (*yap satçı muteahhit*), either to build on new land or, more typically, to pull down an older house and replace it with a higher-rise apartment building on a small urban lot. The new apartment units were then shared according to a predetermined ratio, between the original owner(s) of the old house (or of the land) and the small contractor who would typically sell some of the units in advance to finance the construction. This pattern of urban renewal has visually transformed İstanbul since the 1960s, resulting in dramatic increases of urban density in many parts of the city. In the course of such a speculative apartment boom, designs have also become increasingly generic and the resulting urbanscape increasingly faceless.

Yet what is frequently overlooked in the general criticism of this overwhelming fabric of ordinary apartment buildings in İstanbul and other Turkish cities (the so-called "concrete jungles") is the fact that the 1950s constitutes a unique decade that also produced some of the best examples of postwar modern residential apartment blocks. This has to do, first, with the internationalization of Turkish architectural culture after

Ataköy Housing Development (1957–present) in the foreground, contrasting with the generic fabric of urban apartments to the right

1950. Abandoning the early republican obsession with "national style," Turkish architects became receptive to a wide range of international influences, ranging from the later work of Le Corbusier to the "tropical modernism" of Latin America.[6] Equally significant was the availability of both good-quality imported building materials (once the protectionist policies of the early republic were abandoned) and increasingly, their domestic substitutes (made possible by the state's import-substitution policies). Third, to address the capital shortage, credit was made available to housing cooperatives to finance larger-scale, comprehensively designed housing projects.

The canonic Ataköy Cooperative Development in İstanbul is one of the first such experiments realized with credit from the newly established *Emlak Kredi* Bank (Real Estate Credit Bank), initially intended to provide low-interest, long-term credit for residential construction. Projected as a 50,000-unit housing scheme along the coastal road to the west of the city, Ataköy development started in 1957 and has been expanding since then in multiple phases and with a range of different architectural typologies. While falling short of responding to the housing needs of the urban poor and catering instead to wealthier upper-middle classes, there is wide consensus today that the first phases of Atakoy constitute an architecturally successful experiment by most functional, aesthetic, and social criteria. Different housing typologies (including four-story blocks of interlocking cubes, thirteen-story towers, and seven-story *zeilenbau* blocks served by

Top: Ataköy Housing Development, late 1950s apartment block with Corbusean features

Bottom: Birkan Apartment, Bebek, İstanbul (1955) by Haluk Baysal and Melih Birsel

Top: Housing for the Lawyers' Cooperative (1960–61) by Haluk Baysal and Melih Birsel

Bottom: Low-rise, high-density housing with duplex units on two levels, Yeşilköy, İstanbul (1976) by Haluk Baysal and Melih Birsel

two vertical circulation shafts) were laid out in a carefully landscaped park, respecting proper angles of sunlight and ventilation. Reflecting the characteristic 1950s' aesthetic of the modernist apartment block, Corbusean elements such as *pilotis* and roof terraces were used extensively in conjunction with the paradigmatic surface treatments of "tropicalized modernism" such as sunscreens made of concrete blocks or perforated bricks.

The period starting in 1950 also introduced what architectural historians consider to be the first truly private architectural firms and partnerships (as opposed to architects working for or within the state bureaucracy in the early republican period).[7] The "Construction and Architecture Studio" (*Insaat ve Mimarlık Atelyesi*) of Maruf Önal, Turgut Cansever, and Abdurrahman Hancı, established in 1951, and the partnership of Haluk Baysal and Melih Birsel, established in 1952, can be cited as two of the most successful such practices. Although representing exceptions rather than the norm and ultimately remaining ineffective against the magnitude of İstanbul's housing problem, the sense of aesthetic refinement and careful conceptual experimentation that these architects put into apartment design was unmatched for a long time afterward. For example, Baysal and Birsel's Birkan Apartment in Bebek illustrates the "domestication" or "naturalization" of international style "high modernism" into the familiar, even "ordinary" aesthetic of apartment blocks in Turkey.[8] Meanwhile, their more experimental apartment block for Lawyers' Cooperative (*Hukukçular Sitesi*, 1960–1961), one of the canonic projects of modern Turkish architecture, pays homage to Le Corbusier's l'Unite d'Habitation in Marseilles, working with the section to create duplex units stacked within the main grid of the reinforced concrete frame.[9] Most notably, Baysal and Birsel elaborated the same concept into a flexible schema that could accommodate considerable morphological variation—as, for example, in a later project in Yeşilköy where they transformed the corridor into an open-to-sky two-level street flanked by duplex units, resulting in a most interesting but isolated episode in modern Turkish architecture. It is unfortunate that the potentials of such low-rise, high-density typologies, row housing, or perimeter-block developments were unrealized in Turkey, largely as a result of economic, political, and speculative (i.e., extra-architectural) factors. Ultimately it was not these few architectural experiments of quality but rather the socioeconomic realities of the country that would shape the physical fabric of İstanbul and other Turkish cities. Today we can hardly notice these few custom-designed apartments of the 1950s within the anonymous modern vernacular of lesser examples built with inferior technical and financial resources. By the same token, however, it is possible to argue that precisely by blending into the fabric and not standing out (as the more recent gated residential developments do), they represent the ideal of a more democratic modernization project.

While the apartment boom transformed İstanbul's urban fabric beginning in the 1950s, the outer fringes of the city acquired its first shantytowns or *gecekondu*s, literally "built overnight" illegally, mostly on public land. Throughout the 1950s, the need for urban housing, as a result of massive migration from the countryside, was a monumental social, economic, and political challenge for the DP government.[10] To cite some figures: Turkey's urban population, which grew by 20.1 percent from 1940 to

Examples of first-generation squatter houses (*gecekondu*) on the hills of Arnavutköy, İstanbul

1950, reached a growth of 80.2 percent between 1950 and 1960.[11] Unable to deal with the enormous housing shortage created by massive migration from rural Anatolia, the state largely turned a blind eye to *gecekondu* development, which was, in effect, the poorest migrants' own solution to a problem that the state was not capable of addressing. The earliest *gecekondu*s were typically one-story rural-looking dwellings built by the labor of the family who started living in it as soon as the first room was constructed. Their designs were informed directly by use, and their construction was an incremental process: as the family's finances got better, more rooms or even additional stories were added and more specialized help from builders sought. Over time, especially during election periods, successive governments have pandered to the significant vote base in these communities, giving them title deeds to their houses and bringing the basic infrastructure of roads, sewage, and electricity to their neighborhoods. Especially after the *Gecekondu* Legislation of 1966, most of these earlier *gecekondu*s were granted legal status, triggering the commercialization of subsequent *gecekondu* production and thereby bringing an end to the earlier user-built vernacular process.

Before moving to the next phase, I would like to suggest that this earlier phase of İstanbul's transformation between 1950 and 1980, the period of so-called populist modernism typically associated with the ills of rapid urbanization, especially the much-despised apartment boom (*apartmanlaşma*) and squatter/shantytown development (*gecekondulaşma*), actually contains some important but underappreciated lessons.[12] It is in this period that Turkish architectural culture began to address the defining paradox of modernism, namely, the conflict between a socially concerned view of housing as the central question of modern democracies (a question of shelter) and at the same time, an aesthetic preoccupation with the dwelling as a designed product to accommodate the "good life" (a question of quality). More than ever before, architects realized that the modern dwelling had to be conceptualized as inseparable from the question of urbanism, and by and large they refused to escape either to the "garden city" anti-urbanism of the early republic or to the anti-urban exclusivity of the gated community, which would characterize the next phase. It was a brief moment in time when Turkish architecture was released from its larger-than-life civilizational mission under the sponsorship of an authoritarian state and had not yet surrendered to the demands of the global market and to the fashionable residential formulas of the global theme park. It was a moment to which we look back somewhat nostalgically today.

1980–PRESENT: VILLAS, GATED COMMUNITIES, AND SUBURBAN EXPANSION

The growth of İstanbul's urban population is itself an indicator of the magnitude of the housing issue and the inevitable impact of housing patterns upon the urban landscape: the city grew from a population of 1,167,000 in 1950 to 7,521,000 in 1990, and by all estimates, to more than 10 million at the turn of the twenty-first century.[13] With the pressures of such numbers coupled with the phenomenal social, economic, and cultural transformations in Turkey after 1980, when the late President Turgut Özal opened up the country to global markets, İstanbul's macro form has changed dramatically. The proliferation of five-star hotels, supermarket chains, shopping malls, and office towers has transformed the fabric, the skyline, and the social panorama of the city in ways that would have been inconceivable before 1980. While these developments can be seen as manifestations of a worldwide trend in the postmodern era, the rise of political Islam parallel to globalization has given İstanbul a more complex and uniquely hybrid urban culture. After the municipal (and later national) election victories of Islamic-leaning parties since 1994, the visibility of Islam in public urban space has increased (especially the number of women with the controversial headscarf) precisely at the time that İstanbul has become a world city receiving international recognition as a "hot spot" of global tourism, leisure, and entertainment. In contrast to the more or less homogeneous Turkish society of previous decades, differences of class, culture, and background have become deeper and far more conspicuous since the 1980s. In the way that apartments and *gecekondu*s defined the urban aesthetic of the 1950–1980 period, massive new residential developments have shaped urbanism after 1980, introducing new scales, new architectural typologies, and a new turning point in Turkey's history of modernization.

By the 1980s, it was evident that the dual pattern of housing that had emerged in the previous three decades (namely the generic mid- or high-rise apartment blocks of the middle and upper-middle classes in the city and the small, rural-looking, single-family *gecekondu*s of the poor migrant communities on the urban fringes) could no longer continue as before. The small contractor-initiated apartment boom on small urban lots within the city had used all available space, although fabric renewal by replacing a

High-rise blocks in Atasehir, mass-housing development in a new edge-city on the Asian side of Istanbul

smaller, medium-rise apartment (even a relatively new one) with a taller one as soon as new codes allowed it has been a continuing practice, especially in upper-middle-class neighborhoods on the Asian side of the city. Meanwhile, in the poorer neighborhoods, the old, user-initiated *gecekondu* process did not continue beyond the end of the 1960s: once these areas were included within the boundaries of metropolitan İstanbul and provided with basic infrastructure, the resulting speculative increase of land values made these areas too expensive for further spontaneous occupation by migrant families. Consequently, the quasi-rural, user-built first-generation *gecekondu*s were progressively replaced by higher-rise, multi-unit apartments, now produced by a speculative process of commercialized, profit-driven, frequently illegal, and substandard construction. The resulting pervasive aesthetic of poorer neighborhoods, the "contemporary vernacular of İstanbul," is that of cheaply built reinforced-concrete frame buildings, filled in with brick walls, sometimes inhabited only on the lower floors and unfinished at the top with reinforcement bars sticking out.

Generic view of İstanbul's poorer urban fringes

Such fabric renewal in both the old apartment and *gecekondu* areas through a progressive increase of building heights and densities has been a continuous process since the late 1960s. What is truly new in the post-1980 period is a phenomenal expansion of new construction on the city's periphery in the form of entire residential communities and large-scale housing developments (*toplu konut*), rather than single apartment buildings on small lots. The first important factor behind the emergence of these new residential patterns is the opening up of new suburban land on both the European and Asian sides of İstanbul for residential and commercial development, allowing a dramatic expansion of the boundaries of metropolitan İstanbul. The second and equally significant factor is the flow of new capital and the emergence of new actors in the housing market: big businesses, banks, and large real estate development companies willing to invest in residential construction, especially for projects targeting middle- and upper-income groups, seeking new lifestyles away from the city or at least insulated from its perceived environmental, social, and aesthetic ills.[14] This has given post-1980 İstanbul what many observers consider to be the paradigmatic residential typology of the period: the gated suburban community or "*site*" as the preferred residential choice of middle- and upper-class Turks, illustrating a global phenomenon that urban sociologists call "the new urban segregation."[15] Although private development and construction companies have been the indisputable driving force, the government has also partici-

High-rise housing blocks on the outskirts of İstanbul

pated in these new trends. The establishment of the Mass Housing Administration (*Toplu Konut İdaresi* or TOKI) in 1984, with the aim of providing credit for large-scale production of low- and middle-income housing, has played an important role in the proliferation of standardized, multi-unit, high-rise blocks in İstanbul's peripheral areas. Ongoing publicly funded "urban renewal projects" (*kentsel dönüşüm projesi*) continue to replace entire neighborhoods of first-generation *gecekondu*s with new high-rise housing projects.[16]

A visible architectural consequence of these developments is the shift to much higher rise (twelve to twenty-four stories and more) residential typologies, often built with prefabricated techniques and rationalized construction processes. Today the periphery of metropolitan İstanbul is an ever-expanding belt of new high-rise residential blocks, targeting a wide range of potential buyers from middle income to the high end. Entire new "edge cities" such as Ümraniye or Ataşehir on the Asian side or Beylikdüzü on the European side have emerged, with a surreal urbanscape of mushrooming residential towers, shopping malls, "hypermarkets" (including European franchises such as Carrefour, Migros, etc) and international "megastores" such as IKEA. That many new residential construction remains unfinished or empty supports İlhan Tekeli's analysis that since the 1980s, the production of middle- and upper-income housing has exceeded the demand, not only reversing the picture of the previous period but highlighting the importance of creating demand through newer marketing techniques.[17]

Advertisements for a new gated residential development in Beylikdüzü, İstanbul

A typological and architectural plurality informs these new trends, particularly on the upper-income end of the market. While the first examples of gated suburban communities for wealthier buyers featured single-family villas marketing a new lifestyle close to nature, these were soon followed by denser typologies with clusters of medium- or high-rise blocks in comprehensively designed, gated communities including auxiliary facilities like swimming pools, tennis courts, playgrounds, and shopping areas. A most illustrative example is the transformation of Göktürk to the northwest of the city some 25 kilometers from the center, from village to booming satellite city of gated residential communities and a municipality proudly encouraging such development.[18] Initially a small village and a *gecekondu* area serving the brick manufacturers and coal mines nearby, Gokturk's fate was soon to change, largely due to its favorable location. Not only was it in relative proximity to the city but also it was protected from unchecked growth by virtue of being surrounded by land closed off to development by the "Belgrade Forest" to the north and a military zone to the east. After the administrative status of Göktürk was changed to a municipality in 1993, a private developer, Esat Edin, began building the luxury residential community of "Kemer Country," marking an important first in what would soon be a pervasive trend. In the following decade, land values in Göktürk would increase by 500 percent, and new luxury residential communities, such as "İstanbul-İstanbul" completed in 2000 by a consortium of real estate companies, and the equally exclusive Ay-Tek residences would follow Kemer Country. The publicity brochure of Göktürk Municipality takes pride in the fact that "the design quality of these residences, their high prices and the quality of the infrastructure ensures the maximum homogeneity of its inhabitants."[19] Meanwhile, the original inhabitants (poorer farmers and industrial workers) of old Gokturk are employed as the gardeners, security guards, and cleaning staff of the new gated communities, marking both the new urban segregation characteristic of the post-1980 period and a new symbiotic relationship between different social classes living in close suburban proximity. As such a vivid case of "new urban segregation and symbiosis," Göktürk is now a compelling research laboratory for students of architecture, urbanism, urban sociology, and cultural studies, both nationally and internationally.[20]

As declared above by Göktürk's mayor, without any hint of irony, the new suburban villas and gated residential communities represent an unprecedented new trend in the privatization of space in general, a conspicuous retreat of the wealthy and privileged behind well-guarded perimeters and hermetically sealed SUVs (including, in some cases, the employment of a bodyguard) to better insulate themselves from poorer, less cultivated, and visibly more "Muslim" urban crowds and from the messiness of an increasingly contested public space. In stark contrast to the early republican emphasis on homogeneous national communities and avoidance of conspicuous luxury and ostentatious display of individualism, it is precisely the promise of exclusivity—physical and social separation from the masses—that the potential customers of suburban villas and gated communities are after.[21] New keywords such as pleasure (*keyif*), quality of life (*yaşam kalitesi*), and exclusivity (*ayrıcalık*) feature prominently as effective marketing points.[22] In fact, the term "white Turks" (*beyaz Türkler*), whose connotations of race and class

Aerial view of Göktürk, "satellite city" of gated residential developments in suburban İstanbul

distinction would have been anathema to early republican modernizers, is now a common expression designating the owners of these exclusive residences, a predominantly well-educated, internationally well-connected, technologically savvy, and mostly young population of wealthy professionals, business executives, corporate managers, finance wizards, stock-brokers, journalists, and media celebrities.[23]

Important shifts in the design and production process of residential construction also separate this last phase of Turkish modernization from the urban apartment boom of the 1950–1980 period. Small contractors had built these earlier apartment buildings with limited capital, employing conventional techniques of reinforced-concrete frame construction with brick infill walls and mostly domestic finishing materials. By contrast, large construction firms, often with international design and development teams capable of mobilizing cutting-edge construction technologies, are active on the residential construction scene today. With the entry of large finance capital into the construction sector (such as the role of İs Bankası in the development of two exclusive gated communities on the Asian side of İstanbul, Kasaba and Optimum), the scale, complexity, and corporate structure of residential development have reached a level inconceivable in the earlier periods of Turkish modernization. Whereas the modern apartments of the 1950s and 1960s were entirely the work of Turkish architects, it is not uncommon today to find the stamp of prominent international designers, as for example in Maya Residences in Etiler designed by Skidmore, Owings & Merrill, the American corporate giant whose work in Turkey goes back to the İstanbul Hilton in the early 1950s. Similarly,

Promotion of gated residential communities

Neotraditional architectural style of residential developments (2002) in Kemerburgaz near Göktürk

the third phase of Kemer Country bears the signature of the prominent Florida firm of Duany Plater-Zyberk & Company, marketed to Kemer Country residents as the architects who introduced neotraditionalist "New Urbanism" to İstanbul.[24]

The irony is that whereas the national processes of urban housing production in the earlier phase gave us the modernist apartment blocks of the 1950s and 1960s, the transnational design and construction processes of the 1990s have promoted neotraditional house designs. The most pervasive stylistic choice in the gated suburban community market appears to be some version of the traditional "Ottoman/Turkish house" with tile roofs, wide overhangs, modular windows, and projecting window bays on the upper floor. With rhetorical references to Ottoman wooden mansions or *konaks* (as in the case of "Beykoz Konakları" on the Asian side of the Bosporus or "Fildisi Osmanli Konakları" in Beylikdüzü) and to Ottoman neighborhood units or *mahalles* (as in the case of Kemer Country), these developments package themselves as remedies to the

"Kemer Life" residential development (2006) by Emre Arolat Architects in Kemerburgaz near Göktürk

destructiveness of modern urbanism and a return to the architectural and urban qualities of traditional environments. However, the stylistic references to tradition are often
only skin-deep: a postmodern façade architecture employed to lend distinctiveness and
historical/cultural relevance to what is in fact a generic luxury suburban villa or gated
residential community. Rather than evoking any larger cultural or national significance,
neotraditional architectural style is just another marketing tool, targeting a particular
group and appealing to the tastes, lifestyles, and desires of that group. Not surprisingly
in such a pluralistic market, there is plenty of room for other styles, including a modernist aesthetic. For example, adjacent to the neotraditional "Turkish-style" residences in
Kemerburgaz near Göktürk, it is possible to see Kemer Life, a more recent residential
development designed by Emre Arolat, featuring five-story modern apartment blocks
connected at the ground level by public arcades. Another notable modernist example
is Optimum villas near Ömerli Dam on the Anatolian side of İstanbul, designed by one

of the young stars of contemporary Turkish architecture, Han Tümertekin, and constructed by the collaboration of İş Bankası with EMTA (Integrated Engineering Designs Company). These latter examples testify to a further differentiation within the high end of the housing market, this time to cater to a more discerning, educated, and sophisticated clientele.

At the end of more than a decade of frantic construction around İstanbul, the density in some suburban communities such as Göktürk and Kemerburgaz has reached such levels that they undermine their developers' promises of tranquility, personal space, and connection to nature. No longer finding the exclusivity they have sought, coupled with the practical difficulties of commuting, it is not surprising that the exodus to suburbia seems to be losing its appeal for the wealthiest of İstanbul's inhabitants. Instead, the fortunes of an even newer residential typology are on the rise: high-end lofts and residential towers within the city, complete with their parking garages, shopping malls, and other services. Some of the most popular examples are the Maya Residences in Etiler, Elite Towers in Şişli, and more recently, the highly fashionable "residence towers" of Kanyon and Metrocity malls, as well as those of Levent Lofts and Sapphire Tower by Tabanlıoğlu Architects in Levent, especially after the construction of the subway system connecting these areas to the city center. The impact of these on the skyline of İstanbul and the change of scale in juxtaposition with the older apartment building fabric are dramatic. Meanwhile, the increasing popularity and international appeal of the old Pera-Galata district as the new arts, culture, and entertainment zone of İstanbul have accelerated efforts toward the gentrification of the old urban housing stock in this very dense and cosmopolitan heart of the city. As many old buildings are fixed up for small residences, bars, cafes, and art galleries, real estate values are on a dramatic rise, attracting cosmopolitan Turks and international buyers alike. Collectively, these latest trends may be the harbinger of yet another phase in the ongoing saga of Turkish modernization and its physical expression on İstanbul's urban landscape.

Opposite: Typical suburban villa development of the late 1990s in Kemerburgaz near Göktürk

Above: Aerial view of Levent showing the new shopping malls/office and residential towers next to the older city fabric of generic apartments to the left and the Zincirlikuyu Cemetery in the foreground

Below: "French Street": urban gentrification in the historic Galata-Pera area of İstanbul

Notes

Aspects of this chapter were first addressed in an interdisciplinary symposium on "Turkey's Engagement with Modernity" in Oxford in September 2004 and then presented as a paper in the "Turkish Triangle" conference at the Harvard University Graduate School of Design in April 2005. I thank Hashim Sarkis and Pani Pyla for inviting me to contribute to this volume and to Murat Güvenç at İstanbul Bilgi University, who was a generous and invaluable resource for reworking the paper in 2007.

1   Daniel Lerner, *The Passing of Traditional Society: Modernizing the Middle East* (Glencoe, IL: Free Press, 1958), Cyril E. Black, *The Dynamics of Modernization: A Study in Comparative History* (New York: Harper and Row, 1966), Bernard Lewis, *The Emergence of Modern Turkey* (Oxford: Oxford University Press, 1961), Arjun Appadurai, *Modernity at Large: Cultural Dimensions of Globalization* (Minneapolis: University of Minnesota Press, 1996), and Dilip Gaonkar, ed., *Alternative Modernities* (Durham and London: Duke University Press, 2001).

2   Especially in Lerner, *The Passing of Traditional Society,* and Lewis, *Emergence of Modern Turkey.*

3   Goankar, *Alternative Modernities,* introduction.

4   For an excellent overview of the political economy of housing production in Turkey's republican history, see İlhan Tekeli, "Türkiye'de Konut Sunumunun Davranışsal Nitelikleri ve Konut Kesiminde Bunalım," (Characteristics of Housing Production in Turkey) *Konut '81* (Ankara: Kent-Koop, 1982), 57–101. Also see İhsan Bilgin, "Modernlesmenin ve Toplumsal Hareketliliğin Yörüngesinde Cumhuriyetin İmarı" (Building the Republic in the Context of Modernization and Social Mobility) in Yıldız Sey, ed., *75 Yılda Değisen Kent ve Mimarlık* (Seventy-five Years of Architecture and Urbanism) (İstanbul: Tarih Vakfı Yayınları, 1998), 255–272.

5   Urban planner Murat Balamir writes that rather than being a preferred residential typology, "apartmentalization" in Turkey (*apartmanlaşma*) is the consequence of external factors such as lack of capital, shortage of available urban land, etc. See "Kira Evinden Kat Evine Apartmanlasma" (Apartmentalization from Rental Houses to Flats), *Mimarlık,* no. 260, 1994, 29–33.

6   See Sibel Bozdoğan, "Democracy, Development, and the Americanization of Turkish Architectural Culture in the 1950s," in Sandy Isenstadt and Kishwar Rizvi, eds., *Modernism in the Middle East* (Seattle: University of Washington Press, 2008), 116–138.

7   See Uğur Tanyeli, "1950'lerden bu Yana Mimari Paradigmaların Değişimi ve Reel Mimarlık" (Changing Architectural Paradigms since the 1950s), in Sey, ed., *75 Yılda Degişen Kent ve Mimarlık,* 241.

8   In her "Rethinking Ordinary Architecture in Postwar Turkey" (paper presented to the Docomomo conference, New York, September 2004), Ela Kacel challenges the common opposition between "high" and "anonymous" modernism and convincingly argues how projects like Birkan Apartments "transformed the international into ordinary modern architecture." Also see her "Fidüsyer: Bir Kollektif Düşünme Pratiği," in Müge Cengizkan, ed., *Haluk Baysal—Melih Birsel* (Ankara: TMMOB Mimarlar Odası Yayınları, 2007), 7–31.

9   For another remarkable example of the similarly conceived modernist block of duplex units in Ankara, see Ali Cengizkan, "Cinnah 19: Ütopik mi, Gerçek Modern mi?" (Cinnah 19: Utopia or Real Modern?) in *Modernin Saati* (The Hour of the Modern) (Ankara: Mimarlar Derneği, 2002), 173–187.

10 Charles Abrams, the prominent planner and housing expert who published his famous *Man's Struggle for Shelter in an Urbanizing World* (Cambridge, MA: MIT Press, 1964), came to Turkey for a research trip in 1951 and prepared a report for the United Nations on the conditions and problems of housing and urbanization in Turkey. The same year another report on housing, planning, and building construction was prepared for the Turkish government by an SOM team led by Gordon Bunshaft, who would design the Hilton Hotel the following year.

11 Yıldız Sey, "Cumhuriyet Doneminde Konut" (Housing in the Republican Period), in Sey, ed., *75 Yılda Değişen Kent ve Mimarlık,* 285.

12 The most insightful general analyses of Turkish architecture and housing after 1950 can be found in the writings of Uğur Tanyeli and İhsan Bilgin in Turkish, such as the essays they have contributed to Sey, *75 Yılda Değişen Kent ve Mimarlık.* Unfortunately there are no English translations of these discussions.

13 "Türkiye Ulusal Rapor ve Eylem Planı" (Turkey's National Report and Plan of Action), prepared for the Habitat II Conference in İstanbul, 1996.

14 See Sencer Ayata, "The New Middle Class and the Joys of Suburbia," in Deniz Kandiyoti and Ayşe Sanktanber, eds., *Fragments of Culture* (New Brunswick: Rutgers University Press, 2002), 25–42.

15 See Rowland Atkinson and Sarah Blandy, eds., *Gated Communities* (London: Routledge, 2006), Ayşe Öncu and Petra Weyland, eds., *Space, Culture, and Power: New Identities in Globalizing Cities* (London: Zed Books, 1997). Asu Aksoy and Kevin Robins, Ayşe Öncu, Çağlar Keyder, and others have studied İstanbul's new axes of social, cultural, and spatial differentiation in light of these urban theories. See also Ayfer Bartu and Biray Kolluoğlu, "Emerging Spaces of Neoliberalism: A Gated Town and a Public Housing Project in İstanbul," in *New Perspectives on Turkey,* no. 39, 2008, 5–46.

16 See especially Özlem Ünsal and Tuna Kuyucu, "Challenging the Neoliberal Urban Regime: Regeneration and Resistance in Başibuyuk and Tarlabasi," in Deniz Göktürk, Levent Soysal, and İpek Türeli, eds., *Orienting İstanbul: Cultural Capital of Europe?* (New York: Routledge, 2010), 51–71.

17 Tekeli, "Türkiye'de Konut Sunumunun Davranişsal Nitelikleri ve Konut Kesiminde Bunalım," 91–92.

18 Publicity publication, *Gerçeğe Dönüsen Rüya Göktürk* (A Dream Come True: Gokturk) (Istanbul: Municipality of Göktürk Publications, 2006).

19 Ibid., 77.

20 See a recent study by the students of architecture and urban design, ETH (directed by Kees Christianse and Tim Rieniets), published as *Ausfahrt Göktürk* (Zurich: ETH Research Studio Publication, winter semester 2005–2006).

21 See Şerife Geniş, "Producing Elite Localities: The Rise of Gated Communities in İstanbul," in *Urban Studies*, vol. 44, April 2007, 771–798.

22 For example, "Optimum bir Yaşam" (An Optimum Life), the publicity booklet of the Optimum Houses, an exclusive suburban development in İstanbul by EMTA Integrated Engineering Designs Inc.

23 On the emergence, tastes, and lifestyles of the "white Turks," see Rifat Bali, *Tarzı Hayattan Life Style'a: Yeni Seçkinler, Yeni Mekanlar, Yeni Yaşamlar* (From *Tarz-I Hayat* to Life Style: New Elites, New Spaces, New Lives) (İstanbul: İletişim, 2002).

24 Kemer Country publicity brochures and newsletters throughout the 1990s.

HOUSING/SETTLEMENTS

RACHEL KALLUS

6

STATE-CONSTRUCTED EVERYDAY:
ENVISIONING A PLACE FOR THE
NATIONAL COMMUNITY

In the late 1950s, an experimental neighborhood was initiated by the Department of Construction and Housing in the development town of Kiryat Gat in southern Israel. Defined as an "integrative habitational unit" by Artur Glikson,[1] its architect, the intention was to combine different aspects of urban and regional planning to comprise a residential quarter based on ecological and sociological principles, with the aim of ensuring optimum communal cohesion. Incorporated into the department's declared policy of shifting emphasis from supplying shelter to social absorption and community structuring, the physical setting of the Integrative Habitational Unit (hereafter IHU) was intended to achieve two main national goals: population dispersal and immigrant absorption. It took into account the residential environments required by varied ethnic groups and presented a development model for social integration and an alternative to the abstract and context-neutral constructions of the Department of Construction and Housing in new development towns. The intention was to combine planning policies and architectural design to build "a real place for real people."

This careful localization of the national community that integrated the city and its elements (i.e., the neighborhood) in a broader social, economic, and planning system shows how the urban sub-unit becomes part of the state's development scheme. It exemplifies how national-scale modernization is adapted to the residential level. Coping with immigrants—mainly from North Africa and Asia, who were considered unfit for agricultural pioneering—necessitated solutions for integrating these populations in the cities. The urban sub-unit into which these people were absorbed was thus perceived in

The location of Kiryat Gat

the context of economic development of the region and seen as a bridge between the city and the region, between urban and rural development.

Envisioned nationally but implemented locally, the IHU constructed quotidian day-to-day life in accordance with a national agenda. In its meticulous design manipulations, it translated national goals of economic growth, social cohesion, and territorial control into a closely detailed residential environment. Architecturally, it took into account political goals and their attainment through the design of physical objects—buildings and spaces—complying with the state's hegemonic ideology. Thus the IHU is a social and cultural entity based not only on the understanding of professional practitioners and their sensitivity to formal attributes but also on their profound awareness of a political context.

This text focuses on the IHU in Kiryat Gat, evaluating its attempt to provide, through architecture, a locus for a national community.[2] It discusses how architecture creates the political landscape of the everyday by constructing material and social realities. It considers the notion of "state-constructed everyday"—an everyday reality designed in relation to the politics of the state and its attempts to spatialize national territory. The residential environment is where identity and citizenship are contextualized and mundane daily routines are molded into spatial patterns of forms, materials, and movement. Investigation of the IHU in this context reveals how the residential environment is envisioned by architects and enlisted by a nation-state for reinforcing its hold on land and people alike, thereby exposing the duality of the residential environment as both a personal space and a national domain. Considering the residential environment as a product of architectural practice raises issues concerning development processes and their fundamental assumptions, methods, and implementation.

NATION BUILDING AND CONSTRUCTION OF THE EVERYDAY

From the outset, Israel's spatial design has derived from a double agenda. Outwardly, it was intended to establish ownership and control over national territory, whereas inwardly it was intended to facilitate the creation of a living space in which inhabitants could find their identity and lifestyle, and endow a symbolic meaning on the daily practices endemic to that space. Architecture, especially modern architecture, played a major role, as an effective means by which the environment could be interpreted, modified, and contested.[3] This is certainly not unique to Israel, but the Israeli experience, with its territorial goals and its vast and speedy development, reveals how nation-state modernization has continuously shaped and reshaped the built environment, and underlines the unique role of architecture in this process.[4]

The tension between national and personal space that has characterized Israel's planning agenda from the outset is evident in the first national physical plan, completed in the early 1950s.[5] In accordance with the two national goals of immigrant absorption and population dispersal, the plan details a framework in which all areas of the country are balanced and harmoniously settled.[6] Space is perceived as the mold into which the nation-state is poured, and citizens are the raw materials of its construction. The plan specifies that the primary goal of national planning is "the division of the population according to economic, security, and social requirements." But "dispersing the population across the country is not the *outcome* of economic reality, it is what makes this reality," thus underlining the tension between national and personal space.[7]

Such tension is the basic premise of a "contract" between the state and its citizens, in which the state as a sovereign political entity is legitimized by its people.[8] Housing has been a major instrument through which the state has initiated its sovereignty.[9] Twentieth-century housing, in Israel as elsewhere, operates in tandem with the modern nation-state. It is based on the government's obligation to provide "minimum" living standards for its citizens. At the same time, housing provision is a strategy of nation-state building, playing an important role in reinforcing the relationship between a (sometimes imaginary) community and a territory.[10] Thus in the political entity known as "the state," national identity (i.e., citizenship), though intended to override local affiliations, is still a place-bound concept.[11] The modern nation-state is a sociopolitical construct,[12] relying extensively on physical design—that is, architecture (especially modern architecture),[13] which projects its identity by means of formal institutions.[14]

National traditions,[15] however, are created not only by means of monumental architecture, but also by the architecture of the everyday—the home and the residential environment. Balibar argues that the nation-state derives its collective meaning from a "fictive ethnicity" based on family and school, in which the home and the residential environment play leading roles.[16] Planned neighborhoods are ideal settings for creating a national community because they shape territorial boundaries and construct a sociocultural identity around the living space. This is where conflicts about representation, access, and entitlement of differently empowered groups occur.[17] Here the residential system not only provides shelter, it is also a context in which a complete redefinition of the relationship between the individual and the state happens. The appropriateness of the residential environment is that it can design space and society simultaneously, giving concrete form to national goals while shaping the image and identity of a people. The residential environment is thus an efficient and powerful tool that allows for formal construction of a sense of place by controlling the informal practices of everyday life.

The involvement of the nation-state in the production of everyday life calls for reassessment of the concept of the everyday. In light of current views of the everyday as an analytical category and a conceptual instrument, state-constructed everyday demands rethinking because it reveals the problematic reality of the quotidian—the arena in which territory and identity are manipulated by the nation-state.[18] Lefebvre sees everyday life as a technique used by the state. As he says, "The state is now built upon daily life. Its base is the everyday."[19] Harvey explains how the state uses professionals to legitimize the everyday by ordering its material reality.[20] By virtue of design and construction of concrete projects, sovereignty and hegemony are institutionalized and internalized. Location, identity, and power are established via day-to-day mechanisms of confrontation, compromise, and consent among economic, social, and political forces. The role of professionals (especially architects and planners) in production of the everyday comprises responsibility not merely for aesthetic aspects but also for effective use of spatial and human resources, as well as for translating hegemonic values into affective experience.[21]

Fascination with the everyday is longstanding, but it is currently accepted as a critical practice that resists modernity, usually with regard to political analysis of the consumer society and the nation-state as challenged by its subjects. Lefebvre's theory of the relationship between the everyday and modernism indicates the potential of every-day "spontaneous conscience" to confront the tyrannies of daily existence.[22] De Certeau challenges the monotonies and tyrannies of daily life by stressing the individual's capacity to manipulate situations and create "networks of anti-discipline."[23] These criti-cal perspectives have aroused interest within architectural discourse, mainly for their potential to challenge the profession's involvement in geometries of power.[24] Lessons of the everyday insist on seeing architecture as a "cultural landscape"—the entire mate-rial world that people make and conceive. It stressed a return to "small-*a* architecture" that is concerned with how day-to-day life is experienced in relationship to places and how people inhabit them.[25] Moreover, in a domain that is increasingly linked to global-ization, the concept of the everyday has been seen as an attempt to reconnect to place by offering architectural resistance to commodification and consumption.[26] Faced with "the bureaucracy of controlled consumption" (per Lefebvre), everyday life is seen as a lived experience of a political struggle against the forces of a capitalist economy.

Growing realization of the political consequences of professional practice, although somewhat oblivious to methodological dissimilarities of architectural and political hegemony, has aroused greater awareness of local nuances of power.[27] Elsewhere I have discussed the internal, complex, and multilayered hierarchies of colonization and con-trol, in an attempt to identify how professional practice normalizes mechanisms and systems of power and control through the production of everyday life.[28] The ongoing challenge for professional practitioners within the framework of the nation-state and its ideology is to decipher the political culture of a nation-state and to explain the relation-ship between state apparatus, professional practice, and "ordinary people."

As suggested by Lefebvre, the notion of the everyday must be accepted as both an analytical category and a conceptual instrument, in order to reveal both a *way of under-standing* and a *way of reading* in which "critical knowledge and action...work together."[29] The following discussion examines the role that the residential environment plays in the state-constructed everyday by studying the way in which an urban sub-unit (the neighborhood) is envisioned as a place for the national community. The chronicle of the IHU at Kiryat Gat reveals the intricacies of professional engagement in the blueprint of the state-constructed everyday, and the attempt to integrate national agenda locally through a spatial system that transmutes ideas into the form and the material of every-day life.

As with other mid-twentieth-century housing solutions, the IHU was an attempt to humanize the environment, in reaction to modernist ideas, especially as promoted architecturally by the CIAM (Congrès Internationaux d'Architecture Moderne) and its members.[30] Based on a growing emphasis on spiritual and emotional values in a world dominated by science and technology, the project offered a new comprehension of architecture practice driven by a desire to integrate scientific knowledge with socio-cultural understanding. To appreciate how unique this experimental planned development unit actually was, however, the IHU must be seen in light of hard-line pragmatic modernism, battling with the harsh material, political, and social realities of post-Mandate Palestine, in the newly established State of Israel. Contrasting with this intensity, the IHU seems to present a softer approach despite its scientific rationale. Although not free from professional elitism, bureaucratic oppression, and complicity with a political regime practicing extreme exclusion, the IHU proposes a somewhat more malleable approach to the Israel modernization project. In attempting to foster a sense of community and place and to find the "lost urban space," it humanizes the *machine à habiter* and addresses, to some extent, issues of personal and cultural identity.

In the course of designing the IHU,[31] many analytical schemes were prepared, in which sociocultural intentions were translated into the appropriate architectural considerations, enhanced by the intricate interplay of masses and voids.[32] These studies attempted to shape the spatial configuration of communal activities, define the center of the neighborhood, and suggest various movement patterns. An axial system of paths and an assortment of public open spaces throughout the neighborhood encouraged social exchanges, with communal facilities carefully placed at the center to encourage shared activities. The division of the area into sub-units was to formulate social sub-groupings, where the placement of different building types was used to achieve greater spatial variation.[33] Mixed dwelling units and an assortment of building types were also designed to allow social diversification and intensify urban ambiance. High and low buildings placed side by side increased density, thereby making land use more efficient, but also promoting an urban atmosphere. Distanced from the city center, the neighborhood achieved physical distinction from its surroundings by arranging the buildings as a barrier, supported by open green spaces that promoted a sense of community—a city within a city.

With all of these formal manipulations, the IHU aimed mainly to create a new society, taking upon itself the shaping of a national community. The societal goals, though concentrated at the local level, spelled out agendas at the national level—to integrate immigrants belonging to a range of ethnic groups and promote community cohesion. Housing officials repeatedly claimed that "[the immigrants] must be educated...to [accept] the level of housing that is common in the country...[because] there are customs that cannot be taken into consideration, and it is imperative to educate the occupants to break those habits."[34] Providing a home environment enabled the state

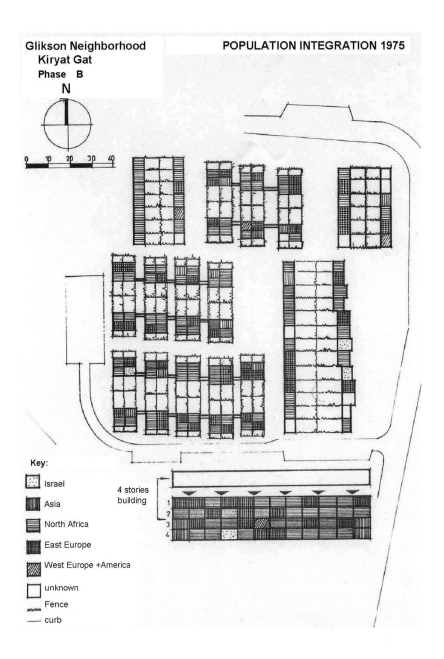

Post-occupancy evaluation of the Integrative Habitational Unit's social integration (source: Slijper and Stoop 1978)

The New Inhabitants

Argentine

Tunisia

Iran

Oman

The Netherlands

Israel

Morocco

England

Romania

Yemen

Ethnic groups to be integrated, as seen by the Department of Housing in its 1950s publication (source: Israel Builds, 1958)

"Melting Pot," a 1950s' caricature by Friedl Stern

to penetrate the personal space of a family and control its most intimate activities. The official intention was that the housing unit would be "an educational tool for proper family life."[35] An official study declared that in planning the apartments, "the ethnicity of the immigrants must not be taken into consideration, since the intention for both the immigrants and the host society is to forge a uniform Israeli style of life."[36] Glikson never questioned the basic premise of these goals, and saw the IHU as the most effective means for attaining them. Spatial concerns investigated through design were fundamentally directed at forming the most suitable residential environment for effective social integration. Such concerns focused on the building, the cluster, and the neighborhood, and how they could become efficient social units activated by physical form and integrated into the city and the region.

Glikson's rationale for such acute state involvement in physical planning was based on his understanding of contemporary professional goals anchored in the reality of modernity. As he argues, "the state in which human life processes resulted in

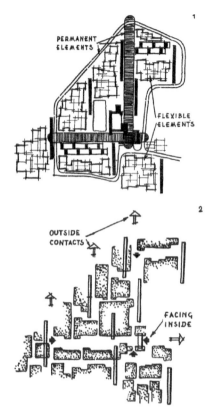

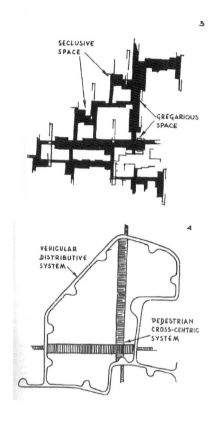

Studies of the center and various movement patterns (source: Glikson 1967)

architecture, without mediation of planning, is a 'paradise lost'. At the present stage, habitation must be consciously planned, and the multiple significance of the man-made environment must be the foremost of the architect's reflections." In compliance with the national program, the notion of the habitat, embodied in the IHU, was "to create an environment that would provide means to rehabilitate, educate, and root the new settlers in their new homes."[38] The residential environment's potential for social rehabilitation and ethnic integration was systematically analyzed in a series of studies, which, despite attempts to relate to a specific locale, constructed a nationally perceived social unit. The IHU was envisioned as a neighborhood where immigrants from North Africa, Asia, and Europe would live together with the Israeli-born. Statistical and sociological data analyzed the demographic characteristics of the different groups, their households, and their housing needs in terms of flexibility, ownership, utilities, and their preferred living conditions. Further data on communal relations, identity, leadership, and assimilation produced dwelling type combinations and housing cluster organizations geared to promote neighborliness. The outlined design preferred subgrouping combinations according to ethnic, socioeconomic, and personal characteristics, demonstrat-

Overall plan of the neighborhood (source: Glikson 1967)

ing the importance of the IHU not only for its specific environs but also as a nationally integrated social unit.[39]

Although essentially an urban sub-unit, the IHU was integrated in the Lakhish region. Lacking any political status, the region was regarded as a planning unit that could overreach administrative definitions and relate to natural and geographic attributes. Regional planning dealt with land use, infrastructures, and settlement growth beyond the city, to achieve an efficient integration of immigrants, both socially and economically. Essentially a rural area, it systematically organized settlements of different sizes, establishing an operational framework to manage economic and social resources. The intention was to create a structural relationship between the small rural settlements in which immigrants lived (principally for geopolitical reasons)[40] and connect them to a larger economic and production unit—that is, the city.[41] The Lakhish region, with Kiryat Gat as its urban center, demonstrated a structural principle in which region, city, and neighborhood formed a hierarchical continuum.[42] The IHU was not simply an urban structural element but also a building block of the larger region, integrating the city and its units in a broader social, economic, and planning system.

A view of the neighborhood in its early years (source: Glikson, 1967)

The intention was to develop the IHU as a basic "environmental unit," based on an architectural approach imperative for "a period of urgent demand for popular housing and of mass-production methods."[43] Unlike the common housing schemes developed at the time that constituted abstract and sterile environments, the IHU was an attempt to create a viable and rooted-in-place urban unit. Contrary to the routine practice of the Department of Construction and Housing, of "building houses and not neighborhoods,"[44] it suggested a strengthening of the "inner link between the house and the quarter...to create truly urban forms of housing."[45] This scheme challenged other state housing developments based on planning stages separated from physical design and implementation. It intention was to overcome the "dichotomy between the designers of the houses and the planners of the overall layout of the towns."[46] This dichot-

THE LACHISH REGION

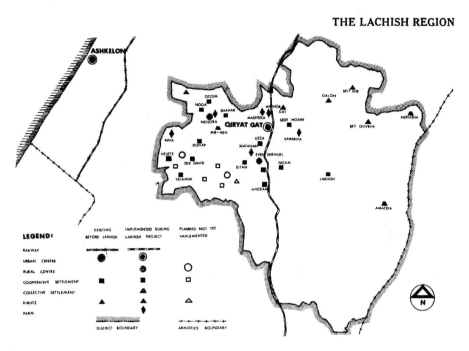

The Lakhish region (source: Glikson, 1967)

omy resulted from dividing planning and architecture into two discrete departments, located in two different government ministries. Separating housing policy decisions from the architectural design development of the houses on location caused the erection of pre-designed standard building typologies on randomly demarcated plots in accordance with land-use schemes, and with no preliminary site development. As one architect of that time described it, "Houses were simply placed on the ground with no regard for topography. If the ground was leveled, the houses stood on stilts; if it sloped, the stilts were of different heights."[47] The IHU's comprehensive approach was intended to resolve such issues.

Tension and integration between architecture and planning are evident in the state's first master plan[48]—a three-dimensional illustration of the physical and spatial qualities of various sites to be developed throughout the country, outlined with only two-dimensional colored land-use schemes. To facilitate future physical development, the plan details the features of various settlements, suggesting how they could be implemented. In retrospect, this attention to detail may be considered the plan's greatest asset, since it envisioned actual places. It has also been the plan's greatest shortcoming—inadequately committed to design interpretations with insufficient guidance for future implementation in place, which follows the plan's overall spatial agenda.[49] This shortcoming was addressed in the IHU, by making no distinction between planning and architecture. Glikson, like other architects of the time, saw himself as architect and planner, operating successfully at the varied scales of the built environment. This enabled him to translate policy into physical design and consequently turn abstract state agenda into spatial concrete framework.

The introduction of the IHU corresponded with a gradual change in the structure of government offices, increasing the planning responsibilities of the Construction and Housing Department and allowing it and its Planning Section to be involved at various levels of urban development.[50] Glikson argued that "the reconstruction of the idea of the town might best commence with environmental units which are large enough to be comprehensive and small enough to be comprehensible."[51] He further argued that "architecture, urbanism, and regional design must all interact in order to form the human habitation,"[52] because "in the construction of a new residential quarter there is an essential distinction between a building and a group of houses."[53] This change in the meaning of a "housing project," from a description of a group of residential buildings to a synonym for urban development,[54] marks a renewed interest in the urban space, based on architectural awareness of the consequences of the modernist city in which the familiar urban space had been practically lost.[55] It suggests an approach to the city that connects policy-making strategies (planning) with formal design tactics (architecture) through the use of analytical methods that characterized the emerging practice of urban design, which was officially defined only about ten years later.[56]

In its vision of the urban space as "a container of social power"[57] the IHU clearly echoes the neighborhood-unit concept.[58] Nonetheless, it was fundamentally different from Perry's unit, which was based exclusively on the function of educational institutions. The IHU was, first and foremost, an architectural unit attempting to achieve social assimilation through effective and comprehensive environmental integration. Its influence on the locale was intended to "create both visual and functional connections with its environs, and the identification of people and places with well-defined interior spaces."[59] This is most apparent in the master plan prepared by Glikson for Kiryat Gat, where the residential quarter is an urban development unit based on pedestrian and vehicular arteries and residential density, integrated in the city through landscape and topography.[60] Studies of the visibility of different parts of the city demonstrate the sensitivity with which the neighborhood was placed in relation to its surroundings, to create the area's terrain.[61] This proves once again that the IHU was not only an element of the urban structure but also a building block of the larger system, intended to link the region's agrarian way of life with the city's agro-production and services in a well-balanced environment.[62]

The terminology used for the IHU (i.e., habitational unit) further suggests a theoretically constructed residential environment. As Eleb points out, the notion of habitat in modernist discussion has replaced prior terms such as "dwelling" or "residence."[63] Although this expression may overcome contradictions with the idea of international solutions, its use in postwar architectural discourse seems to support the notion of a theoretically constructed residential environment that is often divorced from day-to-day living and contradicts the notion of the everyday. This refutes, of course, the IHU's attempt to overcome the neutrality of planned development and "the danger of build-

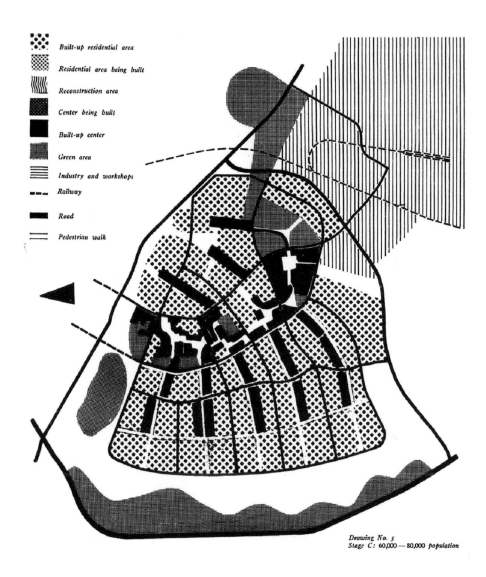

Legend:

- Built-up residential area
- Residential area being built
- Reconstruction area
- Center being built
- Built-up center
- Green area
- Industry and workshops
- Railway
- Road
- Pedestrian walk

Drawing No. 5
Stage C: 60,000 — 80,000 population

Schematic design of Kiryat Gat (source: Stoop 1967)

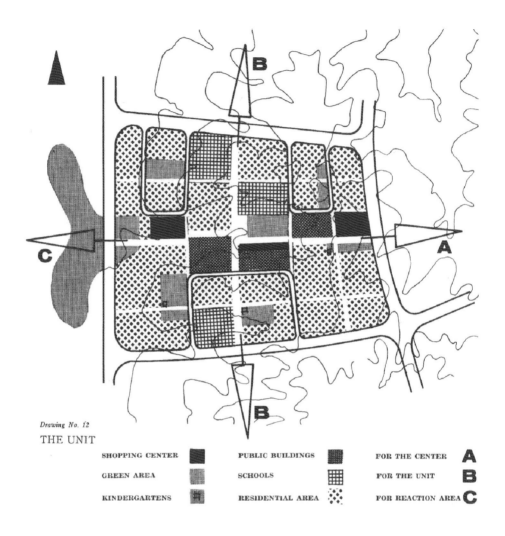

Drawing No. 12

THE UNIT

SHOPPING CENTER ■
GREEN AREA ▒
KINDERGARTENS ▥

PUBLIC BUILDINGS ▦
SCHOOLS ▦
RESIDENTIAL AREA ░

FOR THE CENTER **A**
FOR THE UNIT **B**
FOR REACTION AREA **C**

Schematic design of Kiryat Gat's urban sub-unit (source: Stoop 1967)

ing another nondescript community of the type made all too familiar in other Israeli development towns."[64] But by enlisting a preliminary scientific approach to ensure that "a diversified and realistic program could become the basis of integral planning,"[65] the IHU defined an abstract and homogeneous urban entity that was perfect as a means of adapting national-scale modernization to the residential level.

THE POETICS OF THE EVERYDAY

Studies conducted over the years attempted to evaluate the success of the IHU as a planned development unit, and to measure its effectiveness in regard to population mix, social integration, and community cohesion.[66] These studies consider the IHU as a mere exercise in social engineering, in line with the Israeli doctrine of the "melting pot." Indeed, the neighborhood aimed at social integration and served to shape the individual as part of the national collective. But the IHU was also deeply rooted in form making and in physical design that tried to integrate not only ethnic groups but also the different aspects of the environment. Its meticulously calculated design scheme placed the neighborhood in an environmental system that related buildings to neighborhood, city, and region—all becoming elements for architectural intervention in which social and political goals were attained through designed manipulations of physical objects.

Replete with contradictions, the IHU epitomizes interest in the human condition in the midst of modernism's indifference to the individual and her or his unique place. What is so intriguing is the insistence on contemplation in light of pressing realities; the call for permanency when temporary solutions could easily have alleviated immediate needs; interest in small gestures within a large modernization project; and the striving for continuity and connectedness, against a political terrain of reformulation and of distancing from the past. Although highly praised by the professional community, in reality the neighborhood's everyday existence was quite grim from the outset.[67] Stigmatized as a public housing project populated mainly by immigrants, located in a peripheral development town at a distance from the city center, it has never fulfilled the vision of its planners.[68] Today, with the lowest socioeconomic status and real-estate value in Kiryat Gat, the neighborhood has been listed several times by the Ministry of Construction and Housing for rehabilitation. It continues to be a source of conflict and uncertainty for city officials and residents alike.[69]

Nonetheless, the IHU is a daring project. In a state that is historically unclear about its urban centers and ritually sustains its rural development, the IHU reinstitutes the city's role.[70] IHU's call for humanization of the urban environment was not a reaction merely to international modernism but to the indiscriminate adoption of modern architecture in the Israeli context. As much as its development epitomizes the international debate over modernism and its future, it is grounded in its local context. For Glikson, Israeli architecture faced unique problems that could not be solved by techniques borrowed from elsewhere. Although Israel's architects were struggling to achieve modern standards, he felt that the means at their disposal were those of "backward countries."[71]

His desire for modernity was based in the western world's awakened understanding of the limitations and scarcity of natural resources, in the need to achieve a better balance between progress and development, and in a sensitivity to the human condition. Unlike its American and European counterparts, the IHU is firmly anchored in a decolonized Middle Eastern region endeavoring to reinvent itself according to a modernist rationale. Disregarding the transitional turmoil of a nation-state in the making, the IHU could perhaps be seen as a benign adaptation of modern universal precedents. It evolved, however, in a highly politicized context of constructing the collective identity of a new nation-state under complex geopolitical circumstances. Thus it is the outcome of professional practice operating in a contested terrain of multifaceted layers of colonization.

As a national modernization project formulated at the residential level, the IHU develops as a one-way progression replicating the stages traversed by western societies, usually based on the assumption that economic conditions are indicators of social well-being. According to this logic, economic status is associated with improved technology, increased division of labor, incremental commercial facilities, urbanization, and decreasing traditional authority. Mainstream thinking in the 1950s assumed that higher standards of living would benefit the entire population, ultimately reaching the grassroots via a trickle-down effect—the basic assumption underlining IHU development at the national level, even though it was not seen in such simple and impersonal terms. However, although sensitive to social issues and to the physical environment, it not only ignored the previous inhabitants of the site[72] but did not take into consideration the social and power relationships of the new residents, or their desires and aspirations. The top–down approach generally assumed that better integration would foster social well-being and economic growth. Hence neighborhood development and evaluation of its success were not seen at the personal level, as experienced by the residents, but in conformity with nation-state agendas and in accordance with its own standards.[73]

Ironically, though opposed to modernism as advocated by CIAM, the IHU fully realized CIAM's agenda of working in synergy with the state. Like Le Corbusier, for whom the state was the only authority with enough political power to realize modern architecture, the IHU does not call for political or structural change[74] It embodies a socially constructed allegiance to the state and its hegemonic ideology. Although locally implemented, the IHU was not a small-scale, avant-garde endeavor, but an attempt to shape the institutional practice of the state and its apparatus according to new social and environmental awareness. In its questioning of modernism, the IHU could easily be seen, in the context of critical regionalism, as challenging modernist assumptions of universal progressiveness.[75] In that context, its success is not so much in counteracting the placelessness of modern architecture but rather in relating to a specific locale and its social and political contexts. Rather than employing contextual strategies to achieve a sense of place and meaning, the IHU manifests deep comprehension of a locale and its complex bureaucratic and politicized circumstances. Hence, unlike the critical regionalism that emphasizes topography, climate, light, and tectonic form—all physical elements—the IHU emerged mainly from intense awareness of the political context. Its political insight is not less significant than its architectural achievement. In fact, it was this careful consideration and perception of highly complex bureaucratic and politicized circumstances that enabled the IHU to achieve meaningful architecture and thus become a blueprint for a state-constructed everyday.

Notes

1   On Glikson's work, see *Journal of Architectural and Planning Research*, 21(2), 2004, theme issue: Artur Glikson and the Making of Place: A Look at His Lasting Impact on Planning and Architecture (guest editor Rachel Kallus).

2   This chapter does not discuss the neighborhood in detail. This has been done by others, especially Robert Marans, in "Social and Cultural Influences in New Town Planning," *Journal of the Town Planning Institute*, February (1970): 60–65; "Kiryat Gat, Israel: A New Town," in *The Role of Housing in Promoting Social Integration*, U.N. Dept. of Economics and Social Affairs (New York: United Nations, 1978); and "Neighborhood Planning: The Contributions of Artur Glikson," *Journal of Architectural and Planning Research*, 21(2) (2004): 112–124. Rather, it examines an experimental neighborhood as formulated at a specific historical moment, in the context of circumstances of "nation-state building" and as part of an emerging postwar architectural culture.

3   Rachel Kallus and Hubert Law-Yone, "National Home/Personal Home: Public Housing and the Shaping of National Space," *European Planning Studies* 10(6) (2002): 765–779.

4   Israel is only one example of the use of modern architecture in nation-state building, though modernization that considers the home environment is more widely discussed in the colonial context. See, for example, Monique Eleb, "An Alternative to Functionalist Universalism: Ecochard, Candilis, and ATBAT-Afrique," in *Anxious Modernisms: Experimentations in Postwar Architectural Culture*, edited by Sarah Williams Goldhagen and Rejean Legault (Cambridge: MIT Press, 2000), 55–73. For discussion of the American home in postwar reconstruction, see John Archer, *Architecture and Suburbia: From English Villa to American Dream House, 1690–2000* (Minneapolis: University of Minnesota Press, 2005); Andrew M. Shanken, *194X: Architecture, Planning, and Consumer Culture on the American Home Front* (Minneapolis: University of Minnesota Press, 2009).

5   Arieh Sharon, *Physical Planning in Israel* (Jerusalem: Government Press, 1952 [Hebrew]), 5.

6   These national goals, though conflicting—see Erik Cohen, "Population Dispersal and Intermingling of the Exiles as Colliding Missions," in *Intermingling of the Exiles*, edited by Shmuel Noah Eisenstadt and Abraham Zlotchov (Jerusalem: Hebrew University, Magnes, 1969 [Hebrew]), 143–157)—form the infrastructure of Israel's physical development, its national housing policies, and its various architectural solutions.

7   Ibid., 12.

8   Partha Chatterjee, *The Politics of the Governed: Popular Politics in Most of the World* (New York: Columbia University Press, 2004).

9   The use of housing by the state is most pronounced in settler societies; see Daiva Stasiulis and Nira Yuval-Davis, "Introduction: Beyond Dichotomies: Gender, Race, Ethnicity, and Class in Settler Societies," in *Unsettling Settler Societies*, edited by Stasiulis and Yuval-Davis (London: Sage Publications, 1995), 1–38. It is especially noticeable in nineteenth-century Australia, Canada, and the United States, where housing was instrumental in defining and constructing national territories while giving land benefits to dominant settler groups; for discussion of the American frontier, see Frederick Jackson Turner, *The Frontier in American History* (New York: Holt, Rinehart and Winston, 1962); for discussion of Turner's thesis, see John Mack Faragher, *Rereading Frederick Jackson Turner: The Significance of the Frontier in American History, and Other Essays* (New Haven: Yale University Press, 1999); for discussion of the nineteenth-century Canadian frontier, see Neil Forkey, *Shaping the Upper Canadian Frontier: Environment, Society, and Culture in the Trent Valley* (Calgary: University of Calgary Press, 2003); for Australia, see Liam Anderson and James O'Dowd, "Borders, Border Regions, and Territoriality: Contradictory Meanings, Changing Significance," *Regional Studies* 33 (7) (1999): 593–604. Examples from present-day Sri Lanka (e.g., David Little, *Sri Lanka: the Invention of Enmity* (Washington, D.C.: U.S. Institute for Peace, 1994) and Estonia (e.g., Gershon Shafir, *Immigrants and Nationalists: Ethnic Conflict and Accommodation in Catalonia, the Basque Country, Latvia, and Estonia* (Albany: SUNY Press, 1995) also show how housing policies are used by governments to shape territorial boundaries, and to construct a citizenship identity among hegemonic ethnic groups around the living space. In Singapore and Hong Kong, public housing policies are the basis for planned economic development and maintain the interests of specific hegemonies; see Manuel Castells, Lee Goh, and Reginald Yin-Wang Kwok, *The Shek Kip Mei Syndrome: Economic Development and Housing in Hong Kong and Singapore* (London: Pion, 1990).

10 Benedict Anderson, *Imagined Communities* (London: Verso, 1983).

11 James Holston and Arjun Appadurai, "Introduction: Cities and Citizenship," in *Cities and Citizenship*, edited by James Holston (Durham: Duke University Press, 1999).

12 Kay Anderson, "Thinking 'Postnationality': Dialogue across Multicultural, Indigenous, and Settler Spaces," *Annals of the Association of American Geographers*, 90 (2) (2000): 381–391.

13 James Holston, *The Modernist City: An Anthropological Critique of Brasilia* (Chicago: University of Chicago Press, 1989); Abidin Kusno, *Behind the Postcolonial: Architecture, Urban Space, and Political Cultures in Indonesia* (London: Routledge, 2000); Sibel Bozdoğan, *Modernism and Nation Building* (Seattle: University of Washington Press, 2002).

14 Lawrence Vale, *Architecture, Power, and National Identity* (New Haven: Yale University Press, 1992).

15 Ernest Gellner, *Nations and Nationalism* (Ithaca: Cornell University Press, 1983); Eric Hobsbawm, *Nations and Nationalism since 1780: Programme, Myth, Reality* (Cambridge: Cambridge University Press, 1990); Liah Greenfeld, *Nationalism: Five Roads to Modernity* (Cambridge: Harvard University Press, 1992).

16 Etienne Balibar, "The Nation-Form: History and Ideology," in *Race, Nation, Class*, ed. Etienne Balibar and Immanuel Wallerstein (London: Verso, 1991), 86–106.

17 Peter Jackson and Jan Penrose, eds., *Construction of Race, Place, and Nation* (London: UCL Press, 1993); Homi Bhabha, *Nation and Narration* (London: Routledge, 1990).

18 Henri Lefebvre, *Critique of Everyday Life*, vol. 1, translated by John Moore (London: Verso, 1991 [1947]); Michel de Certeau, *The Practice of Everyday Life*, translated by Steven Rendall (Berkeley: University of California Press, 1984).

19 Henri Lefebvre, *Critique of Everyday Life: From Modernity to Modernism*, vol. 3, translated by Gregory Elliott (London: Verso, 2005 [1981]), 123.

20 David Harvey, *The Urbanization of Capital* (Oxford: Blackwell, 1985).

21 Vale, *Architecture, Power, and National Identity*; Kusno, *Behind the Postcolonial*; and Bozdoğan, *Modernism and Nation Building*.

22 Lefebvre, *Critique of Everyday Life*, vol. 1.

23 De Certeau, *The Practice of Everyday Life*.

24 John Leighton Chase, Margaret Crawford, and John Kaliski, eds., *Everyday Urbanism* (New York: Monacelli Press, 1999).

25 Dell Upton, "Architecture in Everyday Life," *New Literary History* 33.4 (2003): 707–723.

26 Steven Harris and Deborah Berke, eds., *Architecture of the Everyday* (New York: Princeton Architectural Press, 1997).

27 On the politicization of Israeli professional practice, see Eyal Weizmann, *Hollow Land: Israel's Architecture of Occupation* (London: Verso, 2007). For more general discussion on the political aspects of architecture, see Neil Leach, *The Anaesthetics of Architecture* (Cambridge: MIT Press, 1999).

28 Rachel Kallus, "The Political Role of the Everyday," *City* 8(3) (2004): 349–369.

29 Lefebvre, *Critique of Everyday Life*, vol. 1, 189.

30 Best known is the work of Team 10, a group formed within CIAM in the early 1950s to challenge the biological analysis of the environment based on rationalist and mechanistic conceptions of progress, in favor of a sociocultural, creative understanding of the human environment. See Alison Smithson, *Team 10 Primer* (Cambridge: MIT Press, 1968). A work in progress examines Glikson's connection with Team 10 (Rachel Kallus, "The National Community and the International Village: Artur Glikson at the Berlin Team-10 Meeting").

31 For a detailed account of the design stages of the IHU, see the work of Robert Marans cited above.

32 Artur Glikson, "Man, Region, World, Artur Glikson: On Regional Planning," *Ministry of Housing Quarterly* 3 (special publication by Israel's Ministry of Housing in memory of Artur Glikson, 1967): 90–91.

33 The plan consisted of six sub-units, each housing between 175 and 200 families, for a total population of about 1,000 families. The size of each subunit was determined by the optimum absorptive capacity of the secondary services, including a kindergarten, a playground for children between ages five and eight, and a small, demarcated open space for social interaction among the people living around it (Marans, "Neighborhood Planning: The Contributions of Artur Glikson").

34 Haim Darin-Drabkin, ed., *Public Housing in Israel: Surveys and Evaluations of Activities in Israel's First Decade, 1948–1958* (Tel Aviv: Gadish Books, 1959), 80.

35 As formulated in a document from the 1950s.

36 Batsheva Rothschild Foundation, "Research on Housing Patterns for Immigrants, 1957," *Engineering and Architecture* 17 (1959): 186 [Hebrew].

37 Artur Glikson, "The Concept of Habitational Unit," *Le Carre Bleu* 1 (1966): 4.

38 Artur Glikson, "Some Problems of Housing in Israel's New Towns and Suburbs," in Darin-Drabkin, ed., *Public Housing in Israel*, 93–94.

39 Glikson, "Man, Region, World," 87. For detailed accounts of patterns of social integration, see Marans, "Kiryat Gat, Israel"; Joseph Slijper and Asher Stoop, *Program for an Experimental Integrative Neighborhood: The Glikson Neighborhood in Kiryat Gat* (Jerusalem: Ministry of Housing and Construction, 1978, [Hebrew]); Yona Ginsberg and Robert Marans, *Social Mix in Housing: Does Ethnicity Make a Difference?* Working Paper 42 (Ramat Aviv: Tel Aviv University, Center for Urban and Regional Studies, 1977); and Judith Shuval, *Social Problems in Development Towns: A Research Study towards Planning an Experimental Living Unit in Kiryat Gat* (Jerusalem: Israel Institute of Applied Social Research, 1959 [Hebrew]).

40 Adriana Kemp, "Borders, Space, and National Identity in Israel," *Theory and Criticism* 16 (2000): 13–43 [Hebrew].

41 Artur Glikson, *Two Case Studies of Rural Planning and Development in Israel*, Israel Ministry of Housing (revision of material prepared for the United Nations Seminar on Regional Planning, Tokyo, 28 July–8 August, 1958), 1964, 3.

42 This approach follows Glikson's even more ambitious view, of "the house and the world," comprising "the inclusion of any particular place into a series of ever widening frameworks, from the house to the quarter, the town, the region, the world." Glikson, "The Concept of Habitational Unit," 4.

43 Glikson, "Man, Region, World," 82.

44 Robert Benet in Gershon Tzipor, ed., "Discussion of Residential Neighborhoods," *Architecture* 1 (1973): 4–15 [Hebrew]; quote on p. 4.

45 Glikson, "Some Problems of Housing in Israel's New Towns and Suburbs," in Darin- Drabkin, ed., *Public Housing in Israel,* 96.

46 Ibid.

47 Benet in Tzipor, ed., "Discussion of Residential Neighborhoods," 4.

48 Sharon, *Physical Planning in Israel.*

49 Kallus and Law-Yone, "National Home/Personal Home."

50 Glikson was the head of the Planning Unit at the Department of Housing from 1953 to 1957. He went into private practice when the department was restructured and commissioned the design of the IHU as a private consultant.

51 Glikson, "The Concept of Habitational Unit," 8.

52 Ibid., 4.

53 Artur Glikson, *Regional Planning and Development: Six Lectures Delivered at the Institute of Social Studies, The Hague, 1953* (Leiden: A.W. Sijthoff, 1955), 82.

54 Shmuel Shaked, "Artur Glikson's Approach to Housing Problems," in *Ministry of Housing Quarterly* 3 (Israel Ministry of Housing: "Man, Region, World, Artur Glikson: On Regional Planning," 1967): 44–45.

55 Roger Trancik, *Finding Lost Space: Theories of Urban Design* (New York: Van Nostrand Reinhold, 1986).

56 Alex Krieger and William S. Saunders, eds., *Urban Design* (Minneapolis: University of Minnesota Press, 2009).

57 David Harvey, *The Condition of Postmodernity* (Cambridge: Blackwell, 1980), 255.

58 Clarence Perry, "The Neighborhood Unit, a Scheme of Arrangement for the Family-Life Community," reprint in *Neighborhood and Community Planning, Regional Survey of New York and Its Environs,* vol. VII, New York, 1974, 1929.

59 Glikson, "The Concept of Habitational Unit," 2.

60 Gabriela Stoop, "A Master Plan for Kiryat Gat," in *Ministry of Housing Quarterly* 3 (Israel Ministry of Housing publication, "Man, Region, World, Artur Glikson: On Regional Planning," 1967): 71–81.

61 Ibid., 78.

62 Glikson, *Two Case Studies of Rural Planning and Development in Israel.*

63 Eleb, "An Alternative to Functionalist Universalism: Ecochard, Candilis, and ATBAT-Afrique."

64 Glikson, "Man, Region, World," 86.

65 Ibid.

66 Shuval, *Social Problems in Development Towns*; Ginsberg and Marans, *Social Mix in Housing*; Slijper and Stoop, *Program for an Experimental Integrative Neighborhood.*

67 Shuval, *Social Problems in Development Towns.*

68 Marans, "Kiryat Gat, Israel."

69 According to the 1995 national census, the Glikson neighborhood, as it is now called, was ranked 1–4 (20 being the highest) in standard of living and socioeconomic level (Israel Central Bureau of Statistics, GIS presentation of the 1995 census).

70 Erik Cohen, *The City in the Zionist Ideology* (Jerusalem: Institute of Urban and Regional Studies, Hebrew University, 1970).

71 Glikson "Some Problems of Housing in Israel's New Towns and Suburbs," 94.

72 Kiryat Gat was established in 1954 on the site of the town El-Faluja and the village Iraq el-Manshiya, both Palestinian settlements until 1948.

73 Shuval, *Social Problems in Development Towns*; Ginsberg and Marans, *Social Mix in Housing*; Slijper and Stoop, *Program for an Experimental Integrative Neighborhood.*

74 The relationship between architecture and the state was one of the six issues presented by Le Corbusier at the La Sarraz conference in 1928. Berlage's lecture at La Sarraz also dealt with this connection. For further discussion, see Giorgio Ciucci, "The Invention of the Modern Movement," *Oppositions* 24 (1981): 69–91.

75 Kenneth Frampton, "Prospects for Critical Regionalism," *Perspecta: The Yale Architectural Journal* 20 (1983): 147–162; Alexander Tzonis and Liane Lefaivre, "The Grid and the Pathway," *Architecture in Greece* 15 (1981): 164–178.

PANAYIOTA PYLA

7

ARCHITECTS AS DEVELOPMENT EXPERTS:
MODEL COMMUNITIES IN IRAQ AND SYRIA

At the founding conference of the United Nations in San Francisco in 1945, the young Constantinos Doxiadis (1913–1975) was the leader of the Greek delegation. Educated in Greece as an architect, and with a doctorate in planning from Germany, Doxiadis held a government post as the coordinator of reconstruction in Greece at the time of the conference. He spoke about a global housing crisis and resource shortages, arguing that the United Nations could not achieve its goals for international development unless the organization also put systematic emphasis on the planning of the physical environment. In an open letter criticizing the priorities of the United Nations, he warned:

> Legislators, financiers, military men and scientists were asked to give their opinion on the reshaping of the new post-war world, but architects and those responsible for physical planning have been ignored. This, however, is not wise, because the new world will be safe only after it has been reshaped on a new basis.[1]

This letter, which circulated among conference delegates, signaled Doxiadis's debut in the international arena, and his goals were already ambitious: to align modernist visions of social reform with the United Nations' aim to secure world peace through growth and development. Turning to architects and planners, he urged them to reconceptualize their practice according to the new geopolitical and socioeconomic transformations of the post–World War II era. Simultaneously, he criticized the United Nations for overestimating economic criteria for development and for failing to devote enough resources to the design of the physical environment.[2] In his vision of modernization, socioeconomic reform had to move hand-in-hand with a comprehensive and orderly transformation of the physical environment, and this required both the recalibration of development practices and the reinvention of architecture and planning.[3]

In the late 1940s, Doxiadis became the coordinator of the Marshall Plan aid to Greece, and later he participated in United Nations and World Bank Technical Assistance missions to newly established nation-states in the postcolonial world. In 1954 he took part in the International Federation for Housing and Town Planning conference, organized in New Delhi under the auspices of the United Nations; there he met Jaqueline Tyrwhitt and Jacob Crane, who would soon become crucial collaborators of his firm. In 1954 he also traveled to Syria as part of the World Bank's mission, and he would later travel to Pakistan, Jordan, and Iraq. These activities allowed him to nurture a strong network of friends and contacts among development officials in U.S. and international development institutions that would prove to be instrumental for his international success.

As he was establishing himself as a player in the scene of international development consulting, Doxiadis also established a private company that aimed precisely to forge strong links between the design of the physical environment and processes of advancing international development. The name "Doxiadis Associates International: Consultants on Development and Ekistics" clearly conveyed the ambition to transcend the typical tasks of architecture and planning firms, and it rapidly succeeded in collaborating with international funding institutions and national governments to design complexes, infrastructures, urban plans, and regional studies in Ghana, Greece, Iraq, Jordan, Lebanon, Pakistan, Syria, the Sudan, and elsewhere. By the early 1960s, Doxiadis was known as a "busy remodeler of the world" and his journal *Ekistics* was circulating internationally.[4]

"Ekistics" was defined by Doxiadis as an entirely new field, "the science of human settlements." Derived from the word "oikos" meaning "home," Ekistics aimed to synthesize the input of all disciplines that could inform the creation of settlements of any scale. As Doxiadis would later explain in his first book on Ekistics, *Architecture in Transition*, "The architect must now enrich his knowledge so as to be able to cover the related fields and co-operate with the community developer, the urbanist, the planner, the economist, the geographer and the social scientist as a member of a single team."[5] The idea of incorporating the input of social sciences to increase architecture's social instrumentality was of course not uncommon in postwar architectural discourse; social scientists themselves initiated such collaborations in an effort to grasp the impact of the physical environment on human behavior and social patterns.[6] Ekistics, however, aspired to bring these interdisci-

Map on the cover of the journal *Ekistics,* showing Doxiadis Associates activity around the world

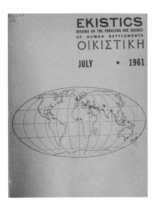

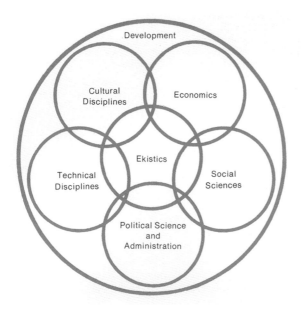

The "Ekistic Circles," a sketch made by Doxiadis Associates illustrating the firm's interdisciplinary ethos
and its primary objective—development

plinary collaborations to new heights, promising to offer a comprehensive response to
human needs.

Ekistics was Doxiadis's way of connecting the professions of architecture and planning with the processes of modernization and development around the globe. Its com-
mitment to industrialization and socioeconomic reform was certainly in tune with the
agenda of American and international development institutions to advance a particular
type of development according to the paradigm of the industrialized West. In the background of such development goals was of course the Cold War's bitter ideological divide.
Doxiadis, however, diligently distanced Ekistics from geopolitical leanings by framing it
as a scientific method aimed at fulfilling the needs of the "common people" and appli-
cable to all societies, "communist and capitalist alike."[7] From the perspective of the
international institutions as well as national governments that funded his projects, such
a claim to scientific neutrality conveniently concealed the pro-Western alliances (and
anticommunist fears) that motivated their modernizing agendas. The technocratic optimism of Ekistics appeared as a promise that social, economic, racial, and ethnic inequali-
ties could be managed away, to make the modernization projects acceptable to (often)
highly diverse societies.

Even if Doxiadis believed that his approach embodied scientific truths with transnational applicability, he promised that his firm would calibrate built interventions
according to the resources and needs of each specific locale. Doxiadis pledged that he
would not act like a "magician planner," who "has all the solutions up his sleeve and he
pulls them out like rabbits."[8] Often implying criticism for the new cities emerging in the

postcolonial world (and sometimes pointing the finger specifically at Brasilia in Brazil and Chandigarh in India), Doxiadis seemed to suggest that his firm would overcome the functionalist, universalist, and ultimately homogenizing preoccupations of other modernist interventions, by embarking on exhaustive surveys and research programs that would "diagnose" (echoing scientific and medical authority) each locale's needs and potentials.[9] This dual claim to scientific legitimacy and cultural sensitivity was particularly palatable to many young governments of the postcolonial world, whose eagerness to modernize their state was accompanied by a desire to champion shared ideals of national identity and pride.

Doxiadis's claims to scientific legitimacy and cultural sensitivity were strengthened by the multinational composition of his group of collaborators and what often appeared as a quasi-Western identity of his own. As *The New Yorker* put it in a long 1963 article devoted to "the Ekistic World":

Doxiadis has the sort of European abilities that are needed—he is up on the latest planning techniques, and he runs his firm with northern (or, "western") efficiency— but, being a Greek, he is free of the imperialist stigma, and, for the same reason, he can do things more cheaply, and often more suitable, for his Afro-Asian clients than a northerner could, because he is more familiar with their customs and standards.[10]

The prejudices behind an argument that set the continents of Africa and Asia, along with the country of Greece, apart from some Western—presumably higher— "standard" are of course a vivid reminder of how much of the postwar drive for modernization was rooted in essentializing worldviews that divided the world into "developed" versus "underdeveloped" cultures and assumed that all cultures were on a linear and predetermined path to progress. It was the belief in these reductionist models of development that allowed mid-twentieth- century development experts to "hurry about the developing world," as the historian Roger Owen put it, while being "much better at talking than listening."[11] Doxiadis tried to distinguish himself from the many Western consultants, advisors, and technicians who were streaming into various parts of the postcolonial world, citing his own experiences with postwar reconstruction in Greece that taught him how to enrich his training and expertise with an intimate understanding of local realities. When he would describe his intervention as strong but necessary medicine, however, this key figure of midcentury architectural modernism seemed to buy into developmentalist worldviews that advocated that different countries had to be brought up to speed with the West—failing to recognize development as a cultural process tied to complex circumstances of specific locales.[12] This essay is an investigation into these complexities and contradictions of Doxiadis's development practices.

The focus is Doxiadis Associates' interventions in Iraq and Syria, which are representative of this firm's modernizing ambitions. Examining rural and urban housing in Iraq and urban plans for Syria, I analyze Doxiadis's concepts of "orderly" physical expansion, his emphasis on nurturing "social balance," and his conceptions of local particularity and cultural difference that attempted to insert architecture and planning into larger national modernization programs—while also aspiring to recalibrate the developmentalist logic of funding institutions.

MODEL COMMUNITIES IN IRAQ

The Iraq Development Board—a quasi-governmental body overseeing an accelerated program of national modernization in Iraq with the support of Western consultants—became the first international client of Doxiadis Associates in 1955 when it solicited the firm to prepare a housing program for the entire country. [13] At that time, wealth from oil industry revenues had created favorable conditions for development in a young nation trying to establish itself before the outside world, and the pro-British government launched a campaign to introduce a new era of political stability.[14] The Iraq Development Board had been overseeing the construction of dams, irrigation and drainage systems, bridges, roads, factories, power plants, housing, schools, hospitals, and public buildings since the early 1950s. Doxiadis was solicited at a point when the Iraq Development Board increased its funding for housing and community facilities, in an effort to provide more readily visible signs of progress and prevent social unrest.[15] The need for gestures of social reform seemed urgent as the increasingly unpopular Iraqi government saw uncomfortably obvious parallels between Iraq and Czarist Russia, and was nervously trying to secure political stability. For similar reasons, British and American consultants also encouraged reform, hoping that Iraq, seen as an important Middle Eastern bastion against communism, would not replicate the experience of Egypt, where a 1952 revolt brought the rise of Gamal Abdel Nasser and his Soviet-allied policies.[16] Doxiadis Associates' initial charge was to create a comprehensive five-year plan for the improvement of housing conditions throughout the country, which would involve the construction of tens of thousands of new houses and the amelioration of even more existing units, the construction of schools, and infrastructure projects. The firm began with interventions in Mosul, Basra, Kirkuk, Mussayib, and Baghdad, and eventually it was assigned additional tasks, including the master plan for Baghdad.

The model community Doxiadis proposed for western Baghdad is paradigmatic of Ekistics' housing principles. The Western Baghdad Development Scheme (a few miles west of the existing city center) was to house a population of 100,000, either through government-funded housing or self-help housing. The scheme was comprised of different "community sectors" of 7,000 to 10,000 people, and each sector provided for administrative, social, educational, health, and other community buildings, shopping centers, green areas, coffeehouses, and mosques within walking distance. Echoing the social and functionalist logic of the "neighborhood units" of the postwar British New Towns, the plan provided for a degree of self-sufficiency in each sector, favoring pedestrian movement. Roads were organized according to a rectilinear pattern that also defined the grid system for standardized housing modules. Even if Doxiadis believed that cities were dynamic and needed to accommodate continual growth, each sector had a rather static quality, with a predetermined size and prescribed dimensions for plots, roads, and public areas. This was the firm's solution for preserving human scale in residential communities within a growing metropolis.

Each community sector was broken down to smaller socio-spatial units arranged hierarchically. The smallest, called "community class I," was constituted by ten to

The Housing Program of Iraq

GOVERNMENT OF IRAQ
DEVELOPMENT BOARD-MINISTRY OF DEVELOPMENT
TECHNICAL SECTION 5
DOXIADIS ASSOCIATES, CONSULTING ENGINEERS

Vocational Schools for Building Trades

GOVERNMENT OF IRAQ
DEVELOPMENT BOARD-MINISTRY OF DEVELOPMENT
TECHNICAL SECTION 5
DOXIADIS ASSOCIATES, CONSULTING ENGINEERS

Left: Doxiadis Associates pamphlet
Right: Doxiadis Associates pamphlet

twenty families of similar income. A group of three to seven such communities made a community "class II," also having a homogeneous economic status. House types, all of which promised the basics of sanitation and safety, also corresponded to the income-based hierarchy. The hierarchical logic continued: An agglomeration of class II communities plus an elementary school was designated a community "class III." Class III communities of different income groups, plus a market and shops, a teahouse and a mosque, could constitute a community "class IV," namely the "community sector" of 7,000 to 10,000. This "community sector," constituted "the basic element" of Baghdad's urban plan and was a prototype for the building block of many cities subsequently designed.[17] Doxiadis Associates' plan for western Baghdad was a plan for a community class V (combining a group of sectors of class IV) that would join other parts of the city, to create a class VI community (Baghdad) that would then join larger regional communities, and so on. Rural communities were also situated in a larger regional schema.

In analyzing his work, Doxiadis tried to contextualize such abstractions of "scales" and "hierarchies" by arguing that the smaller class I, II, and III communities of Baghdad corresponded to sizes found in Iraqi towns and villages.[18] (The eight volumes of "Diaries," which compiled notes, photos, and observations by various Doxiadis Associates employees in Iraq between 1955 and 1958, became a key source in extrapolating guidelines for local habitation patterns, material choices, and aesthetic preferences.)

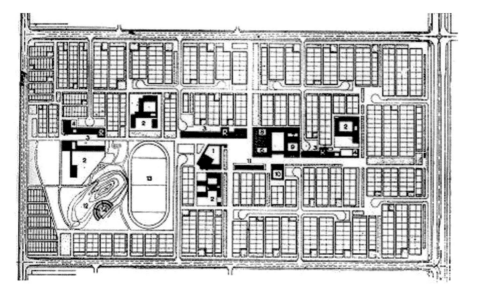

Above: Plan of community sector in western Baghdad. The legend under the full drawing included: 1) mosque, 2) schools, 3) markets, 4) public baths, 5) coffee houses, 6) administration, 8) cultural center, 12) public park, 13) sports ground

Below: Model of community sector in western Baghdad

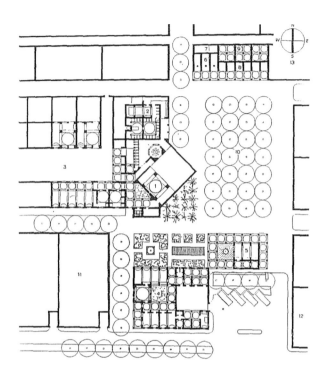

Layout plans

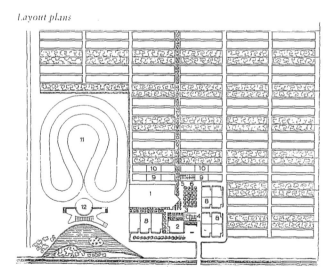

Typical village for Greater Mussayib, 1959

The larger community scales, then, were explained as new phenomena necessitated by advanced transportation and communication technologies. As Doxiadis's close colleague Jaqueline Tyrwhitt pointed out, the multiple hierarchies of communities were an attempt to correct British versions of "self-contained" neighborhoods in New Towns, that prescribed an optimum size of neighborhoods and were already facing criticism for failing to account for people's increasing dependence on the automobile and new industrial needs for mobility.[19] Doxiadis Associates hoped to introduce more flexibility by inscribing each community within larger ones, although their effort remained bounded by a linear hierarchical logic that assumed that communities and subcommunities could neatly fit into each other.

The formal ordering of the community sector had a social agenda behind it: the small homogeneous residential communities (class I and II) were expected to interact (on a "class III" level and beyond) to promote a slow and controlled intermixing of social classes and the gradual "development of social balance amongst the several classes of the citizens."[20] This was Doxiadis Associates' attempt at social engineering, in tune with the Iraqi regime's campaign to eliminate sectarian and tribal divisions. The strategies for nurturing social balance, however, steered away from the city's intricate tribal, nomadic, ethnic, and other social formations that created tight communities inside the city. For all their field reports and on-site analyses, the firm overlooked the specific demographic dynamics in the city (caused, for example, by the emigration of most of the city's Jewish population to Israel after 1947, or the influx of rural population, including many Christians and Kurds from the north and Shias from the south). The proposals were instead confined to vague references to a "proper" grouping among different communities that would presumably create "a healthy community spirit."[21] Translated into formal gestures, "proper" grouping meant, for example, the insertion of middle-class housing between upper- and lower-income neighborhoods, to minimize contact between opposite sides of the economic spectrum. Some residential sectors were even separated with "green spaces" that acted as soft barriers between classes. Such design strategies were apparently Doxiadis Associates' attempt to compromise with government administrators' demands that "different classes of citizens should not be mixed."[22] Even if tribal and ethnic differences were to be brushed aside in favor of a shared sense of modern nationhood, economic class distinctions were preserved. This demand was made repeatedly by government officials, as Doxiadis Associates' diaries show, and the resulting proposal was less about substantive social equity than about an administrative ordering of society. Understood more in visual and aesthetic terms, this kind of rational ordering of both the urban fabric and society echoed many examples of twentieth-century high-modernist urbanism and its grand visions for the rational engineering of social life.[23] The irony in the case of Doxiadis's partnership with the state is that his Ekistics was framed precisely as a rejection of aesthetic preoccupations in favor of a more comprehensive conception of human needs.

A similar aesthetic of order and efficiency characterized rural plans for Iraq. Based on a rather unidirectional view of design as a process that moves "from the national conception to the detail," Doxiadis's team inserted the villages of Iraq within larger territorial schemes of community classes arranged hierarchically. Within each rural center, the layout abided again to Doxiadis Associates' requirements for uniformity and standardization, and rural houses were lined up on a modular grid and according to functional zones. The particular physical and social geographies of the village were practically absent because, as Doxiadis emphasized, the firm was not simply faced with the task of designing a village or two, but "types" of villages and buildings "which can be repeated many times."[24]

As background to Doxiadis Associates' urban and rural proposals were extensive research programs that the firm had launched to examine climatic conditions, sun radiation and wind effects, and geological formations, and to experiment with the orientation of buildings and passive cooling possibilities. Approximating United Nations consultant guidelines to evaluate climatic variations, local materials, and labor, to use them "more fully and rationally," and to increase productivity, temper mechanization, and minimize cost, Doxiadis Associates established guidelines for the selection of materials and construction methods to maximize the economy of housing.[25] Doxiadis Associates also hired local contractors, asking each to use their

Central market in Mosul, on a cover of *Ekistics*

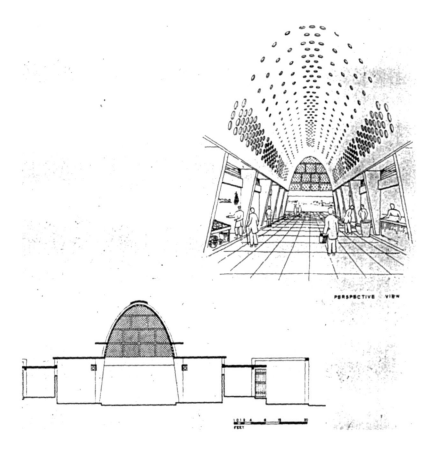

PERSPECTIVE VIEW

FEET

own familiar building technique, and, acting much like UNESCO's "field consultants," they supervised to identify the most economical approach and provide on-the-job training.[26]

In all urban and rural plans for Iraq, Doxiadis Associates attempted to insert local character into the rational methodology of housing by including *hamams,* coffee shops, and mosques in each sector, with the occasional covered market with a roof shape reminiscent of traditional souqs. Another gesture was the introduction of a small public square for each group of ten to fifteen attached houses that was to serve as "a modern substitute for the traditional gathering places of tribal life."[27] Initially these were named "gossip squares," although Doxiadis eventually became uneasy with a term that reinforced cultural stereotypes and replaced it with the more scientific-sounding "community squares of first degree."[28] Such squares were small in scale and informal in character—very different from the huge squares of Chandigarh, with which Le Corbusier tried to replace crowded bazaars and streets; and it was certainly more attentive to the habits and practices of the local past than the boundless public spaces of Brasilia.[29] What prevailed most, however, was an aesthetic imperative of standardization and mass production that left little opportunity to contemplate a more cultured conception of the human subject. Still overpowered by the modular functional plan, the squares, *hamams,* and mosques were stripped of much of their historical and social context and

Gossip square in Mosul

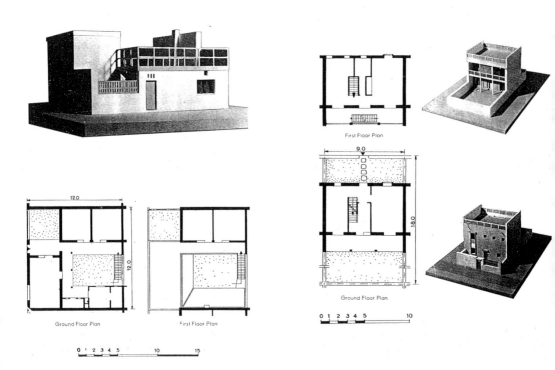

First Floor Plan

9.0

18.0

Ground Floor Plan

0 1 2 3 4 5   10

12.0

12.0

Ground Floor Plan   First Floor Plan

0 1 2 3 4 5   10   15

House types in western Baghdad

seemed to reflect more an orientalist nostalgia than any profound understanding of Iraq's public life, the intense heterogeneity of its society, or the particularity of its aspirations to modernity.

A similar critique could be extended to Doxiadis Associates' studies of local climate and formal vocabularies. Climatic conditions were treated abstractly in terms of solar exposures, wind patterns, and rainfall data, never really becoming an integral part of material choices, spatial conceptions, or larger design sensibilities. Doxiadis Associates may have recognized the open-air courtyard and colonnaded upper gallery as typical of the region's residential architecture, but the firm's own reinterpretations in its standardized housing modules pushed courtyards to the side or the back of each unit. This compartmentalization was in tune with Doxiadis's notion that however important local knowledge systems were, the Ekistics expert had to maintain "enough distance" to not lose sight of the "demands of efficiency."[30] The final housing schemes lost the traditional courtyards' climatic benefits and secluded qualities. Similarly, Doxiadis Associates' attempts to reinterpret wooden window screens with reinforced concrete produced

Experimental housing in western Baghdad

larger patterns of openings that were not nearly as effective in increasing wind pressure, softening sunlight, or providing a sense of privacy. Doxiadis Associates' housing units ultimately compared unfavorably to the old city's mud huts with movable roofs, in terms of their microclimate.[31]

Doxiadis Associates' five-year housing program for Iraq came to an abrupt end in July 1958 when a military coup led by General Abd al-Karim al-Qasim brought the brutal deposition of the Hashimite monarchy and its replacement by a revolutionary republic with socialist leanings. Under these circumstances, Doxiadis Associates' commission was cancelled in May 1959, leaving the Athens-based firm out of the new building boom of Baghdad in the next decade.[32] By the time they left, however, Doxiadis Associates had completed the construction of hundreds of units (some neighborhoods in western Baghdad, but also a few in the northeast side of the city and the Army Canal, which are still referred to by the locals as "Doxiadis's houses"), which would become the precedent for many of the firm's future projects.[33]

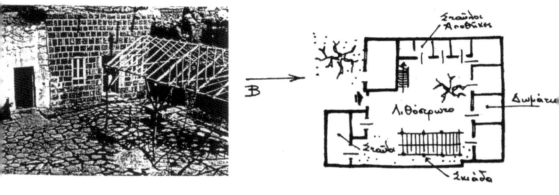

Photos and a sketch plan of a house in the Hauran area
from Doxiadis Associates diaries on Syria

MASTER PLANS FOR SYRIA

Doxiadis Associates' development strategies reached far beyond the design of housing and model communities, to the master planning of entire cities and regions. At
these larger scales, the imperatives of order and efficiency were accompanied by an
emphasis on urban growth, to be facilitated through large-scale functional restructuring. Doxiadis Associates initially tested their strategies in the master plan for Baghdad,
commissioned in January 1958, just a few months before the firm had to pull out of
Iraq. Another opportunity emerged in June 1959, when the government of the United
Arab Republic (established in 1958 after the union of Syria and Egypt) commissioned
Doxiadis Associates to prepare master plans for the Syrian cities of Homs and Hama.
For Doxiadis, who favored a hierarchical design approach that moved from an urban
whole to the individual area, the opportunity to start anew from a master plan was the
ideal beginning point.[34]

When Doxiadis began to collaborate with Syria's Ministry of Municipal and Rural
Affairs, the country was already in the midst of a long-term program of economic development, which involved the creation of irrigation and drainage projects, the improvement of transportation and communications infrastructure, the advancement of the
manufacturing industry, and the opening of previously unexploited lands for cultivation.
Once again, Doxiadis Associates' interventions were seen as a stabilizing force, and as
part of the government's efforts to introduce a new era of stability in a country that had
experienced immense turmoil since its political independence from France in 1946.

Doxiadis had already traveled to Syria during February–April 1954 as a member
of the International Bank for Reconstruction and Development, and he had produced
an extensive two-volume document with notes and photographs on Syria's physical environment that became a key reference for his firm's master plans five years
later.[35] This two volume "diary," as it was called, charted climatic conditions, analyzed
demographic distributions, juxtaposed construction methods of different regions,

considered material choices and costs, and mapped the location and uses of factories, agricultural fields, and archeological sites.[36] It constituted the model for the "Diaries"— such as the Iraq diaries mentioned earlier, that Doxiadis Associates' teams produced for various countries. If the diaries' preoccupation with the comprehensive accumulation of data attempted to showcase Doxiadis's scientific ethos, the abundant photographs of street life and living conditions in rural and urban areas, accompanied occasionally by sketches and comments, revealed another side of Doxiadis's own sensibilities. The attention to the spatial qualities of streets, the appreciation of the play of shade and light, and the careful recording of details of construction all broaden postwar architectural notions of contextualism and regionalism. They also echoed the ideas of Doxiadis's mentor Dimitris Pikionis—who, within the context of Greece, pioneered the denunciation of modernist rationalism and valorized site specificity and sentimentality.[37]

When it came to Doxiadis Associates' proposals for Homs and Hama, social and spatial qualities of the existing dense fabric that Doxiadis captured in his photographs had to be negotiated with the firm's preconceived imperatives for a rational and efficient ordering of the city. So even though the Syria diaries produced by Doxiadis had commented positively on the beautiful old souqs, the markets open to the sky, and the closely packed districts of special crafts, the preliminary report for Homs, for example, concluded that the old city suffered from an "irrational" use of land" and a lack of open space.[38] This judgment seems to have been more influenced by an adherence to prescribed definitions of density than any understanding of souqs, mosques, and courtyards as spaces with a wide range of social purposes. The plan Doxiadis Associates submitted to the government stipulated the creation of public gardens, open recreational spaces, and wider roads, lumping these needs together with the need for upgrading services for water supply, sewage treatment, and other public utilities. In effect, the proposal was presenting the spatial preference for lower densities to be just as urgent as the tackling of sanitation and health issues.[39] What Doxiadis Associates' "Summary of Problems" for Homs seems to have missed was that the old city's urban density had an immense social value, and that the colorful souqs, dark and narrow as they were, provided abundant opportunities for public gathering—even if they did not fit rationalized categories and distribution ratios for buildings and open spaces.[40]

The overall master plans for Homs and Hama promised to set the basis for the future expansion in an orderly fashion and become a symbol and an instrument for creating an efficient, modern city. The first task was to identify an axis of future growth that imposed an overall territorial order. This idea was based on a planning model that Doxiadis Associates was beginning to develop at the time, based on the notion that the most efficient method of urban expansion was to allow the city center to expand continually along an axis to avert congestion. Echoing the open-ended logic of "Linear City" concepts, Doxiadis Associates' model would allow the residential areas and business districts to expand continually along the central core's flanks, and their linear expansion would be controlled by zoning and the siting of public buildings, road systems, and green areas.[41] In the case of Homs and Hama, the central axis of growth was defined along the north-south direction that connected each urban center to the larger cities

THE EXISTING CITY OF HOMS

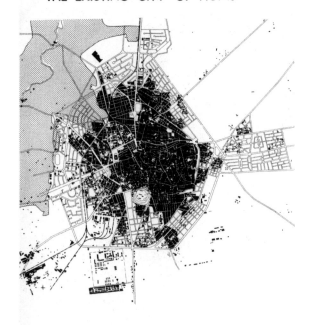

TENDENCIES FOR DEVELOPMENT

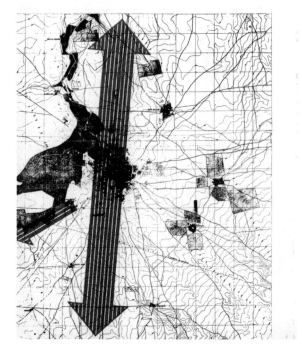

Doxiadis Associates' map for Homs showing the predicted direction of growth

PLAN D'AMENAGEMENT ET D'EXTENSION
LES ESPACES VERTS

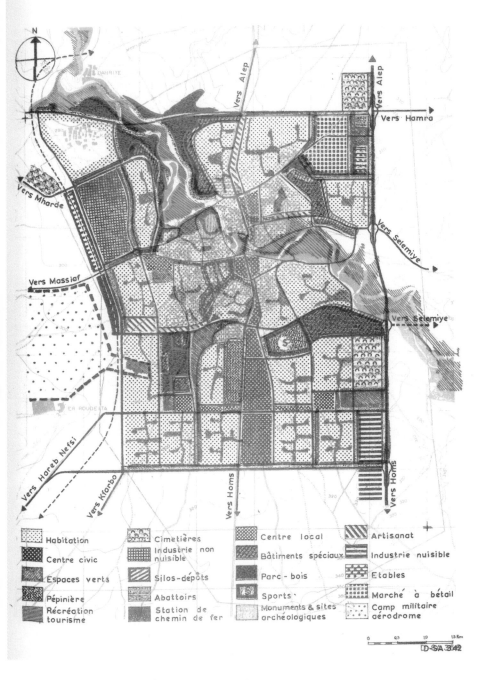

Plan for Hama, highlighting the proposed green spaces

of Aleppo and Damascus. In Homs, that central axis was pushed toward the east of the city to bypass the old dense city, and to extend the city eastward, where there was open land for unhindered expansion. In Hama, the main axis defined by the commercial-administrative center went through the center of the city and over the Orontes River, incorporating the old city center within the city's new, expandable center. Major roads were inserted either parallel or perpendicular to each city's axis of growth to create a regular pattern for the residential sectors. The commercial and administrative center was given a linear shape, and its future growth was to follow the central axis. Industries were confined to the edges of each city outside the directions of future north-south growth. "Green spaces" often filled the gaps between the residential grid and the preexisting geographies of each city.

The master plans also outlined the general principles for residential sectors, suggesting the creation of a hierarchy of communities similar to those in Baghdad. The firm's preliminary proposal suggested the formation of "integrated residential communities" so as to transcend the stark distinctions between rich and poor. [42] But the final reports for Homs and Hama that followed the feedback from the government favored a greater degree of class segregation. For Homs, Doxiadis Associates recommended the distribution of income groups "with the highest income groups along the commercial center and green areas." [43] In Hama, the final plan proposed that "the lowest income groups be located near the industries and the outer parts of the city, while the highest income groups... be next to the green areas and the civic center." [44] Such rigid class distinctions were far from Doxiadis Associates' initial experiments for intermixing income groups. Somewhere between the firm's technocratic postures of neutrality and their assumption that state agendas reflect the population's aspirations, Doxiadis Associates remained confined to local power structures instead of transcending them. One can obviously argue that the final reports´ proposed segregation is not a result of the designers' strategies but a product of state policies and pressures—part of an ongoing give-and-take between Doxiadis Associates and its client. This is one of the ironies in the firm's collaborations with state modernization practices: The celebrated goal to cater to human needs was reduced to a class-based distribution of services.

As in Baghdad, the master plans for Homs and Hama were not implemented, and after Doxiadis Associates' departure, modernization plans changed direction in both Iraq and Syria, becoming more self-conscious in their anti-Western claims and leaving no room for the kind of universalism Doxiadis advanced. Even local architects (like Mohamed Makiya and Rifat Chadirji in Iraq who had previously collaborated with Doxiadis Associates) began to shift direction to abandon the technocratic and universalist ethos of Ekistics in favor of more explicit valorizations of local cultural roots.[45] Ekistics too eventually changed direction in the 1960s, to plans that were not about national modernization but global transnational networks. The firm's work did, however, maintain an emphasis on physical environment as key to global socioeconomic development.[46]

PRELIMINARY MASTER PLAN OF HOMS

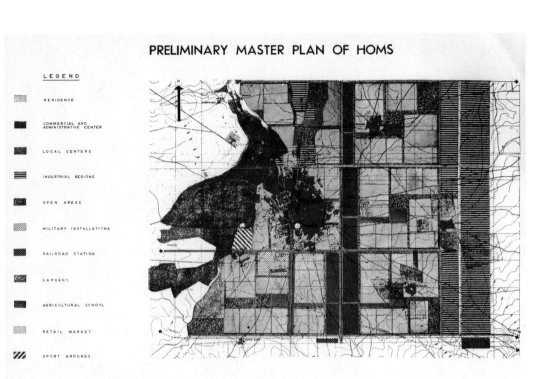

LEGEND

RESIDENCE

COMMERCIAL AND
ADMINISTRATIVE CENTER

LOCAL CENTERS

INDUSTRIAL REGIONS

OPEN AREAS

MILITARY INSTALLATIONS

RAILROAD STATION

GARDENS

AGRICULTURAL SCHOOL

RETAIL MARKET

SPORT GROUNDS

DISTRIBUTION OF INCOME GROUPS

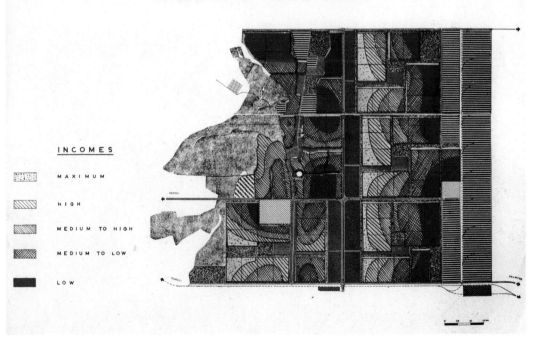

INCOMES

MAXIMUM

HIGH

MEDIUM TO HIGH

MEDIUM TO LOW

LOW

Doxiadis Associates' final master plan for Homs, juxtaposed with the final proposal for the distribution of income groups

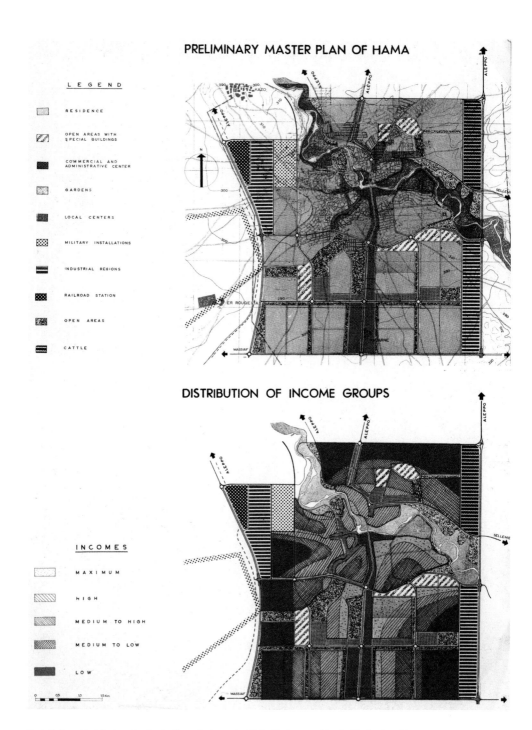

PRELIMINARY MASTER PLAN OF HAMA

LEGEND

RESIDENCE

OPEN AREAS WITH
SPECIAL BUILDINGS

COMMERCIAL AND
ADMINISTRATIVE CENTER

GARDENS

LOCAL CENTERS

MILITARY INSTALLATIONS

INDUSTRIAL REGIONS

RAILROAD STATION

OPEN AREAS

CATTLE

DISTRIBUTION OF INCOME GROUPS

INCOMES

MAXIMUM

HIGH

MEDIUM TO HIGH

MEDIUM TO LOW

LOW

Doxiadis Associates' final master plan for Hama, juxtaposed with the final proposal for the distribution of income groups

REFLECTIONS

Doxiadis Associates' prolific practice in the late 1950s was instrumental in linking architectural modernism with postwar development. Their effort to transport architecture to a domain of development managerialism was characterized by many paradoxes: Their optimism for promoting social equality competed with the firm´s alignment with state agendas, which often supported existing hierarchies. Their aspiration to promote transnational equality missed the geopolitical imbalances among their supposed beneficiaries. And even if Doxiadis and his firm emphasized the importance of local particularity, this was often lost in the execution, overshadowed by a fixation on grand ordering. Still, Doxiadis Associates' attempt to contemplate the dilemmas of Iraq's and Syria's post-imperialist identity compares favorably to rigid appropriations of local heritage—see, for example, Frank Lloyd Wright's orientalizing references in his scheme for the Opera House in Baghdad, not to mention the later Ba'ath regime's populist distortions of both countries' cultural heritage[47]—that entirely missed the ambiguities in concepts of local tradition. Despite its shortcomings, Doxiadis Associates' plans were significant in contemplating the role of architecture/planning in the messy realities of postcolonial nationhood. And even if Doxiadis Associates approximated United Nations development policies, they did not fall into their logic, because they situated their developmentalist ambitions within a nexus of contemporary architectural-planning debates that remained wary of rationalist reductionism. Doxiadis may have been fascinated by the modernist dream of initiating widespread social reform, but he also questioned the elitism of the profession. It was through this combination of developmentalist optimism with socio-architectural concerns that Doxiadis and his firm formed their peculiar conception of modernization, full of nuances, which constitutes a fascinating page in the history of postwar development.

Notes

1   Doxiadis, "To Architects and to All Who Are Interested in Physical Planning for the Reconstruction of the World in the United Nations" (Athens, October 12, 1945): 371.

2   Ibid. Doxiadis often recommended that the United Nations establish a distinct agency for human settlements, but it was not until 1963 that the idea materialized with the establishment of the United Nations ad hoc committee on housing planning and development.

3   Doxiadis made similar arguments about the role of architecture-planning in international development in Doxiadis, "Report by C.A. Doxiadis, Expert, Greece," *Mass Housing in Rapidly Developing Tropical and Subtropical Areas,* International Council for Building Research Studies and Documentation (Rotterdam, 1959), 1–38, esp. pp. 6–7.

4   See *Life,* "Busy Remodeler of the World," October 7, 1966.

5   Doxiadis, *Architecture in Transition* (London: Hutchison and Co., 1963), 96–97.

6   For more on the alignments of postwar architectural and planning discourse with social sciences that emerged in that era, see, for example, Hashim Sarkis, "Dances with Margaret Mead: Planning Beirut Since 1958," in *Projecting Beirut: Episodes in the Construction and Reconstruction of a Modern City,* edited by Peter Rowe and Hashim Sarkis (New York: Prestel, 1998).

7   Doxiadis, "The Science of Ekistics," *Architektoniki* 3:13 (1959): 9–72, quotation on 13.

8   Doxiadis, "The Rising Tide and the Planner," *Ekistics* 7: 39 (January 1959): 4–10, quotation on p. 6.

9   Ibid.

10   Christopher Rand, "The Ekistic World," *The New Yorker* (May 11, 1963): 49–87, quotation on 53.

11   Roger Owen, "Foreword," in Hashim Sarkis, *Circa 1958* (Beirut: Fares Foundation, 2003), p. 11.

12   On planning legislation in India, which had applied several aspects of the British planning system, Doxiadis argued, "Are we sure when we mention English legislation and schemes and present them as

an ideal for all the other countries, that the countries are ripe enough to consider this legislation and try to imitate it... We cannot jump immediately to the higher level of planning that has been reached by the countries with much greater experience."On the other hand, we cannot say that we will require the 200 years that England, for example, has required to reach this stage, We may be able to cover the same distance in 50 years instead of 200--or maybe 30 or 35 years, but certainly, we cannot eliminate completely the intermediate stages... our problem is not how to imitate the more advanced countries--and I am speaking also with experience of and in the name of, I think on this occasion, my own country (Greece)--but how to study the problem of land use and land development which in every phase is going to be balanced with the abilities of our country to implement it. C.A. Doxiadis, "Comments on Land Use Controls and Planning Implementation," Proceedings of the Southeast Asia Regional Conference, Meeting of the International Federation for Housing and Town Planning, New Delhi, February 1–7, 1954 (Government of India Press, 1957), 427–428. Excerpts reprinted in Ekistics 4:27 (December 1957), quotation on 129.

13   For a more extensive analysis of Doxiadis Associates' operation in Iraq, see Panayiota Pyla, "Back to the Future: Doxiadis's Plans for Baghdad, 1955–58," Journal of the History of Planning 7:1 (February 2008): 3–19, which also appeared in a slightly different version in "Nation-Building in Baghdad, 1958," in Modernism and the Middle East: Politics of the Built Environment, edited by Sandy Isenstadt and Kishwar Rizvi (Seattle: University of Washington Press, 2008).

14   For the board's funding and activities at the time, see, for example, Fahim Qubain, The Reconstruction of Iraq: 1950–57 (New York: Frederick A. Praeger, 1958), pp. vii and xi; Ishan Fethi, "Contemporary Architecture in Baghdad," Process Architecture (May 1985): 112–132; and Kathleen Langley, The Industrialization of Iraq (Cambridge, MA: Harvard University Press, 1961), p. 81. For a more recent critical discussion of the Board's social agenda, see Joseph Siry, "Wright's Baghdad Opera House and Gammage Auditorium: In Search of Regional Modernity," Art Bulletin (June 2005): 265–311.

15   Waldo Bowman, "A Modern Mesopotamia is Molded," Engineering News-Record (December 12, 1957): 34–54, quotation on 36.

16   The Economist, "Development in Iraq: Special Survey," CLXXXIII, 5939, June 22, 1957, fourteen-page supplement after p. 1076. Summary reprinted in Ekistics 5:28 (January 1958): 45–48.

17   "The National Housing Program of Iraq," Architectoniki 13 (January–February 1959): 42–46.

18   Doxiadis, "Architecture, Planning, and Ekistics: Abstract of the Third Part of a Lecture Series Given at the Massachusetts Institute of Technology, Spring 1957," Ekistics 7:42 (April 1959): 293–296.

19   Doxiadis's close colleague Jaqueline Tyrwhitt pointed to the pitfalls of New Towns and the advantages of Doxiadis's reinterpretation of neighborhood units in "Outline of Background Paper for Expert Group Meeting on Planning and Development of Satellite and New Towns, 1964," Harvard University, Frances Loeb Library (vertical files). For the broader United Nations debates on New Towns, see United Nations, Planning of Metropolitan Areas and New Towns (New York: UN, 1967).

20   Doxiadis Associates, "Iraq Housing Program," Doxiadis Associates Pamphlet no. 5, September 1959. For a summary of the firm's goals for the Iraq project, see Architectoniki 13, 1959, and Doxiadis Associates, "A Regional Development Program for Greater Mussayib, Iraq, 1958," Ekistics 6:36 (October 1958): 149–186.

21   Doxiadis Associates, "Iraq Housing Program."

22   The demands of Iraqi officials are recorded, for example, in Doxiadis Associates, Iraq Diaries, v. 1 (1955) [Archive Files 23873, Constantinos Doxiadis Archive].

23   Among the systematic critiques of modernist urbanism, and a key exposition of the technocratic utopianism of high modernism in many realms of practice, is the work of James Scott, Seeing Like a State: How Certain Schemes to Improve the Human Condition Have Failed (New Haven: Yale University Press, 1998).

24   Doxiadis, "Plans for Village in Mussayib by Professor Fathy" (21 July 1958): 1–2, quotation on 1. For an example of how the firm's emphasis on standardization shaped the architecture of rural houses specifically, see the description of the debates between Doxiadis and one of the members of his team, Hassan Fathy, in P. Pyla, "Hassan Fathy Revisited: Postwar Discourses on Science, Development, and Vernacular Architecture," Journal of Architectural Education 60:3 (February 2007): 28–39.

25   United Nations, FAO, Inter-Agency Working Party on Housing and Related Community Activities, "Extension of Low-Cost Housing and Related Community Facilities," January 1959. Reprinted in Ekistics 7:44, 458–466, quotation on 458. See also the report on the 1963 Committee on housing Building and Planning, in which Doxiadis participated. According to this report, one of the tasks of the UN Committee on Housing building and Planning was to develop practical proposals to assist developing countries on such matters as "low cost housing in different climates or cultures, improved building materials and their better use, and ways of promoting acceptance and adoption of efficient organizational and building techniques." UN ECOSOC, Committee on housing Building and Planning, "Provisional Agenda, Jan. 1963" [UN Documents E/C.6/1]

26   UNESCO promoted the idea of "field consultants," from the late 1940s. UNESCO, "Report of the Reconstruction and Rehabilitation Commission," UNESCO c/11/Rev. 1, 22 (January 1947): 6. By the 1960s, education and training became very important. The UN Special Fund, the World Bank, the International Monetary Fund, and Private organizations like the Ford Foundation, promoted training programs for officials in public administration, and financial and

economic fields. See Barbara Ward, "The Decade of Development: A Study in Frustration," first published in 1965 by the Overseas Development Institute, then in *Two Views on Aid to Developing Countries* (London: Institute of Economic Affairs, 1966).ref on 31-32.

27 "Special to the *New York Times* from Baghdad, Iraq, May 14, 1958," abstracted in *Ekistics* 5: 33 (June 1958): 280–282; quotation on 281.

28 C.A. Doxiadis, "Gossip Square," in *General Reports* (December 1956–57). For a more extensive discussion on this topic, see Panayiota Pyla, "'Dedicodou Meydane' Hakkinda Dedicodular: Siradan Bir Kamusal Alanin Tarihini Ortaya Dokmek" [Gossip on the 'gossip square': Unpacking the histories of an unglamorous public space], *Dosya* 27 [Special issue on "Architecture and Everyday Life] (December 2011): 19-24.

29 From James Holston's argument about the pitfalls of the modernist city's urban density, one can argue that the figure-ground relationships in Doxiadis Associates' plan compare favorably to those encountered in Brasilia. See Holston, *The Modernist City: An Anthropological Critique of Brasilia* (Chicago: University of Chicago Press, 1989), 119–136.

30 Doxiadis, "Pakistan Diary 20," 1954. See also Doxiadis Associates, "A Regional Development Program for Greater Mussayib, Iraq, 1958," *Ekistics* 6:36 (October 1958): 169, paragraph 38.

31 John Gulick. «Baghdad: Portrait of a City in Physical and Cultural Change,» *Journal of the American Institute of Planners* 33, 4 (1967): 246–255, quotation on 252.

32 In the 1960s local firms took on a huge volume of work, and after the creation of the first school of architecture in Iraq in 1959, the number of local professionals grew dramatically.

33 A summary of the buildings that were completed appears in Doxiadis Associates, "Progress of the Housing Program," *Monthly Report 46*, Document Prepared for the Government of the Republic of Iraq (Athens, May 1959). Also see Gulick, p. 253. For current reflections on the reception of the project, see Vasiliki Siouti and Paschalis Koroneos, "The Greek Mission in Iraq" [In Greek] *Epsilon* 630 (May 4, 2003):76–82, quotation on 76.

34 A similar opportunity would appear in the design of Islamabad, which gave the maximum freedom for a comprehensive master plan.

35 The diaries accompanied Doxiadis's report on Syria, submitted to the International Bank for Reconstruction and Development. This report served as a reference for the World Bank's *Community and Development.*, fiche 91

36 The journal *Ekistics* also devoted extensive coverage to Syria's overall development. See, for example, Charles Issawi, "Economic Revolution in the Middle East," *The Listener* (BBC), vol. LVIII, no. 1484, September 5, 1957, 333–335. Reprinted in *Ekistics* 4:25 (October 1957): 99–100. See also A.J. Meyer, "Harvard University Seminar on Economy of the Middle East, October 10, 1957," *Ekistics* 4:25 (October 1957): 101.

37 Demetris Pikionis, who guided Doxiadis's early training in architecture, was a vigorous critic of modernist rationalism, which he believed threatened to strip architecture from a "plethora of virtues" and "sentiment." Pikionis's own projects passionately emphasized site-specificity. Even if Doxiadis, from early in his career, was more interested in the efficiency of urban plans and the mass production of houses than the aesthetics of a single edifice or the intricate particularities of a landscape, Doxiadis often recognized Pikionis as one of his major influences. Jaqueline Tyrwhitt refers to Pikionis as one of the three major influences in Doxiadis's early life. Tyrwhitt, "Background to C.A. Doxiadis's Ecology and Ekistics," *Ekistics* 266 (January 1978): 12–19, esp. 13–14. This was also confirmed by another close associate of Doxiadis, Panayis Psomopoulos, in an interview with the author, Athens, 27 July 2005.

38 Doxiadis Associates, "Plan for the City of Homs, Syria: Summary of Preliminary Report No. 3 Prepared for the Government of the United Arab Republic, Province of Syria," reprinted in *Ekistics* (1958), quotations on 278 and 274.

39 See "Summary of Problems" in Doxiadis Associates, "Plan for the City of Homs, Syria," 278–279.

40 Doxiadis Associates, "Plan for the City of Homs, yria," quotations on 278–280.

41 This urban model was at still at its beginning stages in the plans for Syria. It was further developed and implemented in the planning of Islamabad, and Doxiadis would later call this planning concept "Dynapolis." For more on the connections of Dynapolis to Linear City concepts, see Pyla, «Back to the Future," 3–19.

42 Doxiadis Associates, "Plan for the City of Homs, Syria," quotation on 278.

43 Doxiadis Associates, "The Future of Homs and Hama," *Doxiadis Associates Monthly Bulletin* 11 (Athens: Doxiadis Associates, 1960), 4. [HFA PP 13B].

44 Ibid., 6. Also Doxiadis Associates, "Rapport Final sur le Plan d'Emenagement et Programme de Developpement de la Ville de Hama, Preparé pour le Gouvernement de la Republique Arabe Unie, Province Syrienne," Doxiadis Associates Archive, Document Dox-SA 7, 24 April 1961.

45 See, for example, Rifat Chadirji, *Concepts and Influences: Towards a Regionalized International Architecture, 1952–1978* (London and New York: KPI, 1986).

46 For more on Doxiadis Associates' practice from the 1960s onward, see Panayiota Pyla, "Planetary Home and Garden: Doxiadis's Environment-Development Politics," *Grey Room* 36 (Summer 2009): 6–35.

47 For Wright's proposals for Baghdad, see Siry, "Wright's Baghdad Opera House and Gammage Auditorium"; and Neil Levine, *The Architecture of Frank Lloyd Wright* (Princeton, N.J. : Princeton University Press, 1996). For reflections on Saddam Hussein's interventions in the 1980s, see William Brantley, "The Search for Baghdad," *Urban Land* 63 (2004): 49–55.

IOANNA THEOCHAROPOULOU

8

IMPROVISING URBANISM IN POSTWAR
ATHENS (1952–1974): TECHNIQUES AND
PROCESSES OF ANOTHER DEVELOPMENT

The opening scene of every traditional *Karagiozis* shadow-puppet theater performance is always framed by two buildings: on the left, the Greek hero's hut, and on the right, the Ottoman ruler's palace. The hut is always tilting, unstable, supported by an old tree trunk, with holes in the roof, while the ruler's palace is large, splendid, and beautifully maintained. Beyond the opposition between the Greek (oppressed) and the Turk (oppressor), these two representations succinctly encapsulate one of the most fundamental aspects of modern Greek society: the split between "official" and "unofficial" culture, "high" and "low," or what some anthropologists have termed the "Romeic" (inward-looking, retaining continuities with Ottoman times) and the "Hellenic" (outward-looking, trying to relate to the West and to express continuities with an idealized ancient world).[1]

The origins of *Karagiozis* as a character are in fourteenth-century Ottoman culture; every play is about the poor, ugly, physically deformed Karagiozis (he has one extremely long arm) and his struggle to keep himself and his family fed and sheltered. In each performance, by some ruse he convinces the ruler that he is something he is not: a baker, a pharmacist, a captain, a doctor. He then proceeds to improvise, blundering his way through, claiming each profession for his own until he is caught and punished, though not before he has made fun of the authorities and managed to have a meal or two.

What might this urban (anti)hero and his techniques for survival have to do with informal housing development in postwar Athens? I propose that these images may help us think about Athenian postwar architecture and urbanism—though not because they have any apparent similarities. Rather, in very different ways, they both allow us

Karagiozis shadow-puppet theater stage showing the hero *Karagiozis* and his family traveling from their shack, on the left, to the Ottoman ruler's palace or sarai, on the right.

Athens, ca. 2002. Photographs of the contemporary Athenian landscape showing *polykatoikia* buildings by Panos Kokkinias.

to understand some important characteristics of Greek modernity. Karagiozis's strug-gle to survive might be a fruitful catalyst for opening up the question of how urban development worked in Athens in this period. Articulating the opposition between feast and famine, traditional shadow-puppet theater is especially fitting in exploring a similar opposition in the building practices of postwar Athens that seemed to oscil-late between great restrictions on the one hand and large financial and social profit and achievement on the other.

In proposing an analogy with Karagiozis's theater, I want to argue that the kinds of building practices or modes of performance of those involved in housing construc-tion during the post-World War II period, like Karagiozis's theater, relied on specific tech-niques of improvisation. I discuss three such techniques as they manifested themselves in building practices of postwar Athens: the ruse, status reversal, and parody.[2]

The concept of improvisation is useful when thinking about postwar Athens, where a great deal of building took place in an improvised or informal manner. Like all improvisation, this urban performance was about a set of actions that were modified opportunistically according to particular circumstances. By the term "informal," I refer to buildings that were constructed in a semi-illegal or marginally legal fashion, defying urban plans and completed mostly without input from architects. Even when designed with some involvement from architects, Athenian postwar housing development was very often at least in part improvised, as parts were routinely changed to satisfy indi-vidual owners after the permit was issued, thus eluding laws and regulations.

After an introductory section where I give some background on the evolution of Athenian urbanism, I explore how postwar development relied on improvisation tech-niques, or as Michel de Certeau might say, culturally specific "ways of operating."[3] Only by understanding these kinds of processes can we begin to explore the peculiarities of Athenian urbanization. Or to put it another way, the landscape of another urban history becomes visible only if we begin to understand these processes.

ATHENS: A SHORT HISTORY OF THE *POLYKATOIKÌA*

Architects and historians have endlessly rehearsed Athens's problems and missed opportunities, but with few exceptions have not found ways to appreciate the city's positive aspects, especially with regard to its informal character.[4] Athenians are used to everyone's disappointment with their city: it is noisy, polluted, sprawling, and not par-ticularly friendly. One of the most striking things about Athens in the postwar period, and the reason for much critical dismissal, is that planning, in the Western European sense, mostly failed here; the city is primarily composed of minimally planned, often illegal development.

Athenian postwar urban development consisted of small-scale (five- to six-story) apartment blocks, collectively known as the *polykatoikìa*—from *"poly"* (many) + *"katoikia,"* a modern word originating from the ancient root *"oikos," "oikia,"* meaning "dwelling," "household." Formally, the *polykatoikìa* looks modern, even though only

Polykatoikia apartment blocks in advertisements of the publisher's lottery in *Apogevmatini* newspaper, November 13, 1961. The main image shows photographs of typical postwar *polykatoikia* apartments. The cartoons surrounding the image reinforce the point of the caption: "Luck Bank... all lottery ticket holders are eligible to win houses-cars-cash" showing *polykatoikia* apartment blocks and cars (on top), cash (on the left), and modern appliances (on the right).

about 5 to 15 percent of postwar production were constructed with any involvement by architects.[5] Formal sources for the *polykatoikia* include architect-designed prewar modernist buildings. Horizontal ownership, and with it the first housing apartment buildings, was introduced with the first Building Regulation of 1929 under the Eleftherios Venizelos government. These buildings were designed by trained architects and were of high structural and aesthetic quality. They were owned largely by the upper-middle classes.

Made of reinforced concrete skeletons with brick or other masonry infill, the postwar *polykatoikia* has wide openings, white unadorned façades, flat roofs, simple linear cantilevered balconies and, in upper-class neighborhoods, roof gardens and *pilotis*. In short, the *polykatoikia* utilizes a simplified modernist aesthetic, without deploying the

Middle-class *polykatoikia* building from 1957 featuring an apartment on the third floor advertised as a lottery prize. Note that the labels on the second floor indicate that the building was constructed by two civil engineers, Stefanos D. Anastasiadis and Nikos P. Stamoulis.

Examples from interwar *polykatoikia* apartment blocks from the upper-class area of Kolonaki: 1) 26 Loukianou Street, designed by architect Renos Koutsouris, and 2) Patriarchou Ioakeim 45 and Ploutarchou Streets, designed by architect Konstantinos Kouropoulos, who was also the owner. Both date from 1933.

intellectual complexity of architect-designed examples from Europe or from the local interwar modernist tradition.

Constituting the most dominant building form of the postwar period, this housing type was produced most often by small builders and developers.[6] Unlike the development experts working elsewhere in the Middle East during this period, in Greece the term "developer" [*ergolavos*] had a different meaning, closer to "small builder" or "head of small construction team." There were two broad types of developers: the largely uneducated developer-contractors who had come from the provinces in search of work and who usually (though not always) had a background in building trades, and the middle- or upper-middle-class engineers who were more likely to work with architects—though a few architects worked as developers themselves.

Unlike postwar development and reconstruction in Northern Europe, Athens avoided state-funded and state-planned housing almost completely. None of the postwar master plans—and there were many—were ever put into practice.[7] The U.S. Marshall Plan, administered after the end of the war, was used primarily for the reconstruction of the countryside as well as for major infrastructural works. Housing was delegated to the private sector. State involvement in housing, which was never great in Greece, in fact fell to 5 percent between 1959 and 1968, and to 3 percent between 1969 and 1972.[8]

The whole logic of state planning and with it, state-organized housing development, remained culturally alien to Greece until the twentieth century. When Athens was founded as a modern city in the early 1830s, planning was introduced by Bavarian and foreign-educated Greek architects, with some success.[9] Yet it was not of the local culture in any natural way, and perhaps this was why it failed to be properly implemented even then. It may have been too Western European when there were two distinct and not altogether equivalent cultures coexisting in Athens. In the words of theater scholar Theodoros Chatzipantazis, those were the "urban-European" and the "popular-eastern Mediterranean."[10]

These two cultures were in fact quite antithetical in many respects. This situation remained largely unresolved until the twentieth century. In this sense, blaming individual developers for "ugly" *polykatoikìa* development or blaming the state for its inefficient mechanisms for implementation only skims the surface of this national phenomenon. Rather, we have to look to older cultural and historical processes and structures, or ways of operating, to understand why things evolved as they did.

More specifically, the three major factors identified by scholars as important for the birth of the concept of planning in Europe around the first half of the nineteenth century—the problems of growing industrial cities, the rise of social planning and increased intervention by professionals, and the invention of the modern economy—were not articulated in the same ways in nineteenth-century Greece as in the rest of Europe.[11] There were no growing industrial cities. Industrialization begun late in comparison with Western Europe (in the early twentieth century), and industry has never played as large a part in the Greek economy as elsewhere in Europe. Since there were no large industries and large industrialists, the idea of social planning was never a major discourse.

In addition, professionalization happened late in many fields, including architecture. The School of Architecture within the National Metsovion Polytechnic School in Athens was not founded until 1917—almost ninety years after the inception of the Greek state. Until then, courses in architecture were taught at the School of Engineering (founded in 1887).[12] The first graduates in architecture from a Greek university started practicing in the early 1920s. Yet the majority of buildings continued to be executed by engineers with some architectural knowledge, especially the so-called practical engineers.[13] The latter had very little formal education. Instead they had on-site training, updating a tradition of master-craftsmen and worker teams spanning centuries in Ottoman-occupied Greek areas.

Rather than diminishing, this tradition grew in strength following the 1922 population exchange with Turkey: at that point, in an effort to address the refugee crisis by creating jobs and housing, the government created what architects called "semi-professionals" by founding state-run schools for their education. This situation became worse for architects when, during the German occupation in 1941, the government renamed these "semi-professional" schools as Schools for Sub-Engineers [*Sxoles Ypomixanikon*], which operated in different guises through the 1960s.[14] During the postwar period, with an urgent need for housing, middle-class clients were much more likely to entrust their properties to practical engineers or other non-architects than to architects, who were still perceived as being the least necessary actors.

Another important particularity of Greek urbanization was the large extent to which it was craft-based.[15] As design historian Victor Margolin has suggested, the separation of professionals and nonprofessional designers into distinct categories became manifest with the onset of industrialization in European countries.[16] Before that, "everyone made things," or at least decisions about things. Since there was no such sudden or overall "successful" process of industrialization in Greece, it was difficult for Greek society to accept the idea of a clear distinction between professionals and nonprofessionals. This fact helps to explain the feeling of mistrust the general public often has toward professionals, which results in their routinely trying to sidestep them, even to this day.

The invention of a modern economy was also formalized and articulated very differently in Greece than in Western Europe. Specifically, urbanization happened in different ways in Greece, where rather than being defined by polarized and dependent relationships between urban bourgeois and proletariat classes, there was instead a strong polarization between capital city and countryside. In addition, there were no strong market towns, no regional university centers, and no strong independent guild system. In sum, there was no strong urban culture by the nineteenth century—at least not to the same extent as in Europe. As a result there was also no well-defined urban architectural tradition, public or private.

In the twentieth century, the tension between planning and what we could call individual development became even more dramatic. Not only were whole segments of the city plan consistently put together by individuals, but the government agencies in charge of planning were repeatedly constituted only to be abolished or reconstituted under other guises and with different titles. The event that transformed the evolution of Athens's urban fabric was the influx of refugees following the War of 1922 and population exchanges with Turkey. At this time, Athens's population of about 300,000 people suddenly almost doubled with the arrival of 250,000 refugees; the city's housing needs also doubled overnight. Again the government did little to help, although it did produce some limited prototypical modernist housing.[17]

Demand for housing continued to be pressing. Between 1923 and 1928, vast new areas sprang up on the edges of the existing official city plan, developed mostly by a new breed of small entrepreneurs, according to architectural historian Kostas Biris, mimicking the housing development initiated by the government for refugees.[18] These businessmen, whether owning small plots of land or working with individual owners at the limits of the city plan, cunningly put together their own proposals for "self-functioning settlements."[19] Remarkably, they would typically succeed in having their plans approved by the Ministry of Public Works after the plots had already been divided, whether meeting the requirements set out by law or not. Biris writes:

> [These small businessmen] would then place outrageous advertisements in the daily press, selling what was ostensibly farmland or even mountainous inaccessible land as plots fit for building. Thus in the space of a decade the new areas of Kypriadou, Psychiko, Ilioupoli, Cholargos and Gargitos were created. Of these only Psychiko and Ilioupoli had known designers (Alexandros Nikoloudis and Aristomenis Valvis respectively).[20]

As in the 1920s and 1930s, in the years following World War II and the Greek Civil War (1946–49) there was a massive influx of population into Athens. This time it was internal migration: with the devastation of the Greek countryside, people were keen to move from rural areas into cities, where they could start their lives anew. Athens's population grew from 1,378,586 inhabitants in 1951 to 2,530,207 in 1971. With this population growth, an intensive period of new building development began.

This new development resembled that of the 1920s and 1930s in some important respects: it was not properly regulated, few architects were involved, and most buildings were constructed by small teams of contractors/developers. These developers, whether small builder-contractors or engineer-entrepreneurs, worked as heads of construction teams rather than as typical businessmen. Neither group owned the land before starting construction. Small builder teams usually did not have their own tools, nor did they have the capital to pay workers in advance. The social distance between most contractors and construction workers was not so great: often they had been construction workers themselves or had also recently arrived from the countryside.

The tradition of small construction firms went hand-in-hand with small-scale private land ownership. Rather than the large plots of land and large construction businesses of Northern Europe, Athens is characterized by small plots, often only 6 meters wide at the street façade. Yet this way of doing things also "worked as a mechanism of sharing income to the benefit of the lower and middle class layers of the population."[21] To understand this more fully, one needs to turn to the financial process prevalent in this period and to a lesser extent today.

Production of the majority of postwar *polykatoikìa* buildings hinged on the so-called *antiparochì* financial system.[22] Relying on negotiated exchange, this system allowed an owner of land or an existing residential property to negotiate a percentage with a contractor to construct a *polykatoikìa*. No money needed to change hands in advance; rather, the original owner would gain one or several apartments in the new building in exchange for his land, depending on the negotiated terms. Advertising individual apartments and selling them (often before their construction had begun) allowed new buyers to suggest changes to typical floor plans to suit their needs, and contractors could gradually obtain the necessary cash for completing construction. If there was an existing building on site, it would simply be demolished.[23] This process also allowed eluding or shifting the terms of the building permit, and many buildings, especially on the city outskirts, were constructed without permits.

Sidestepping the banking system, this way of "self-financing" resulted in the direct channeling of savings by the lower and middle classes toward housing. Even those with no property or savings to start with were able to benefit from this process, as they found ample employment in construction. Others married into families that owed some land or a building that could be "exchanged." The huge demand for urban apartments during this period provided many incentives to save, particularly through the dowry system.[24]

An important difference from the economic crisis brought about by the influx of refugees from Asia Minor during the 1920s was that during the 1950s and 1960s, internal migrants were incorporated "more or less automatically" into the working class of cities and what was left of the prewar middle class that had diminished during the occupation and Civil War.[25] These migrants could find employment—sidestepping the obligatory evidence that one was not a communist (the so-called Certificate of Social Beliefs)—in *polykatoikìa* construction. For this was also the Cold War period, and Greece was seen by England and America as an important bulwark state against the spread of communism.

Yet the reliance on small builders and entrepreneurs contributed to the ineffectiveness of organized state-controlled planning. This phenomenon was usually assessed in negative terms in the postwar period; a revealing headline reads: "Athens: The Planning Monster."[26] Another headline from 1955 announced that the capital was in "uncontrolled," "irresponsible" hands: "The Disfigurement of Athens: Land Encroachers and Other Shrewd, Cunning People Appropriate Public Space and Destroy the City's Appearance."[27] These provocative titles reflect a perception not only of a lack of planning but of an organic anomaly, a "pathological," even "anti-natural" result due to a kind of chaotic and even monstrous situation.[28] One often reads similar stories in the papers to this day; we might say that ever since the early twentieth century, domestic *polykatoikìa* construction has been obsessively discussed and criticized, all the while filling every available urban space.

The majority of this informal or unplanned housing was of a relatively decent, even high standard. It was certainly of far better quality than the shantytowns that surrounded cities in developing countries elsewhere.[29] First noticed by an anthropologist in 1986, this fact usually eludes critics who have a hard time assessing this development as "architecture." Relentlessly repetitious, even banal in an architectural sense, this development invites us to search for other modes of interpretation. The next section presents some ideas based on a closer look at the context of Greek social and cultural life.

When looking around Athens today, we encounter a uniform landscape. The ecology of this landscape is the result of a complex game between authorities and developers. Like *Karagiozis,* the ways in which this game was played reveals a lot about Greek social and cultural life. Anthropologist Mary Douglas has noted that a humorous situation "consists of a victorious tilting of uncontrol against control, it is an image of the leveling of hierarchy, the triumph of intimacy over formality, of unofficial values over official ones." She also sees "a correspondence between the structure of the joke and the structure of the social organization in which the joke takes place."[30] The reversal of hierarchies has some positive sides, some of which we can begin to see through humorous yet deeply rooted cultural artifacts such as the *Karagiozis* theater.

More specifically, it is generally acknowledged that everyone who wanted to build in Athens during the postwar period utilized some ruse to get around certain institutions: from the small builder who may have cheated on the amount of iron used as reinforcement for concrete, to the developer who may have sold apartments to unsuspecting customers without owning the land upon which they were built. The comedy in some of these cat-and-mouse acts, and the official and non-official language used to describe them, evokes the shadow theater character once again. Thus the popular ironic use of such terms as *oikopedofagos* [literally "land-eater" or "landstealer," "encroacher"], *mneimeiofàgos* ["monument-eater"],[31] *oikopedemborio* ["plot-commerce"], *polykatoikiàs* ["*polykatoikia*-maker"], *antiparochitzìs* ["part-exchanger"], and *emporospitàs* ["house-trader"] bring to mind the famous antihero's insatiable hunger for crafty sleights-of-hand and for made-up, almost nonsensical language. For those who can understand them, these terms immediately evoke the cultural and social specificity of the postwar period.

In a sense, it is as if the way these processes worked, especially the financial process of *antiparochì*, encouraged—almost institutionalized—a certain way of doing things. If not exactly a ruse, the part-exchange financing system was akin to it. Dependent as it is on negotiation, it was a shifting, unfixed way of operating that encouraged craftiness (if not deviousness), since the more adept one was at negotiating, the more apartments one was able to gain in a new *polykatoikìa* in return for an old house. And if not exactly the opposite of organized planning, usually thought of as a series of rational, rule-bound, official processes, this kind of local process and its accompanying accepted mode of behavior were far from it.

There was an ongoing game between construction and state regulation. Developers consistently tried to circumvent regulations, but the regulations were also changed to benefit developers, especially in times of elections. Foreigners were endlessly fascinated with Athenians' apparent disregard of municipal law and unusual ways of addressing construction. As travel writer Kevin Andrews exclaimed in 1967:

Squatter's rights are confirmed if a house is roofed during the night: 30,000 such sprang up during a few weeks of 1963 while the police were anticipating the *coup d'etat* that hangs over every general election. If one is highly placed or well enough connected, it is quite easy, up on Lykavitos where the limit is two storys out of respect for one of the world's rare views, to build a broad-beamed skyscraper with ritzy penthouses and then get somebody in Parliament to change the law.[32]

The postwar "urban anarchy" was not without precedent in Greek everyday life, as the practice of sidestepping of regulations existed since at least the 1920s and 1930s. Yet in both times it was not simply the "weak" (refugees and the urban poor) who used their traditional craftiness to get by and avoid regulations. The state and its officials often deployed similar techniques for their own ends—to get votes, to satisfy supporters, or simply to make some extra cash. This is most clearly illustrated by the fact that "amendments" could be built into the building code. These amendments begun to appear in 1929 with the first code to be enforced.[33] The 1955 building code in turn allowed even more such amendments. It prescribed *deviations* [*parekliseis*] of up to 10 percent of anticipated surface area in central Athens and 5 percent in areas surrounding the center, essentially making central areas more vulnerable to urban anarchy.[34] This building code legalized all illegal construction up to that point, a populist move that was repeated later by the junta government.

Far from being totally distinct from any official way of doing things, this resulting "para-urbanism," in historian Dimitris Philippidis's terms, existed not only in parallel with official urbanism but also worked symbiotically with it, each satisfying specific and complementary interests.[35] For instance, after 1923 no one was legally allowed to parcel up agricultural land and sell it as buildable urban land. However, Philippidis writes, "between 1957 and 1977 about 1.5 million of these pieces of previously classified agricultural land were sold as urban plots, with the State's tacit approval."[36]

Thus rather than trying to scrutinize postwar urbanism aesthetically—"the postwar *polykatoikia* has no aesthetics," critics have often written—one needs to focus on processes and landscape: small events that add up, forming patterns based on repetition and small variation. These processes range from bureaucratic rules that monitored height and width of buildings (the building codes) to specific construction and improvisation techniques.

Although these processes may have contributed to making the urban landscape of Athens "monotonous" and "homogeneous," they also reveal some deeply ingrained cultural characteristics. To explore this notion, let me return to *Karagiozis*. As *Karagiozis* "becomes" someone else in each play, he has to imagine a suitable way to behave and to dabble in official language and terms clearly foreign to him. For instance, when necessary, he can even take on the profession of a midwife:

I will *become* a midwife, with a degree from Paris, ex-professor […] I will mimic a woman's voice, walk like a woman and other such delicate things. Yes sir, I can learn all this for 30 sovereigns! That's no small reward.[37]

Karagiozis, who has no trade or profession (he is totally illiterate), each time declares proficiency in yet another field: from barber to airplane pilot, scholar, lion-tamer, skier, midwife, and astronaut. His goal is to relentlessly trick the Ottoman authorities—always failing, and always trying again. The theme of trickery and the false claim of mastery of a profession is parodied, among other places, in the popular comedy from 1960, *Ta Dervisopaida.*[38] Like the puppet-theater hero *Karagiozis,* the two protagonists in this film were two men just in from the provinces who claimed proficiency in every conceivable building trade. They even called themselves "master builders." But as the audience soon discovers, neither of them knew how to put two bricks together. Causing chaos on the *polykatoikìa* building site, they were soon chased away by the head supervisor, causing hilarious small accidents while on the run. But the trickery didn't stop there: whereas the two protagonists told the developer that they were expert builders, he in turn told his clients that the new neighborhood was to have many nonexistent amenities—a practice quite common at that time.

As with film characters, *Karagiozis*'s characteristic ruse is related to the mythological *mêtis.* Classical scholars have described *mêtis* as combining "flair, wisdom, forethought, subtlety of mind, deception, resourcefulness, vigilance, opportunism, various skills, and experience acquired over the years," arguing that it is an "extraordinarily stable [characteristic] throughout Hellenism."[39] In a different context, Michel de Certeau described this characteristic in *The Practice of Everyday Life.* For him *mêtis* embraces "a spectrum of behaviors, from know-how to trickiness."[40] It is exactly this spectrum of behaviors, these ways or processes of doing things, that shaped the development of the Athenian urban landscape.

Aside from the ruse, another cultural technique or process equally important to our understanding of postwar informal development is the ambiguity, intentional confusion, sometimes even reversal of categories between high- and low-class status, educated and uneducated, wealthy and poor. In the *Karagiozis* puppet theater, these ambiguities are purposefully exaggerated as our hero stumbles his way through what are often hilarious instances of status reversal where "he is transformed from a poor uneducated man of low status into a skilled educated man of high status."[41]

Such a confusion of categories, especially between formal/officially approved and informal/partly or wholly not approved was consistently retained in postwar Athens, where a majority of construction was produced in an improvised manner by people without formal training. This goes against our usual understanding of the role of "experts" in modernization processes. In the Greek context, this was more evidence of the lack of clear boundaries between different areas of professional expertise. A group of women builders working in a clearly non-architect-designed *polykatoikìa* indicates a reversal of traditional gender roles—something that was not common, yet it did seem to exist.

The idea of a confusion of categories through a ruse was repeatedly explored in popular films—always comedies. Examples include a sense of confusion as to what was private and what was public property, or where one was allowed to build. This theme is explored in *Fos, Nero, Tilefono* (Electricity, Water, and Telephone) by Kostas Stanjalis

Polykatoikia construction by a group of women builders with a male supervisor, Athens, ca. 1959. Although we don't have precise information about women builders, it seems that some women were involved in construction during this period.

from 1966 and *Enas Veggos gis oles tis doulies* (One Veggos for All Odd Jobs) by Dinos Katsouridis from 1970. Both films are about how a poor character from the countryside is put in a situation where he has to claim expertise in different trades and ends up working in real estate. He is then instructed to sell land on mountainous or other inaccessible areas that actually belong to the state. Far from a fictitious situation, this practice was also quite common, as newspapers from that period confirm.[42]

Although *polykatoikìa* housing did not exactly reverse "high" and "low," it certainly blurred any clear separation. It is not hard to distinguish between a *polykatoikìa* in a wealthy neighborhood from one in a poor one based on the quality of materials used, yet the basic diagram of unadorned white façades, reinforced concrete frames, flat roofs, and large window openings can be found in both. The lower-middle classes tended to build with developers rather than architects, but architects would often do basic design work and sign their names on planning permits to gain income. Dimitris Philippidis has commented on the fact that

> businessmen took advantage of engineers [and architects] in many forms: aside from the humiliating fee discounts and the charge of 10% of the legal fee they could gain from selling their professional stamp on drawings, there was also the practice of commissioning only the façade of a *polykatoikìa* to an architect. This practice ... meant an amazing typification of the *polykatoikìa* especially in the postwar period.[43]

Thus rather than standardization of construction techniques and materials as found elsewhere in Europe and the Middle East, in Athens there was a unique repetition of formal façade characteristics with few variations, which brings us to the last process under discussion, that of parody.

PARODY, OR THE TYPE AND THE STEREOTYPE

It is worth reemphasizing that the tradition of nonprofessionals working in building trades existed since Ottoman times, extending to the twentieth century. Specifically the practice of "façade design," as historian Kostas Biris has shown, was rife during the 1920s and 1930s, when modernism was introduced to Greece.[44] At that time, popular neoclassical façades in humble houses were routinely converted to "modernist" ones. This indicates the extent to which architecture was considered an important part of national identity: to become "modern"—which was extremely desirable, especially as it was linked to a dream of becoming more "European" than Eastern Mediterranean— meant that buildings had to suddenly look "modern" also.

Where did Athenian postwar *polykatoikìa* developers look for their examples to emulate? The modernist apartment blocks built during the early 1930s were surely one inspiration. Yet postwar development retained links with the rural vernacular, especially in building techniques and ways of working with materials. After all, the village literally came to the city during this time: proportions of urban and rural populations were reversed, from 38 and 48 percent respectively in 1951, to 53 and 35 percent by 1971.[45] In terms of techniques of production, even though the postwar builders' work was not identical to "traditional" stone building, one could argue that it was an updated version. The construction techniques were relatively simple, always craft-based and using minimal equipment. Making use primarily of wood and concrete mixed on site and carried up narrow ladders in small tin buckets, this work was easily learned, with few changes for the first postwar decades.

Was postwar *polykatoikìa* housing then a form of popular or vernacular art, or popular civilization? It is hard to distinguish between authentic and non-authentic popular expressions, since there remains little authentic folk tradition in the pre-industrial nineteenth-century sense. Nor can we accept that popular culture is about an autonomous expression of a people's genius. Rather, it is more about how people use an object or event or performance. I propose that the postwar *polykatoikìa*—like popular theater—was such a popular expression. This is not to say that it was beautiful or naïve, like pre-industrial popular art. Nor was it particularly formally interesting, as many architects have noted. In its improvised and unplanned processes of construction, it was closer to a vernacular craft-based way of doing things, and particularly of utilizing resources.

This returns us to *mêtis,* which is also about resourcefulness as well as an economy of means, or in de Certeau's words, "obtaining the maximum number of effects from the minimum force."[46] Economy is a well-known and fundamental characteristic in vernacular architecture in terms of both materials and forms. The postwar *polykatoikìa* presents a surprising continuity with the vernacular in its sense of economy, its diagrammatic simplification, and seemingly endless repetition, as well as in its culturally preestablished patterns of life.

Anthropologist Alki Kyriakidou-Nestoros uses an interesting example to illustrate the shift from pre-industrial to industrial popular culture: multicolored plastic everyday eating utensils that in the postwar period replaced hand-made ones are as "authentic" as the older models because "they retain the old types or forms as well as the old names of things... without any particular effort from those who use them"[47] In a similar vein, architect Dimitris Pikionis, writing in 1935 about toys being sold in Aiolou Street, an area of Athens near the city market that is lined with inexpensive shops and street peddlers, had observed that urban life and its new conditions might bring about new popular art forms. Illustrating his text with a black-and-white image of spinning tops, tin animals, and shadow-theater characters, Pikionis noted that:

> "Aiolou Street" is a symbolic term. It signifies all these areas where the feeling of popular tradition [*laiki paradosi*] comes into a creative contrast with the terms of contemporary life. This is the kind of contrast through which new authentic forms of popular art are born.[48]

Is the *polykatoikìa* then simply a parody of modern architecture or a new, equally authentic and valid urban popular form? I suggest that the *polykatoikìa* of the postwar period was both. In most cases the *polykatoikìa* has been left out of architectural history books that tend to focus on individual architects' creations, but architects' contributions, although important, formed only a small percentage of total building production. Yet the *polykatoikìa* is interesting as a popular urban form, visibly modern, that successfully replaced or updated rural building culture. Because the processes of production (including what I call improvisation techniques) and the apparently chaotic, unplanned fashion through which it rapidly spread through urban space were a result of particular cultural characteristics, people felt a deep sense of familiarity toward this urbanism instead of the initial alienation that characterized the introduction of modern architecture elsewhere in Europe.

The tension between familiarity and architectural innovation brings us to parody, the last characteristic that I draw on from the *Karagiozis* puppet theater. To return to the analogy drawn from Kyriakidou's work, on one level the multicolored plastic utensils are also a parody of the hand-made ones: they are an attempt at imitation that is so poor that it may seem ridiculous. Similarly the Athenian *polykatoikìa* at first sight seems "modern." It is still common for many non-architects to use the term "Bauhaus" to describe it. Yet despite any apparent similarities such as flat roofs, horizontal lines, modern materials, and lack of ornamentation, it is also dissimilar in some important ways. The *polykatoikìa* is an extremely simplistic version of modern architecture, lacking the latter's political and aesthetic agenda.

In addition, it was received and interpreted without the fundamental project of a radical break that modern architecture depends on. If modern architecture was about the notion of *type*, the *polykatoikìa* is a stereotype, but an "enabling" one.[49] Like all stereotypes, the *polykatoikìa* "conformed to a fixed or general pattern."[50] Yet the postwar *polykatoikìa* used things for purposes other than those initially intended, in ways that had popular appeal. This may begin to explain some of the antagonism of architects and planners. Rey Chow's discussion of Derrida's misunderstanding of Chinese writing has helped us see that stereotypes are not necessarily "forms of entrapment and victimization," but can be the cause of "fundamental signifying or representational process[es] with real theoretical and political consequences."[51]

The postwar *polykatoikìa* was enabling in that it enabled the transformation of rural migrants into urban dwellers, with urban aspirations and a modern way of life. It therefore contributed in fundamental ways to the modernization of Greek society. Like the American balloon frame, the *polykatoikìa* was successful at the level of a simply reproducible process as well as that of a desirable popular symbolism.[52] It effectively responded to the interaction between a building's formal aspects and the consumer's understanding of them. Yet in its attempt to become modern too fast, too cheaply, Athens espoused a stereotypical notion of modern architecture, becoming both a parody of and a successful experiment in "a modern city par excellence."[53]

CONCLUSION

Postwar *polykatoikìa* urbanism does not fit neatly into an idea of modern architecture in terms of "high" architectural history, particularly an idea of architecture centered on architects. This kind of urban development, much like the popular shadow-puppet theater, articulates and makes explicit many of the tensions underlining Greek culture and society. Not clearly "high" or "low," architect-designed or not, totally modern or totally vernacular, the *polykatoikia* should be seen as nothing less than a powerful crystallization of postwar Greek culture.

Although based on a capitalist mode of production, the *polykatoikìa* operates in a distinct way, specific to the postwar context in Greece: there were no large firms, no capital in advance, and almost no involvement from banks or other lending institutions. Interweaving the desire of newly urbanized populations striving to survive and prosper in the city with the financial, social, and cultural processes identified here, the resulting building becomes a vehicle for postwar society to remake itself. Allowing for widespread transformations in everyday life, the *polykatoikìa* and its mechanisms of production offer a compelling example of the ways architecture can shape society. The history of the *polykatoikìa* adds new layers of complexity and provides us with a richer background against which to view the "informal" as a phenomenon that now accounts for one third of urban habitation around the world.

Notes

I am grateful to the Council on Library and Information Resources (CLIR) and the Mellon Foundation for generously funding a major part of my Ph.D. dissertation research from which this chapter is drawn. An earlier elaboration of this chapter was published in *Paradigmata*, the Greek Pavilion Catalogue, Ninth International Architectural Exhibition, Venice Biennale 2004.

1   Michael Herzfeld, "Within and Without: The Category of 'Female' in the Ethnography of Modern Greece," in *Gender and Power in Rural Greece*, ed. Jill Dubisch (New Jersey: Princeton University Press, 1986), 217–218. Although the Ottoman and Hellenic are obviously not the same, they function in the same way in this example, as a foreign "other" culture. Michael Herzfeld has also discussed the Hellenic and Romeic aspects of Greek culture in his book *Ours Once More: Folklore, Ideology, and the Making of Modern Greece* (New York: Pella Publishing Company, 1986).

2   This interpretation and the use of the term "improvisation" was initially inspired by scholarly work on the Karagiozis theater. See in particular Yiannis Kiourtsakis, *Proforiki Paradosi kai Omadiki Dimiourgia, To Paradeigma tou Karaghiozi* [Oral Tradition and Group Creativity] (Athens: Kedros Publications, 1983); for a discussion of *Karagiozis'* links to the European carnival tradition, see Yiannis Kiourtsakis, *Karnavali kai Karagiozis. Oi rizes kai oi metamorfoseis tou laikou geliou* [Carnival and Karagiozis: The Roots and

Metamorphoses of Popular Laughter] (Athens: Kedros Publications, 1985). See also Theodoros Chatzipantazis, *I eisvoli tou Karagiozi stin Athina tou 1890* [The Invasion of Karagiozis in Athens ca. 1890] (Athens: Stigmi Publications, 1984).

3   Michel de Certeau, *The Practice of Everyday Life* (Berkeley: University of California Press, 1984), xix–xx.

4   Some important exceptions to the general pessimistic attitude toward Athenian urbanism have been invaluable to my work. Among these are anthropologist Peter S. Allen's essay, "Positive Aspects of Greek Urbanization: The Case of Athens by 1980," *Ekistics* 53, no. 318/319 (1986); Kenneth Frampton's "Introduction" to the Greek edition of his *Modern Architecture: A Critical History* (Athens: Themelio Publications, 1987); and Hashim Sarkis's "On The Beauty of Athens," in *Isopolis: Addressing Scales of Urban Life in Modern Athens*, edited by Peter G. Rowe and Hashim Sarkis (Cambridge, MA: Harvard University Graduate School of Design, 1997), 98–105.

5   Theano Fotiou, "Architectonika protypa stin sygxroni Athina: I periptwsi tis astikis polykatoikias, I morphologia tis polis," [Architectural Prototypes in Contemporary Athens: The Case of the Urban Polykatoikia, the Morphology of the City] in *I Neoelliniki Poli* [Modern Greek City], edited by Guy Bourgel (Athens: Exantas Publications, 1989), and Dimitris Philippidis, *Neoelliniki Arxitektoniki* [Modern Greek

Architecture] (Athens: Melissa Publications, 1984). Both Fotiou and Philippidis discuss the minimal involvement of architects, giving slightly different statistics.

6 Some well-known and well-documented examples of postwar *polykatoikia* buildings by important architects include Nikos Valsamakis's *polykatoikia* buildings on Semitelou Street (1951) and Vassilissis Sofias Avenue (1955), and Takis Zenetos's *polykatoikia* on Amalias-Daidalou Streets (1959).

7 For an account of planning and its limitations up to the 1960s, see Kostas Biris, *Athens: From the Nineteenth to the Twentieth Centuries [Ai Athinai apo ton 190–200 aiwna]* (Athens: Melissa Publications, 1966). Aside from being a historian, Biris was also an architect and planner who worked for the City of Athens for almost forty years (1925–65) and produced some of these master plans himself, only to see his attempts frustrated. Between 1945 and 1951, Constantinos A. Doxiadis was responsible for the Greek Ministry of Reconstruction. He had a hard time implementing his innovative planning ideas, although he did have a great deal of success in soliciting foreign aid, rebuilding the devastated Greek countryside, and recognizing the importance of rebuilding and expanding infrastructural networks. Sadly, Doxiadis was abruptly removed from his post, and his work from that period has remained largely unappreciated. See also Dimitris Philippidis, *Gia tin Elliniki Poli: Metapolemiki poreia kai mellontikes prooptikes* [About the Greek City: Postwar Accounts and Future Possibilities] (Athens: Themelio Publications, 1990). In addition, Giorgos Sarigiannis has outlined the conflicted relationship between the various agencies responsible for urban planning in the twentieth century in "Planning in Greece from 1949 to 1974," transcripts of the second History of the City and City Planning Conference, University of Thessaly, 2000. I wish to thank Mihalis Lefatzis for showing me a copy of these transcripts.

8 From Vassilis Kotzamanis and Thomas Maloutas, "I kratiki epemvasi ston tomea tis ergatikis-laikis katoikias" [State Involvement in the Sector of Worker/Social Housing], *The Greek Review of Social Research*: 56 (1985).

9 For more on nineteenth-century Athens, see Biris, *Athens: From the Nineteenth to the Twentieth Centuries*; Manos Biris, *Misos Aiwnas Athinaikis Arxitektonikis, 1875–1925* [Half a Century of Athenian Architecture, 1875–1925] (Athens: TEE Publications, 1987), and in particular Eleni Bastea, *The Creation of Modern Athens: Planning the Myth* (Cambridge: Cambridge University Press), 2000.

10 Chatzipantazis, *I eisvoli tou Karagiozi stin Athina tou 1890*, 19.

11 Reference to these three factors appears in Arturo Escobar, "Planning," in *The Development Dictionary, A Guide to Knowledge as Power*, edited by Wolfgang Sachs (New Delhi: Orient Longman, 1997; reprint 2000), 176–195.

12 The upper-middle classes could also go and study architecture abroad in places such as France, Germany, and Italy.

13 Echoing the initial closeness in the fields of engineering and architecture in terms of education, architects are still simply called "engineers," as are experts from all other technical fields. Despite the existence of the School of Architecture, practical engineers took on most of the building work in large urban centers even after architects organized themselves into an association (1922) and began to complain publicly about the lack of recognition of their expertise. After the government allowed practical engineers to issue planning permits for so-called simple buildings following the Asia Minor catastrophe, the situation worsened. According to architect Vassilis Tsagris, writing in the journal of the Architects' Association, from 4,000 permits issued in 1934, 3,400 belonged to practical engineers. During the postwar period the situation became more complicated, but did not change much: Even as architects resented the government's definition of "simple" buildings and continued to fight for recognition, according to historian Dimitris Philippidis, "in 1957 from 18,461 building permits issued only 1,921 (10%) belonged to architects." Philippidis, *Neoelliniki Architectoniki*, appendix A, 414.

14 This new school type quickly became baptized as "small polytechnic" in colloquial language. Its graduates were legally allowed to design and build "simple" constructions, defined as one- to two-story buildings in reinforced concrete. The definition of "simple" construction quickly became a point of great contention for architects, who rightfully complained against the idea that one- or two-story buildings (which form the majority of construction in the Greek countryside) did not need the attention of architects.

15 On this topic, see also Jean-Louis Cohen, "Constructed Landscapes between North and South," in *Landscapes of Modernization: Greek Architecture, 1960s and 1990s,* edited by Yannis Aesopos and Yorgos Simeoforidis (Athens: Metapolis Press, 1999), 16.

16 Victor Margolin, "The Product Milieu and Social Action," in *Discovering Design: Explorations in Design Studies,* edited by Richard Buchanan and Victor Margolin (Chicago and London: University of Chicago Press, 1995), 124.

17 The so-called refugee housing was designed by talented architects such as Kimon Laskaris and Dimitrios Kyriakos (Alexandras's Avenue 1933–35). On the reception of refugees and refugee housing, see also sociologist Vika D. Gizeli's fascinating book, *Koinwnikoi metasxhmatismoi kai proeleusi tis koinwnikis katoikias stin Ellada, 1920–30* [Social Transformations and the Origins of Social Housing in Greece, 1920–30] (Athens: Epikairotita Publications, 1984). See also "Apartment Blocks for Refugees" under "Buildings" in the collection *20c Architecture, Greece,* edited by Savas Condaratos

and Wilfred Wang (Munich, London, New York: Prestel Publications, 1999), 149.

18 Biris, *Ai Athinai Apo tou 19ou eis ton 20n Aiona*, 286–287.

19 Ibid., 286–287.

20 Ibid.

21 Sophia Antonopoulou, *O metapolemikos metasximatismos tis Ellinikis oikonomias kai to oikistiko phenomeno, 1950–1980* [The Postwar Transformation of the Greek Economy and the Housing Phenomenon, 1950–1980] (Athens: Papazisis Publications, 1991), 20.

22 The term *antiparochì* (from *anti* = against + *parochì* from the verb *parecho,* to provide) is usually translated as "part-exchange."

23 The speed with which this process worked, combined with people's desire for housing and developers' and owners' needs for cash, meant that many nineteenth-century neoclassical houses and other historic domestic architecture vanished quickly.

24 The dowry was officially abandoned in 1983, though it was on the wane for years before that; yet it is still an important part of Greek culture in less rigid ways. In those years daughters had to have a dowry to get married. The most desirable dowry was an apartment in a *polykatoikia.* Thus the dowry system was an important way of transferring funds from the village to the city. Indeed, nonprofessional women played an important role in postwar urbanization: see my essay "The Housewife, the Builder, and the Desire for a *Polykatoikìa* Apartment in Postwar Athens," in *Negotiating Domesticity: Spatial Productions of Gender in Modern Architecture,* edited by Hilde Heynen and Gulsum Baydar (London: Routledge, 2005), 65–83.

25 Anthropologist Peter S. Allen attributes this fact to the following particularities of Greek postwar urbanization: the enormous economic growth during the postwar period, which meant an overall rise in the standard of living for millions of people, thereby improving the work opportunities available to those who came to the city; the "selectivity" of migration (i.e., the poorer went abroad to places such as Germany, the United States, and Australia); those who did come to the city usually arrived after employment had been secured, and they spoke the language and stayed with family members. Another important fact cited by Allen was that migrants held on to properties and other assets in their places of origin that provided them with a sense of security. See Allen, "Positive Aspects of Greek Urbanization," 190.

26 Headline from *Vradyni* newspaper, Athens, 7 March 1957; from the Canellopoulos Archives, E.L.I.A. (Hellenic Literary and Historical Archives), Athens.

27 Headline from *Kathimerini* newspaper, Athens, 5 April 1953; from the Canellopoulos Archives, E.L.I.A. (Hellenic Literary and Historical Archives), Athens.

28 The terms "pathological" and "anti-natural" are from Gustavo Esteva, "Development," in *The Development Dictionary,"* 11.

29 Peter S. Allen quoting Kemal H. Karpat, *Gecekondu: Rural Migration and Urbanization* (London: Cambridge University Press, 1976): "A United Nations study of 23 countries in these three continents [Asia, Africa and Latin America] shows 35 percent of the total urban population in squatter settlements and provides a list of 40 cities averaging well over 30 percent of their populations in shanty towns, noting that the highest percentages are found in India, Brazil and in Turkey. A recent newspaper report notes that 'the average Turkish city dweller lives in a 'gecekondu', and 'about 60 percent of the inhabitants of Ankara and Istanbul are gecekondu dwellers,'" Allen, "Positive Aspects of Greek Urbanization," 188.

30 Mary Douglas, "The Social Control of Cognition: Some Factors in Joke Perception," in *Man III* (1968): 366, quoted in Danford Loring, "Humour and Status Reversal in Greek Shadow Theatre," *Journal of Byzantine and Modern Greek Studies* 2, (1976): 110–111.

31 This term originally used by Kostas Biris refers to those who routinely demolished fine examples of nineteenth century architecture to build postwar *polykatoikìa* buildings. See *Zygos* magazine no. 4, 1956.

32 Kevin Andrews, *Cities of the World: Athens* (A.S. Barnes and Company, South Brunswick and New York, 1967), 13.

33 The 1929 law was soon followed by two equally influential events, the introduction of the first "General Building Code" (*GOK*) of the same year, and the decree about maximum heights of 1934. This decree was voted on the suggestion of architects primarily to ensure a small scale of construction so that the modern city would not end up overwhelming and even hiding the Acropolis hill. Buildings in the center of Athens were not to exceed 14 meters in height.

34 For more details on the building decrees, see Christophoros P. Sakellaropoulos, "Modern Architecture and the Politics of Urban Reconstruction, Athens 1945–1960" (Ph.D. dissertation, National Polytechnic University, Athens, 1993), 230 and 241.

35 Philippidis, *Gia tin Elliniki Poli,* 192. Scholars from different fields have used similar terms to explore the social and political situation of the postwar period such as "para-State" [*parakràtos*], "para-Constitution" [*parasyntagma*], and "para-economy" [*paraeconomìa*] (the latter still widely in use today) to describe parallel and not altogether legal processes that take place with the government's tacit agreement.

36 Philippidis, *Gia tin Elliniki Poli,* 195.

37 This fragment is from "O *Karagiozis* Mami" [*Karagiozis* Midwife], from an anonymous flier published in Athens by Keravnos and Pallas Athena bookstores, which had their own in-house *Karagiozis* publications. It is attributed to the

Karagiozis-player Kostas Manos. From Kiourtsakis, *Karnavali kai Karagiozis*.

38 The title of the film "Ta Dervisopaida," directed by Stelios Tatasopoulos, is etymologically related to the Turkish term "dervish." In Greek popular culture, "dervish" is something akin to the term *maggas*—a street urchin, street-smart, cunning. The title is purposefully ironic in this comedy because the two protagonists were not as street-smart as they wanted to believe. The film opens with one of the most common images from that time, *polykatoikia* housing under construction. We see workers having lunch on newly poured concrete cantilevered balconies and hear a voiceover that declares that "a new city is being created."

39 Scholars believe that this characteristic is known to apply to situations that are "transient, shifting, disconcerting and ambiguous, situations which do not lend themselves to precise measurement, exact calculation or rigorous logic." See Marcel Detienne and Jean-Pierre Vernant, *Cunning Intelligence in Greek Culture and Society*, translated by Janet Lloyd (Chicago: University of Chicago Press, 1991), 1–54. See also Jean-Pierre Vernant, quoted in De Certeau, *The Practice of Everyday Life*, 81.

40 De Certeau, *The Practice of Everyday Life*, 81.

41 The term "status reversal" was coined by anthropologist Danford Loring, writing about *Karagiozis*. Loring argues that status reversal is important in that "the disorder, blurring of boundaries, and confusion of categories which characterize Greek shadow theatre dissociate many elements of Greek culture and society, forcing the audience to examine these individual elements in new and atypical combinations. The theatre's humor and status reversal force its spectators to reconsider the categories according to which their perception of the universe is structured. In this way they more deeply understand and identify with their culture and society." From "Humour and Status Reversal in Greek Shadow Theatre," 110–111.

42 For example, this is discussed in the newspaper articles cited in notes 25 and 26.

43 Philippidis, *Neoelliniki Architectoniki*, 418.

44 Kostas Biris, writing about small-scale housing during the mid-1920s to the late 1930s, noted that: "Single-family houses of one, two or three floors were built by [practical engineers] in the cheapest possible way [...] Only if there was reinforced concrete in floors [...] there was a need for planning permit and specific structural calculations. If there was a question of architectural form, those practical people would delegate the work to some draftsman of façades [*fatsadoros*] who for a small sum would compose a façade with improvised or well-known decorative motifs that would be executed by the *pastadoros*." The latter term means the technician who worked with plaster,

especially decorative plaster, the etymology stemming from *pasta*—paste. Biris, *Athens: From the Nineteenth to the Twentieth Centuries*, 294.

45 These figures refer to the period between 1951 and 1971 and are from Richard Clogg, *A Concise History of Greece* (Cambridge: Cambridge University Press, 1992), 149.

46 De Certeau, *The Practice of Everyday Life*, 82.

47 Alki Kyriakidou-Nestoros, *Laographika Meletimata* [Folk Studies] (Athens: Etairia Ellinikou Logotexnikou kai Istorikou Arxeiou, 1989), 90–91.

48 Dimitris Pikionis, "Ta paihnidia tis Odou Aiolou" [The Toys of Aiolou Street], from *Dimitris Pikionis Keimena* [Dimitris Pikionis: Texts] (Athens: Morfotiko Idryma Ethnikis Trapezis, 1985). This text was originally published in the first issue of *The Third Eye* (October 1935), the important literary and artistic magazine that Pikionis coedited.

49 Rey Chow shows how Derrida's misunderstanding of Chinese as an ideographic language in fact helped him come up with his groundbreaking critique of Western phonocentrism. "The point, in other words, is not simply to repudiate stereotypes and pretend that we can get rid of them, as liberals tend to do, but also to recognize in the act of stereotyping (such as Derrida's fantasy about Chinese inscription) a fundamental signifying or representational process with real theoretical and political consequences. In our increasingly global, cross-cultural contacts, this signifying or representational process can only become more critical." Rey Chow, "How (the) Inscrutable Chinese Led to Globalized Theory," *PMLA*, January 2001, vol. 116, no. 1, publications of the Modern Language Association of America, 71.

50 From the definition of "stereotype," *Webster's 3rd International Dictionary*, c. 1950.

51 Chow, "How (the) Inscrutable Chinese Led to Globalized Theory," 71.

52 The invention of the balloon frame brought about a huge rise in construction in America from the nineteenth century onward: "If it had not been for the knowledge of the balloon frame, Chicago and San Francisco could never have arisen, as they did, from little villages to great cities in a single year." Solon Robinson, *New York Tribune*, 18 January 1855, quoted in Siegfried Giedion, *Space Time and Architecture: The Growth of A New Tradition* (Cambridge: Harvard University Press, 1941), 270. Unlike the balloon frame that relied on a certain level of industrialization, *polykatoikia* construction remained craft-based until at least the mid-1970s.

53 This phrase is from Frampton's "Introduction" to the Greek translation of his *Modern Architecture: A Critical History*, 14.

Contributors

Panayiota Pyla is Associate Professor of Architecture at the University of Cyprus, and previously served on the faculty of the University of Illinois at Urbana-Champaign. She holds a Ph.D. in the History-Theory of Architecture from the Massachusetts Institute of Technology (2002). Among her works is the guest editing of *Design and Culture* on "Sustainability's Prehistories" (November 2012), and her article "Hassan Fathy Revisited," which received the *Journal of Architectural Education*'s best article award (2007).

Eleni Bastéa is Regents' Professor of Architecture at the School of Architecture and Planning and Associate Director of the International Studies Institute at the University of New Mexico. Her books include *The Creation of Modern Athens: Planning the Myth* (2000), *Memory and Architecture* (2004), and *Venice without Gondolas* (poems, 2013).

Elizabeth Bishop co-edited *Imperialism on Trial: International Oversight of Colonial Rule in Historical Perspective* with R. M. Douglas and Michael D. Callahan during 2006. Recently, *Ab Imperio* published «The Local and the Global: The Iraqi Revolution of 1958 between Western and Soviet Modernities," and she is completing a monograph on the 14 *Tammouz* revolution.

Sibel Bozdoğan is a Lecturer in the Graduate School of Design of Harvard University (since 2000) and holds a professional degree in architecture from the Middle East Technical University, Ankara, Turkey (1976), and a Ph.D. from the University of Pennsylvania (1983). She has taught history-theory courses at Rensselaer Polytechnic Institute, MIT, and Istanbul Bilgi University. Her *Modernism and Nation Building: Turkish Architectural Culture in the Early Republic* (2001) received the 2002 Alice Davis Hitchcock Award of the Society of Architectural Historians, and she has recently published *Turkey: Modern Architectures in History* (2012, co-authored with Esra Akcan).

Aslihan Demirtas is the principal of Aslihan Demirtas Design and Research Studio, an interdisciplinary studio based in New York and Istanbul. She holds a Bachelor of Architecture degree from the Middle East Technical University in Ankara, Turkey, and a Master of Science in Architectural Studies from MIT.

Vilma Hastaoglou–Martinidis is Professor Emerita of the School of Architecture, Aristotle University of Thessaloniki, Greece. Her recent books include *Volos, Portrait of the City from the Nineteenth to the Twentieth Centuries* (2007), *Jewish Sites in Thessaloniki: Brief History and Guide* (2009), and *Ottoman Monuments of Thessaloniki* (forthcoming).

Rachel Kallus is an Associate Professor of Architecture and Town Planning at the Technion and heads the Social Hub for Community and Housing. Her research concentrates on the sociopolitical production of the built environment, focusing on ethno-nationally contested spaces. She is the author of numerous writings in books and academic journals on the social and cultural aspects of the built environment and its production.

Ioanna Theocharopoulou holds degrees from the Architectural Association in London and from Columbia University (MSc AAD, Ph.D.) Her research focuses on urban history and theory, and the history and theory of sustainable design. She cofounded the ongoing ECOGRAM conferences on cities and sustainability at the Graduate School of Architecture, Planning, and Preservation at Columbia, in 2008. Her writing has appeared in numerous publications. She is now completing her manuscript for *Builders and Housewives: Constructing Postwar Athens,* which expands on the material presented here. She teaches at the School of Constructed Environments, Parsons the New School for Design.

Neyran Turan is an architect and currently an Assistant Professor of Architecture at Rice University. She is founding editor of the Harvard University Graduate School of Design (GSD) journal *New Geographies,* which focuses on contemporary issues of urbanism and architecture. Turan is also a cofounder of NEMEstudio, a research and design collaborative based in Houston. Turan received her doctoral degree from Harvard GSD, and she holds a masters degree from the Yale University School of Architecture.

Illustration credits

The Aga Khan Program for Islamic Architecture at Harvard and MIT

Based at Harvard University and the Massachusetts Institute of Technology, the Aga Khan Program for Islamic Architecture (AKPIA) is dedicated to the study of Islamic art and architecture, urbanism, landscape design, and conservation, and the application of that knowledge to contemporary design projects.

The goals of the program are to improve the teaching of Islamic art and architecture, promote excellence in advanced research, enhance the understanding of Islamic architecture, urbanism, and visual culture in light of contemporary theoretical, historical, critical, and developmental issues, and increase the visibility of Islamic cultural heritage in the modern Muslim world. Established in 1979, AKPIA is supported by an endowment from His Highness the Aga Khan. AKPIA's faculty, students, and alumni have played a substantial role in advancing the practice, analysis, and understanding of Islamic architecture as a discipline and cultural force.

The Aga Khan Program at the Harvard University Graduate School of Design

Established in 2003, the main aim of the Aga Khan Program at the GSD is to study the impact of development on the shaping of landscapes, cities, and regional territories in the Muslim world and to generate the means by which design at this scale could be improved.

The program focuses on the emerging phenomena that characterize these settings and on issues related to the design of public spaces and landscapes, environmental concerns, and land use and territorial settlement patterns. The process entails a study of their current conditions, their recent history (from World War II to the present), and, most important, the exploration of appropriate design approaches. The program sponsors new courses, option studios, faculty research, workshops, conferences, student activities, and publications. It is supported by a generous grant from the Aga Khan Trust for Culture.

OTHER TITLES IN THE AGA KHAN PROGRAM BOOK SERIES

Two Squares: Martyrs Square, Beirut, and Sirkeci Square, Istanbul,
edited by Hashim Sarkis, with Mark Dwyer and Pars Kibarer

A Turkish Triangle: Ankara, Istanbul, and Izmir at the Gates of Europe,
edited by Hashim Sarkis, with Neyran Turan

Han Tumertekin: Recent Work, edited by Hashim Sarkis

The Architecture and Memory of the Minority Quarter in the Muslim Mediterranean City, edited by Susan Gilson Miller and Mauro Bertagnin

Desert Tourism: Tracing the Fragile Edges of Development, edited by Virginie Picon-Lefebvre and Aziza Chaouni

The Superlative City: Dubai and the Urban Condition in the Early Twenty-first Century edited by Ahmed Kanna